Rigging Math Made Simple
Third Edition

Delbert L. Hall, Ph.D.

with contributions by

Brian Sickels

Spring Knoll Press
Johnson City, Tennessee 37601

Copyright and Liability

Rigging Math Made Simple, Third Edition

Written by
Delbert L. Hall, Ph.D.

with contributions by Brian Sickels

Published by
Spring Knoll Press
Johnson City, Tennessee
www.SpringKnollPress.com

Cover Design by Andrea E. Hall

ISBN-10: 0692309896

ISBN-13: 978-0692309896

Printed in the United States of America

FirstClassBooks
7200 Interstate 30
Little Rock AR 72209

Received by:

Luhar Bhasin
42 Lake Pleasant Dr
Staatsburg, New York 12580-5678

Amazon Order Number: **112-5040948-2835402**
Shipment Number: **2200814**

SKU	Title
GTM-G-3191-000236	Rigging Math Made Simple, Third Edition

Returns Policy:
· For issues with your order, please contact us prior to initiating a return.
· For general returns, initiate a return through your order on Amazon, and you will receive a prepaid return label.

Return Notes:
· Please include your Order ID: 112-5040948-2835402. We are not responsible for issuing a refund if the item is unidentifiable.
· If the return is no fault of FirstClassBooks, the cost of the return label will be subtracted from your refund.
· Keep the tracking information for your shipment until your refund is completed.
· Please do not mark the item "Return or Sender" or "Refuse."
· In all cases the book must be returned in the condition advertised or received. If the book was received in worse condition than advertised you must notify us prior to the return.
· Please note used access cards will not be accepted for returns.
· Orders returned after 30 days may not receive a refund.

How to contact us:
1. Go to Your Orders.
2. Find your order in the list.
3. Select Problem with order.
4. Choose your topic from list displayed.
5. Select Contact seller.

TO REORDER YOUR UPS DIRECT THERMAL LABELS:

1. Access our supply ordering web site at **UPS.COM**®
   or contact UPS at 800-877-8652.
2. Please refer to label #0277400801 when ordering.

Table of Contents

Acknowledgements

First, I want to thank Brian Sickels for his help with this edition. Brian not only wrote two of the new lessons for this edition: Lesson 24: Chalk Markings and Arena Floor Layout and Lesson 25: Angled Truss, but has also been invaluable as a technical editor for the entire book. Others who have been of help in the writing of new lessons include: Simon Captain Howdy, Jim "Doc" Doherty of IATSE - Local 8, Ben Kilmer, Alex French and Mark Pollock. Also, thanks goes to Eric Rouse for making suggestions and bring some new formulas to my attention. A special thanks goes to Steve Rees. Steve has been a proof-reader for all three editions of *Rigging Math Made Simple*. Many others have been helpful in making the third edition of *Rigging Math Made Simple* possible. I am grateful to everyone who has been of help in any way.

Finally, I want to thank all of the people who purchased the first two editions of *Rigging Math Made Simple*. This book has been far more successful than I ever imagined and I truly appreciate the fact that so many people have told me how much this book has helped them learn rigging math.

-Delbert

About the Author

Delbert Hall, Ph.D., is head of the design and technical theatre program in the Division of Theatre and Dance at East Tennessee State University, where he has taught since 1986. Dr. Hall received his Ph.D. from the University of Florida, his MFA from the University of North Carolina at Greensboro, and his B.S.Ed. from Western Carolina University. He was the U.S. Institute for Theatre Technology - Southeast Region's Outstanding Educator in Theatrical Design and Technology for 2000-2001, and received an Outstanding Achievement Award for special effects rigging from the Kennedy Center for the Arts in 2000. He is also a member of IATSE - Local 699.

Delbert has been rigging performer flying effects and aerial dance apparatus for more than 34 years. He is an ETCP certified rigger (Theatre) and an ETCP Recognized Trainer. Delbert regularly teaches workshops on rigging and rigging math and is the originator of *RigCalc*, a rigging calculator app with versions for Android and Apple iOS devices.

Delbert also does destructive testing of hardware used in the entertainment industry and fabrics used in aerial dance in order to better understand how these items break and at what loads.

Preface

The job of an entertainment rigger is to safely suspend objects (scenery, lights, sound equipment, platforms, and even performers) at very specific locations above the ground. The type, size, and location of the structural members from which these objects must be suspended vary greatly from venue to venue. Additionally, the size, weight, and location of each object varies from object to object. To ensure that each object is safely suspended at the proper location, math is essential. Sometimes this math is very simple, and sometimes it can be complex.

One reason catastrophic failures occur is because the load placed on a structural member or a piece of hardware exceeds the breaking strength of the structural member or piece of hardware. While a structural engineer must determine the strength of the structural members and the manufacturers determine the strength of the hardware, the rigger is responsible for knowing the forces that will be exerted on each rigging point and piece of hardware. Because the forces placed on each rigging point and piece of hardware are determined not only by the weight of the object (its static load) but also how the rigging is done and dynamic loads. Entertainment riggers must be able to calculate all of these loads/forces.

There are plenty of entertainment riggers who do not know how to do much math, but these are the people doing exactly what they are told to do and not the ones figuring out what to do. If you want to be a top-notch rigger, you have to know math.

Math does not have to be hard. It is a lot like baking. You need a good recipe, and then you just have to follow it - EXACTLY. The purpose of this book is to provide you with the recipes for solving rigging problems. Once you learn the recipes, you will be able figure out many rigging problems.

This book is more than a list of formulas. It will also help users grasp some of the principles behind the physics of rigging. By understanding these principles and the math behind them, entertainment riggers should be able to look at many rigging situations and determine if it is "obviously safe," or "obviously unsafe," without actually doing any math. However, there are many cases where the load is just uncertain, or the answer is not obvious, and the math needs to be done.

This book may be of particular interest to individuals who wish to become a certified rigger. Many of the mathematical problems and other information presented in this book are intended to prepare individuals for the types of questions they might encounter on a certification exam – in both theatre and arena rigging.
The lessons in this book are not intended to replace "hands-on" rigging experience. Remember, nothing can take the place of practical experience. However, the book does cover some basic rigging principles, especially the ones based on physics and math.

Getting Started

Now, before you start going crazy and screaming, "I can't do math!" - relax. Most rigging math is no more complicated than doing simple addition, subtraction, multiplication and division - the stuff you learned to do in elementary school. What's more, you can even use a calculator to help you do the math. I highly recommend the TI-30XA scientific calculator for this rigging primer. This calculator is inexpensive (under $15), available at Walmart and nearly all office supply stores, and is easy to use. But why a "scientific calculator?" Well, there are a few rigging problems that are just a lot quicker and easier to solve by using scientific functions than by using "simple math." The examples in this primer will take you through examples, step by step. So, get yourself a TI-30XA scientific calculator.

If you are not familiar with this calculator, I have provided a few notes on how to use the TI-30XA scientific calculator in Appendix 2.

What to Expect

Each lesson begins with a general explanation of the problem, where you would encounter this type of rigging problem, and how you would go about solving the problem. Some rigging problems are best understood graphically, so in many cases there will be an accompanying drawing or schematic of the problem. This is then followed by the formula (equation) used to solve the problem. (It should be noted that there are sometimes several equations, or variations on an equation, which can be used to solve a particular problem. If you know a different equation than the one that I am using, and that equation works for you, use it.) Next, I will work through a sample problem in detail and show how to get the correct answer. Finally, at the end of most lessons, there are some sample problems to solve. The answers to these problems can be found in Appendix 1.

Some problems are pretty simple, while others may require multiple steps (calculations). It is a very good idea to have scratch paper and a pencil at all times so that you can record the solutions to each step as you work them out.

At the end of each lesson, there are sample problems for you to solve. The answers to these problems are found in Appendix 1.

Another tool that you may find useful is a rigging web app that works on any device with a web browser. *PocketRigger* available from http://www.springknollpress.com/PocketRigger.html. After you have solved all the problems at the end of each lesson, you may want to create your own problems to solve. *PocketRigger* is a good tool to use to check your math and ensure that you are solving these problems correctly.

Some of the math covered in the later portions of this book is intended more for reference/knowledge than for everyday rigging. These calculations are more complex and not part of *PocketRigger*. I recommend creating a spreadsheet on your computer where you enter the formulas and use them to solve these problems.

Conventions

Each formula (equation) in the lessons includes variables. The most common variables used in this book are:

L = Leg of a bridle or Leg supporting one end of a beam (truss). Note: Sometimes this will refer to length of the Leg and at other times tension on the Leg.
H = Horizontal distance
V = Vertical distance (height)
D = Distance (usually a horizontal distance)

In many cases you will see a number (most often either a "1" or a "2") following the letter (L1, L2, H1, H2, V1, and V2 are common variable names) in problems involving bridles. The number is used to designate which of the two bridles is being referenced. The accompanying schematic will also aid in helping you understand the problem. Other common variables such as "Load" and "Span" are fairly self-explanatory.

Last, I have already stated that we will work through a sample problem in each lesson, but in the early lessons, where I tell you precisely which keys to press on your calculator, I denote the non-numeral keys to be pressed by putting them in square brackets. [X] the multiply key, [÷] the divide key, and [SIN] the sine key, are some of the keys that I indicate in this fashion.

This is Just the Beginning

If after reading this book you want to learn more rigging math, it is strongly suggested that you purchase Harry Donovan's *Entertainment Rigging: A Practical Guide*. Donovan's book is an in-depth study of arena rigging techniques, including math. Also, Jay Glerum's *Stage Rigging Handbook* is an excellent book on theatrical rigging and belongs in every entertainment technician's library. Finally, arena riggers may want to read Fred Breitfelder's *Bridle Dynamics for Production Riggers.*

<u>One Last Thing</u>

Practice, practice, practice is the best way to learn the formulas. I have created a cheat sheet with many of the formulas used in this book – Appendix 3. You can tear it out or copy it, and keep it handy for when you need to refresh your memory on a particular formula. Good luck and enjoy the lessons.

<u>Addendum (Second Edition)</u>

The biggest change to the second edition has been the addition of a unit on "Advanced Rigging." This unit deals with how rigging math is used in "real world" situations and information on apps and software for doing rigging math. One lesson even explains how to download Excel spreadsheets from our website, and how to use it. Of course all of the math used in these spreadsheets comes from lessons in this book.

Having rigging apps and spreadsheets does not mean that knowing the math is obsolete. These aids just help you do it faster. Knowing the math principles behind the apps and spreadsheets will always be important because they help you understand the meaning of results of the calculations, not just the numbers.

As you advance as a rigger, you will understand that math is more than numbers, it is about what those numbers represent, and how to best use them to your advantage. Rigging is both an art and a science, and they must work together.

I always say in my workshops and seminars that a good rigger is proud of his work and eager to show it off to anyone who wants, or is willing, to see it. A rigger who knows his stuff should be happy to explain why he rigged something a particular way, and that may mean explaining the math behind the decisions. Again, if the rigger really knows his stuff, he can easily explain the rigging. And the ability to explain the rigging is a sign of professional – someone to be respected.

Finally, I have created a FaceBook group so interested riggers can discuss rigging math. The link to join this new group is: https://www.facebook.com/groups/1383812178507795/

<u>Addendum (Third Edition)</u>

The third edition adds more rigging calculations, for both theatrical and arena riggers - eight new lessons. Arena riggers will appreciate Lesson 24: Chalk Markings and Arena Floor Layout and Lesson 25: Angled Truss. Theatre riggers will like Lesson 31: Counterweight Bricks, Lesson 32: Pullout Capacity of Lag Bolts, Lesson 33: Drawbridge Problem and Lesson 34: Allowable Loads on Pipe Battens. If you are really interested in learning math, Lesson 34: Trigonometry, is for you. And, if you are interested in getting your rigging certification, Lesson 35: The ETCP Certified Rigger - Formula Table, will be of particular interest.

Not only are there new lessons, but many of the old lessons have been revised or expanded. New, simpler, methods for solving some rigging problems have replaced methods from previous editions of this book. Also added is a new Appendix on shackles. In all, there are almost 100 pages of new material in this edition. Plus, there are new files (spreadsheets) for you to download and use.

I really hope you enjoy this new edition and you find the material both fun and enlightening. And as always - Rig Safe.

Unit I:

Conversions

Lesson 1:

Converting between Imperial and Metric Units

This unit only has one lesson, but it is a lesson with many parts – formulas – that will help you convert between metric and imperial units of measurements. The reason it is a single lesson is that all of the formulas in the lesson are based on the same principle. Once you understand the principle, and memorize the "magic numbers," solving the problems is simple.

There are two tricks to converting between metric and imperial measurements. The first trick is to memorize the "magic numbers" for each pairing. These numbers will be given below. The second trick is to remember that you simply multiply or divide the known number (measurement) by the magic number for that conversion to get the unknown number (measurement). Based on my "magic numbers," you always **multiply** when you convert Metric to Imperial and you always **divide** when you convert Imperial to Metric. Keep this in mind as you go through this lesson.

How you remember the magic numbers will be different for different people. I will explain how I remember them in each part, but my method may not work for you.

Note: The number in parentheses (xx.xx) in the equations below is the answer to the problem.

Converting between Meters and Feet

The magic number to remember for converting between feet and meters is **3.28** (1 meter = **3.28** feet). So,

Meters to Feet

Meters $\times$ *3.28 = Feet*

Example: 5 meters is equal to how many feet?

[ON/C] 5 [X] **3.28** [=]   (16.4)

(Note: 5 is the known number and 3.28 is the magic number)

Feet to Meters

Feet / 3.28 = Meters

Example: 60 feet are equal to how many meters?

[ON/C] 60 [÷] **3.28** [=]   (18.29)

How I remember **3.28**: I know that a meter is more than 3 feet (actually a little more than 39 inches) that gives me the 3. How much more than three feet? Those three-plus inches are a little more than ¼ of a foot, and 0.28 is a little more than 0.25. After doing some equations, 3.28 just looks right, so I remember it.

Converting between Centimeters (cm) or Millimeters (mm) and Inches

The magic number to remember for converting between centimeters or millimeters and inches is **3937** (1 centimeter = **0.3937** inches) and (1 millimeter = **0.03937** inches). So,

Centimeters to Inches

Centimeters × 0.3937 = Inches

Example: 30 centimeters are equal to how many inches?

[ON/C] 30 [X] 0.3937 [=]   (11.81)

Inches to Centimeters

Inches / 0.3937 = Centimeters

Example: 3 Inches are equal to how many centimeters?

[ON/C] 3 [÷] 0.3937 [=]   (7.62)

Converting from millimeters to inches and inches to millimeters is exactly the same as converting from centimeters to inches and inches to centimeter, except a millimeter is 1/10th as large as a centimeter, so just move the decimal place of the magic number one place to the left (use 0.03937 instead of 0.3937).

Millimeters to Inches

Millimeters × 0.03937 = Inches

Example: 15 mm are equal to how many inches?

[ON/C] 15 [X] 0.03937 [=]   (0.59)

Inches to Millimeters

Inches / 0.03937 = Millimeters

Example: 0.35 Inches are equal to how many millimeters?

[ON/C] 0.35 [÷] 0.03937 [=]   (8.89)

How I remember **3937**:   I remember that a meter is a little more than 39 inches long, so that is where I get the 39. Since I like repetition it would be cool if the magic number was 3939, but I know it is not – it is a little off – a little less (2 to be exact). So, 3937 it is.

Converting between KiloNewtons (kN) and Pounds

A kiloNewton is a measurement for force, and the breaking strength of rock climbing hardware is commonly rated in kiloNewtons (kN). The magic number for converting between kiloNewtons and pounds is **224.8** (1 kiloNewton = **224.8** pounds). For practical purposes **225** will do fine and might be easier for you to remember. So, let's use **225** in our examples.

KiloNewtons to Pounds

KiloNewtons × 225 = Pounds

Example: 53 kiloNewtons are equals to how many pounds?

[ON/C] 53 [X] 225 [=]   (11,925)

Pounds to KiloNewtons

Pounds / 225 = kiloNewtons

Example: 2000 pounds is equal to how many kiloNewtons?

[ON/C] 2000 [÷] 225 [=]   (8.88)

How I remember **225** and **224.8**: 225 is just an easy number to remember. In converting between metric and imperial, "2" seems to come up a great deal. In this case it is ".2", and I subtract it from 225 to get 224.8.

Converting between Kilograms and Pounds

The magic number for converting between kilograms (kg) and pounds is **2.2** (**1 kilograms = 2.2 pounds**). Both parts of this number are "2", so that should be easy to remember.

Kilograms to Pounds

Kilograms × 2.2 = Pounds

Example: 6 kilos are equals to how many pounds?

[ON/C] 6 [X] 2.2 [=]   (13.2)

Pounds to Kilograms

Pounds / 2.2 = Kilograms

Example: 2,000 pounds is equal to how many kilograms?

[ON/C] 2,000 [÷] 2.2 [=]   (909.09)

How I remember **2.2**: This is easy - repetition.

Note: The term "Kip" should not be confused with "Kilogram." A "Kip" is simply an abbreviation for 1,000 pounds ("K" meaning thousand).

Sample Problems – Lesson 1

1. 3 meters = _____ feet?

2. 8 meters = _____ feet?

3. 14.6 meters = _____ feet?

4. 17 feet = _____ meters?

5. 2 feet = _____ meters?

6. 5.5 feet = _____ meters?

7. 20 centimeters = _____ inches?

8. 120 centimeters = _____ inches?

9. 55 centimeters = _____ inches?

10. 24 inches = _____ centimeters?

11. 4 inches = _____ centimeters?

12. 17.5 inches = _____ centimeters?

13. 6 millimeters = _____ inches?

14. 44 millimeters = _____ inches?

15. 21 millimeters = _____ inches?

16. 1.5 inches = _____ millimeters?

17. 0.375 inches = _____ millimeters?

18. .8 inches = _____ millimeters?

19. 12 kiloNewtons = _____ pounds?

20. 0.7 kiloNewtons = _____ pounds?

21. 23 kiloNewtons = _____ pounds?

22. 5000 pounds = _____ kiloNewtons?

23. 175 pounds = _____ kiloNewtons?

24. 3600 pounds = _____ kiloNewtons?

25. 14 kilos = _____ pounds?

26. 145 kilos = _____ pounds?

27. 325 kilos = _____ pounds?

28. 3500 pounds = _____ kilograms?

29. 210 pounds = _____ kilograms?

30. 450 pounds = _____ kilograms?

Unit II:

Pulley Math

Lesson 2:
Resultant Forces

<u>Understanding Resultant Forces</u>

Let me begin this lesson by discussing pulleys. Everyone knows that a pulley is used to change the direction of a rope or cable. What is less understood is the load that is exerted on a pulley and beam to which the pulley is attached when a pulley system is used in lifting a load. The term "resultant force" is commonly used to refer to the load on the pulley and its supporting beam. It should be understood that the load/force on the beam is seldom equal to the load being lifted. This force can be a fraction of the load being lifted or as great as twice the load being lifted. The determining factor is how much the rope or cable bends around the sheave of the pulley as it changes direction.

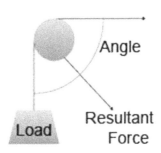

Also note that the direction/angle of the resultant force bisects the two lines. So if the angle of the cable is 90 degrees, the resultant force is at 45 degrees.

The equation for computing the resultant force is:

$$Resultant\ Force = Load \times \frac{sine\ of\ angle}{sine\ of\ (angle/2)}$$

Don't let this formula scare or confuse you. This equation can be broken into two parts: The first part is the load being lifted, and the second part, the scary and confusing part, is the multiplying factor (MF). The MF is the sine of the angle divided by the sine of half the angle as shown by the formula:

$$\frac{sine\ of\ angle}{sine\ of\ (angle/2)}$$

This MF is based on the angle of the rope/cable going into the sheave compared to the angle of rope/cable after it exits the sheave. Below are some examples of "angles" in order to help you understand them better.

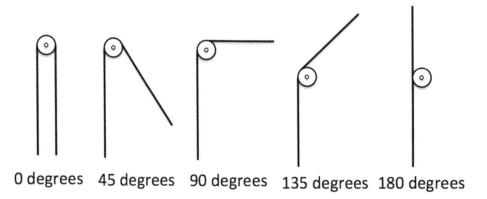

0 degrees   45 degrees   90 degrees   135 degrees   180 degrees

So, using this equation, let's work through a problem.

Example: What is the resultant force on a beam when the load being lifted is 200 lb and the angle of the cable is 90 degrees?

First, let's compute the multiplying factor.

[ON/C] 90 [SIN] [÷] 45 [SIN] [=]   (1.41)   *Note: Since I could calculate* $\frac{90}{2}$ *in my head (45), I did.*

Now, I multiply the MF (the result of my last calculation) by the Load.

[X] 200 [=] (282.84) lb   Note: Since I wanted to use the result of my last calculation in this one, I did not press the [ON/C] to clear that result.

Using the same Load, try different angles. You will discover that the greater the angle, the lower the MF; and the smaller the angle, the greater the MF.

Note: If the angle is zero degrees, this formula does not work since you cannot divide by zero. Luckily, anytime your angle is zero degrees, your MF is automatically 2, which is easy to remember. In fact, you should "know" the MFs for many of the common angles. Here is a list:

Angle (degrees)	MF
0	2.0
90	1.41
120	1.0
180	0.0

IMPORTANT: Do not confuse the Resultant Force (the tension on the pulley and the structure supporting the pulley) with the tension on the rope/cable. If the load that is being lifted weighs 200 pounds, then 200 pounds is the tension on the rope/cable, even if the Resultant Force on a pulley and supporting beam is different.

One last thing: if you do not know the angle, you can calculate it using the formula:

$$Angle = Arctangent\ of\ \left(\frac{Offset}{Distance}\right)$$ Note: An example of this is shown in Lesson 4.

Resultant Force at Zero Degrees

When the angle of the line is zero degrees, such as with a block-and-tackle, use the following rules to find the resultant force on the beam:

- If the working end of the line is coming off of a <u>stationary</u> pulley, then

   Resultant Force = Load + force need to support the load

- If the working end of the line is coming off of a <u>moving</u> pulley, then

   Resultant Force = Load - force need to support the load

Let's look at some examples.

Example 1   Example 2

In both of these examples we have a 2:1 mechanical advantage, but the result forces on the beams are considerable different. Assuming the load in both examples are 100 pounds, let's calculate the load on the beam.

In Example 1, the working end of the line is coming off a moving pulley, so we use the formula: *Resultant Force = Load - force need to support the load.* Because this is a 2:1 MA, the force needed to support the load is 50 pounds. *So,*

Resultant Force = 100 - 50

Resultant Force = 50 pounds

In Example 2, the working end of the line is coming off a stationary pulley, so we use the formula: *Resultant Force = Load + force need to support the load.* Again, the force needed to support the load is 50 pounds. *So,*

Resultant Force = 100 + 50

Resultant Force = 150 pounds

Let's look at two more examples.

Example 3   Example 4

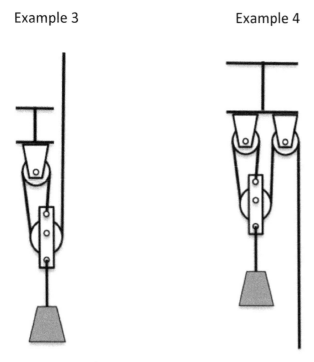

In both of these examples we have a 3: 1 MA. If the load is 100 pounds, then it take 33.33 pounds to support the load. Let's calculate the Resultant Force on the beams for these examples.

In Example 3, the working end of the line is coming off a moving pulley, so:

Resultant Force = 100 - 33.33

Resultant Force = 66.67 pounds

In Example 4, the working end of the line is coming off a stationary pulley, so:

Resultant Force = 100 + 33.33

Resultant Force = 133.33 pounds

Note: http://www.thecrosbygroup.com/html/default.htm#/en/calc/snatchblockrigcalc.htm contains a calculator that can be used to determine the force on a beam in these types of rigs.

Horizontal and Vertical Forces on an Anchor Point

At the beginning of this lesson I said, "the direction/angle of the resultant force bisects the two lines. So if the angle of the cable is 90 degrees, the resultant force is at 45 degrees." This is very important here because you need to know the angle of the Resultant Force in order to calculate the Horizontal and Vertical forces that the Resultant Force puts on the anchor point (the beam supporting the pulley).

Let's look at two examples:

Example 1.

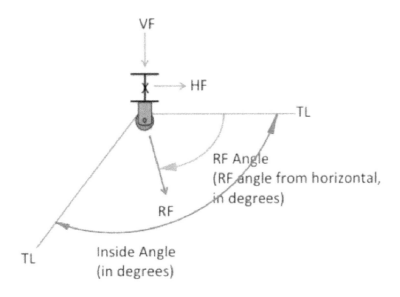

Below is the legend for this diagram.

TL - Tension on Line (Equal to the weight of the Load on Line)
RF - Resultant Force
HF - Horizontal Force on point
VF - Vertical Force on point

The two equations you need are:

$$HF = RF \times COS \ of \ RF \ Angle$$

and

$$VF = RF \times SIN \ of \ RF \ Angle$$

So, let's solve Example 1.

If *Load* = 100 lb and RF *Angle* = 50 degrees
TL = 100 lb
RF = 128.55 lb
HF = 82.63 lb
VF = 98.48 lb

Example 2.

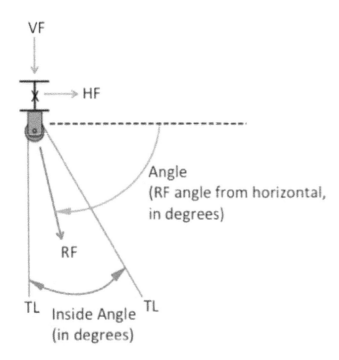

If *Load* = 100 lb and RF *Angle* = 75 degrees

TL = 100 lb

RF = 193.185 lb

HF = 50 lb

VF = 186.6 lb

Note: For this type of problem, you must always measure the RF angle from the horizontal line that is on the same side of the pulley as the RF.

While you may not commit these formulas to memory, knowing the Horizontal and Vertical forces can be very useful in many rigging situations, so remember where they are found in this book so that you can find them when you need them.

Sample Problems – Lesson 2

1. What is the resultant force on a beam when the load being lifted is 300 lb and the angle of the cable is 45 degrees?

2. What is the resultant force on a beam when the load being lifted is 330 lb and the angle of the cable is 135 degrees?

3. What is the resultant force on a beam when the load being lifted is 175 lb and the angle of the cable is 50 degrees?

4. What is the resultant force on a beam when the load being lifted is 300 lb and the angle of the cable is 15 degrees?

5. What is the resultant force on a beam when the load being lifted is 200 lb and the angle of the cable is 180 degrees?

Lesson 3:
Mechanical Advantage

In Lesson 2 you learned that when a rope or cable passes around a pulley a resultant force occurs. If the angle between the entering and exiting parts of the line is less than 120 degrees, then the resultant force is greater than the tension on the line. You also learned if that angle is zero degrees (the line makes a 180 degree turn), then the resultant force on the pulley and whatever structural member is supporting it is twice the load being lifted. At first glance, doubling the load seems to be a bad thing, and it can be. However, you can use the principle of resultant forces to your advantage to make it easier to lift a load. We call this mechanical advantage.

In Lesson 2 we were only dealing with "fixed" or "stationary" pulleys. This means that they are attached to a structural member and do not move – other than their sheaves rotating. In this lesson, we will look at pulleys that are intended to physically move when a load is lifted. These pulleys are sometimes called "running" pulleys. Look at the two examples below and ask yourself, "Is there a pulley in motion (is there a running pulley)?" If the answer is "No" then there is no mechanical advantage. If the answer is "Yes" then there is a mechanical advantage, and you will need to figure out how much.

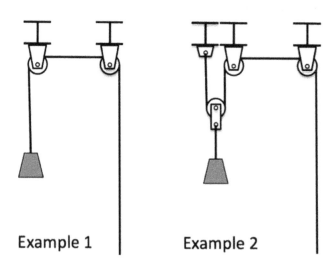

Example 1   Example 2

Before we learn to figure out how much mechanical advantage exists, let's look at how mechanical advantage is expressed. Typically, mechanical advantage is expressed as a ratio, such as 2:1. The number on the left is the "result" of the "effort" of the number on the right. In this example, 2 pounds can be supported for every 1 pound of effort. So, 300 pounds of load can be supported with only 150 pounds of effort. If the mechanical advantage (MA) is 5:1, 300 pounds can be supported with only 60 pounds of effort.

Wow, mechanical advantage is great. But not perfect. You do not get something for nothing. What you give up is speed of lifting. With a 5:1 MA the person doing the lifting must pull 5 feet of rope in order to lift the load 1 foot. So, mechanical advantage is wonderful if you need to lift a heavy load, but DO NOT have to lift it quickly.

Sometimes you see mechanical advantage listed as a single number, such as 2 or 5. These are simplified version of 2:1 and 5:1. Think of them as 2 divided by 1 equals **2**, and 5 divided by 1 equals **5**. This abbreviation works well until you get to complex mechanical advantages such as 3:2 (3 pounds can be supported for every 2 pounds of effort, which we will discuss later in this lesson).

Computing Mechanical Advantage

Computing mechanical advantage is almost as easy as counting, but first you have to know "what" to count. The "what" is the number of parts of the lift line that are applying a force on the running pulley. Because mechanical advantage is created by the running pulley, that is where you must look.

A helpful "Rule of Thumb" for quickly determining mechanical advantage is to count the number of parts of the lift line that are applying force on the running block.

Remember, it does not matter if the load being lifted is connected directly to the running pulley or to a secondary line that is connected to the running pulley (and that line passes over other pulleys). The mechanical advantage is created by the number of lift line parts (the one the operator pulls) acting upon the running pulley.

Look at the three examples below. Identify the running block in each example and count the number of parts of the lift line that are acting upon it. Despite the number of pulleys in each system, they are all examples of 2:1 MA because the running pulley is acted upon by only two parts of the lift line.

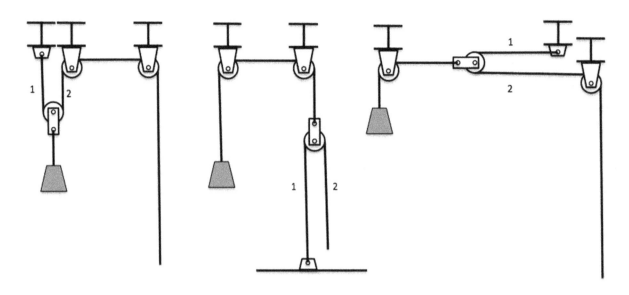

A 2:1 MA is about as simple as you can get. When you have an "odd" amount of MA, one part of the lift line must connect directly to the running pulley. See the examples of a 3:1 MA and 5:1 MA below.

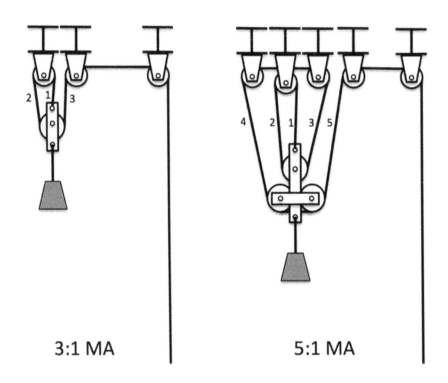

3:1 MA   5:1 MA

Below are two examples of complex 3:1 mechanical advantage rigging.

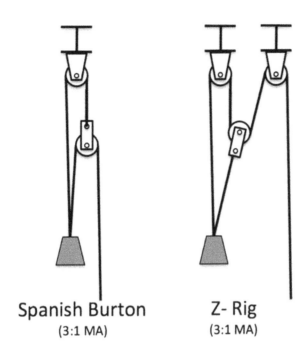

Spanish Burton
(3:1 MA)

Z- Rig
(3:1 MA)

To figure out the MA of these systems you need to think of each one as a two-part system that is interlinked (the MAs added to reveal the total MA). Below is a diagram of the two parts of the Spanish Burton. What is confusing is that some components are used in <u>both</u> sub-systems in different ways but at the same time.

The pulley shown in the diagram in the left (below) functions as a stationary pulley, so the line passing through it and to the load has a 1:1 mechanical advantage. The diagram on the right shows this same pulley as a moving pulley and the two parts of the line passing through it. This creates a 2:1 mechanical advantage that acts upon the line attached to the top of this pulley. This line travels to the load to create a second lifting line with its own mechanical advantage. Since both of these actions are occurring at the same time, we have to add the two mechanical advantages. Therefore, the total mechanical advantage is 3:1.

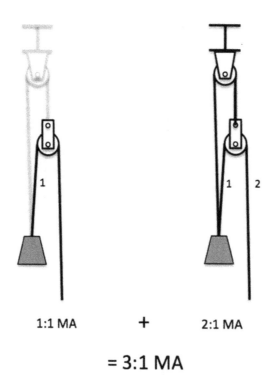

1:1 MA   +   2:1 MA

= 3:1 MA

After you have studied this system, try to figure out how the Z-Rig works.

Sometimes two lines may be used to create the mechanical advantage, as in the example below:

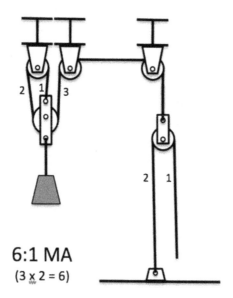

6:1 MA
(3 x 2 = 6)

Mechanical Advantage/ Mechanical Disadvantage

Earlier, I described the MA ratio by saying, "The number on the left is the 'result' of the 'effort' of the number on the right." This implies that there are two parts to every MA system. When we wanted to create a simple mechanical advantage (2:1, 3:1, 4:1, 5:1 etc.), we were only concerned with creating the "result" since our natural effort is 1. What if 2:1 is too much MA (too slow) but 1:1 is not enough MA? Is there a way to rig something in between (1.5:1)? Of course we would not express it this way, since "1.5" is not a whole number and there is no way to rig a "half" of a MA. But 3:2 is the same ratio as 1.5:1, and we can rig a 3:2 MA.

To understand these ratios a little better, let's look at it graphically. Look at the drawing below. Remember when I said, "Because mechanical advantage is created by the running pulley, that is where you must look." Well, what is the dividing line between the two parts of the system? It is the colon (:). On one side is a 3:1 MA and on the other is a 1:1 MA (no mechanical advantage). When you combine these halves (multiply the two left halves of the ratios together and then the right halves of the ratios together), the result is 3:1.

Note: Anytime you multiply any ratio by 1:1, you get the original number.

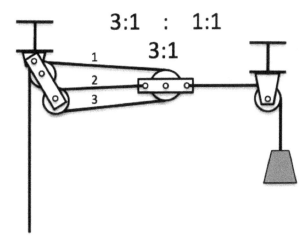

So, to get a 3:2 MA, we need to have a 3:1 MA on one side and 1:2 MA on the other (3 x 1 = <u>3</u> and 1 x 2 = <u>2</u>, so 3:2).

What is a 1:2 MA? It is a mechanical disadvantage (MD) – where the result is less than the effort. In this example, it means that 1 pound of load can be supported for every 2 pounds of effort. In effect, it divides our efforts in half. And half of 3 is 1.5, exactly what we wanted. This system would look like:

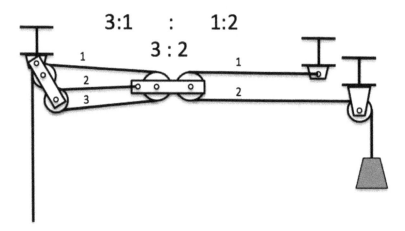

This is one example of a "compound" mechanical advantage system. A compound mechanical advantage system is where you have one simple mechanical system acting upon another simple mechanical advantage system. Sometimes one of the systems is mechanical disadvantage, as above, and sometimes it just multiplies the mechanical advantage of the first system.

Tracing the Forces

The best way to figure out the mechanical advantage or mechanical disadvantages of any system, no matter how complicated, is to "trace the forces" from the load to the operator, and then compare the two numbers. Below is a fairly convoluted mixture of MA and MD systems. Begin with a load of 100 pounds and trace the forces back along every part of the line until you reach the operator. By comparing these numbers, we can discover the ratio.

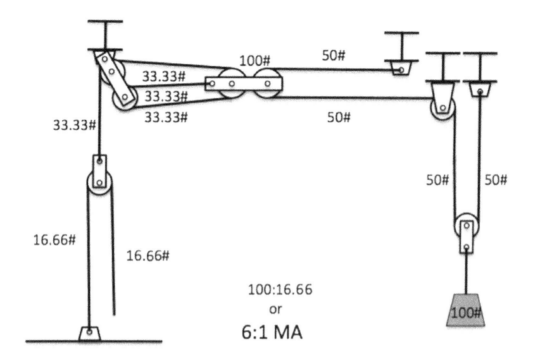

"Tracing the Forces" means, starting with the "known" load (in this case 100 lb), working backward (toward the operator) labeling the force on each part of the line as you go. Remember, the force on a line does not change just because it passes around a pulley. The force only changes as a result of a moving pulley. The goal is to determine the amount of force that the operator must apply in order to support the load on the other end of the system. Dividing the weight of the load by the amount of force needed to support it gives you the MA of the system.

Sample Problem – Lesson 3

What is the force on each part of the line and the mechanical advantage of the system below?

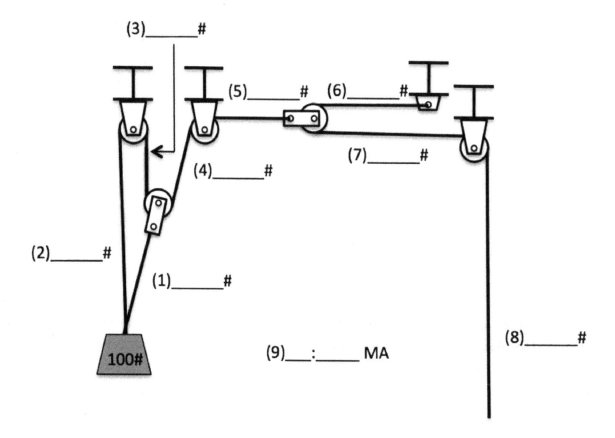

(3)_____#

(5)_____#   (6)_____#

(4)_____#

(7)_____#

(2)_____#

(1)_____#

(8)_____#

100#

(9)____:_____ MA

Lesson 4:

Fleet Angles and D:d Ratios

Fleet Angles

In an ideal world, when a cable runs over the sheave in a loft block (or any other type of block or pulley), the cable should be perfectly perpendicular to the axle. If this were true, then the cable would align perfectly with the groove in the sheave, and its fleet angle would be 0 degrees. We do not live in a perfect world, and when a cable runs between the head block and a loft block (for example), the cable might not be perfectly aligned with the groove in one or both sheaves. If this is the case, the cable can cause the groove to wear since the cable is harder than the sheave. The farther out of alignment (a fleet angle greater than zero), the more (and faster) the sheave will wear. Stage rigging manufacturers specify that the blocks or pulleys used in stage rigging should be installed so that the fleet angle of the cable is no greater than 1.5 degrees. This raises the question, "How can you tell if the fleet angle is 1.5 degrees or less?" That is the subject of this lesson.

To start, we need to establish a line with a zero degree fleet angle (the dotted line in the diagram below) to the groove of the sheaves – the dotted line in the diagram below. This assumes that both sheaves are parallel to each other. Once this is done, we compare the "Offset" (measurement) to the "Distance" between the sheaves.

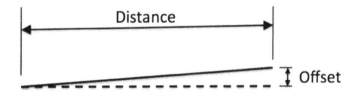

An often used rule of thumb for finding the Maximum Allowable Offset (based on 1.5 degrees) is that you are allowed 1 unit of "Offset" for every 40 units of "Distance."

A better and almost as simple equation for solving this type of problem is:

Maximum Allowable Offset (in inches) = Distance (in feet) × 0.314

Note: You can remember 0.314 by remembering that it is Pi, with the decimal moved one place to the left. So, 3.14 becomes 0.314.

Using this equation, let's calculate the Maximum Allowable Offset when the Distance between the sheaves is 25 feet.

Maximum Allowable Offset = 25 X 0.314 = 7.85 inches

Computing the actual fleet angle

If you want to know the actual fleet angle (in degrees), you must know both the Offset Distance and the Measurement Distance. Then, plug these numbers into the following equation:

$$Angle = Arctangent\ of\ \left(\frac{Offset\ Distance}{Measurement\ Distance}\right)$$

So, if the Offset is 6" (0.5 feet) and the Distance is 25 feet, the fleet angle is:

$$Angle = Arctangent\ of\ \left(\frac{0.5}{25}\right)$$

Note: On the TI-30XA calculator, arctangent is denoted as "TAN-1" and is entered by using the [2nd] and [TAN] keys.

Angle = Arctangent of 0.02

$$Angle = 1.145\ degrees$$

D:d Ratios

When we speak of the D:d ratio, we are speaking of the diameter of the sheave's tread (D) compared to the diameter of the fiber or wire rope that runs over the sheave (d).

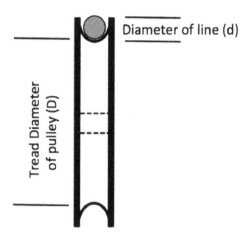

This ratio affects the strength of the line, as well as its lifespan. The smaller the D:d ratio, the sharper the bend and the greater the stress on the line. Both fiber and wire rope manufacturers have "Recommended D:d Ratios" for their products.

Most manufacturers of fiber ropes recommend a minimum D:d ratio of 8:1, although it is common to see ropes passing over sheaves with a D:d ratio of 4:1 or smaller. The minimum recommended D:d ratio for 7x19 and 6x19 construction wire ropes (the most common constructions used in entertainment rigging) is 30:1. Wire ropes with 7x7 construction are stiffer and have a recommended minimum D:d ratio of 40:1. Several sheave manufacturers make sheaves for wire ropes that have D:d ratios of 40:1, 20:1, and smaller. Ratios of 16:1 and smaller significantly decrease the lifespan of the cable. Using a sheave with a D:d ratio that is greater than the recommended minimum D:d ratio will give the rope a greater lifespan.

The sharpness of the bend on the rope also decreases the breaking strength of the rope. The listed breaking strength of a rope is based on a "straight pull." When a rope is forced to bend around a sheave, the tension on the outside of the bend is greater than the tension at the core of the rope, thereby reducing the breaking strength. The table below shows the strength efficiency rating of 7x19 and 6x19 construction wire ropes, based on various D:d ratios.

D:d Ratio	Strength Efficiency	D:d Ratio	Strength Efficiency
40:1	95%	6:1	79%
30:1	93%	8:1	83%
20:1	91%	4:1	75%
15:1	89%	2:1	65%
10:1	86%	1:1	50%

To determine the minimum recommended diameter of sheave for a particular diameter of wire rope, use this equation:

Sheave diameter (in inches) = "D" factor of the D:d ratio × diameter of the rope

Example: What is the minimum recommended sheave diameter that should be used with a ¼" diameter 7x19 GAC?

Sheave diameter = 30 × 1/4"
Sheave diameter = 30/4
Sheave diameter = 7.5 inches

One more thing about sheaves
_____

Just as important as the D:d ratio is the diameter of the rope compared to the size of the groove in the sheave. This is particularly important for wire rope. The groove in the sheave should be slightly larger than the diameter of the rope. The groove should support between 120 and 170 degrees of the circumference of the rope. If less than 120 degrees of the rope's circumference is supported (the groove is too large), the rope will "flatten" on the sheave's tread, and damage the rope. Be sure that the groove is properly sized for the diameter of rope that you are using.

Sample Problems – Lesson 4

1. What is the maximum allowable offset for a cable at 40 feet?

2. What is the maximum allowable offset for a cable at 10 feet?

3. What is the maximum allowable offset of a cable at 25 feet?

4. What is the maximum allowable offset of a cable at 60 feet?

5. What is the maximum allowable offset of a cable at 50 feet?

6. What is the fleet angle of a cable whose offset is 8" at 30 feet?

7. What is the fleet angle of a cable whose offset is 4" at 8 feet?

8. What is the fleet angle of a cable whose offset is 13" at 40 feet?

9. What is the fleet angle of a cable whose offset is 9" at 20 feet?

10. What is the fleet angle of a cable whose offset is 5" at 50 feet?

Unit III:
Bridles

Bridles:
Introduction

Sometimes there is a structural member directly above the location where you need a supporting line and sometimes not. When there is no structural member directly above the needed point, bridles are often used to create a single rigging point in the desired location. Bridles are usually hung in pairs in a "V" shape, but sometimes they are arranged in groups of three or even four legs. The point where these legs converge is called a bridle point. The length of each bridle leg is determined by the horizontal and vertical distances that the bridle point is from its respective anchor point on the structure above. While positioning is one purpose for a bridle, bridles can also be used to distribute the load across several points, thereby putting less force on any single point.

In Lesson 2, we saw how the vertical and horizontal forces on the line produce a diagonal Resultant Force. With a bridle, each leg is the resultant force and creates both horizontal and vertical forces on the structure to which the leg is attached. There are a few more differences. With a pulley, the forces on the "in" and "out" lines are ALWAYS the same, and the resultant force is ALWAYS halfway between the horizontal and vertical lines. With a bridle, only under very specific circumstances are either of these true.

In the bridle below, the legs are nearly vertical (the slight angle is used here in order to make both legs visible). If the legs were absolutely vertical, 100% of the load would be in a vertical direction and the weight being suspended would be equally divided between the two legs. And since the anchor points are directly above the load, there would be no load/force in the horizontal direction. Therefore, if the load being suspended weighs 100 pounds, the tension on each bridle leg would be 50 pounds.

The anchor points on the bridle below are farther apart. Once again, the combined vertical force on the anchor points must equal the weight of the suspended load. But, because the load is NOT directly below either anchor point, there is also a horizontal force on the anchor points. (It should be noted that the horizontal force on the two anchor points, no matter what it is, must be equal to each other in order for the load to not swing.) The ratio of the vertical to horizontal distances (or the angle of the bridle) is a controlling factor in the tension on each bridle leg.

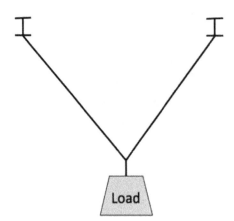

The table below shows how the tension increases as the ratio of the horizontal and vertical distances gets greater and the bridle becomes flatter. These tensions assume a 100-pound load.

Angle from vertical	Bridle Tension on each leg (lb)	Horizontal Tension on each leg (lb)
30	58	29
45	70	50
60	100	87
80	288	284
89	2,865	2,865
89.5	28,648	28,648

Note: If the bridle legs are of equal length, then the vertical load on each leg is 50 pounds.

So, it is important to realize that the closer the legs are to vertical, the less horizontal force on the beams, and, therefore, there is less tension on the bridle legs. Conversely, the flatter the legs (closer to horizontal), the greater the tension on the legs. With a little practice, by knowing the load being supported and estimating the angle of the legs, you can make a reasonably close estimate of the tension on the legs.

Now, that you have a basic understanding of the forces on bridles, let's get to the math.

Lesson 5:
Two-Point Bridles

Bridle Lengths

As stated earlier, bridles are typically hung in pairs and converge to create a new anchor point (the bridle point) somewhere between two existing anchor points. While bridles can have more than two "legs," this lesson will only deal with the two-legged variety. Each leg of a bridle can hang from different heights, be different lengths, and be at different angles. Since we will be computing the lengths of both bridle legs, we will call one Leg 1 (L1) and the other one Leg 2 (L2).

In order to compute the length of each leg, we will need to know a) how low the bridle point is below the anchor point for that leg of the bridle (vertical distance), and b) how far the bridle point is away from the anchor point for that leg of the bridle in a horizontal distance. See drawing below.

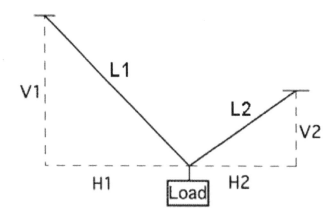

By knowing the V and H lengths, we can compute the length of L (the hypotenuse of the right triangle) by using the Pythagorean Theorem $A^2 + B^2 = C^2$, only we will use $V^2 + H^2 = L^2$, converted into the equation $L = \sqrt{H^2 + V^2}$

So, let's do it.

Example: Calculate the lengths of L1 and L2 where, V1 = 10', H1 = 4', V2 = 6, and H2 = 3'.

L1 = 10 [X²] [+] 4 [X²] [=][√x̄]

L1 = 10.77 feet

L2 = 6 [X²] [+] 3 [X²] [=][√x̄]

L2 = 6.7 feet

When working with any type of bridle problem, I like to draw a diagram, similar to the one above, and label the known distances. I find it much easier to solve most rigging problems when I can "see" what it looks like graphically. Try it, and see if it helps you.

<u>But what is the angle of the bridle?</u>

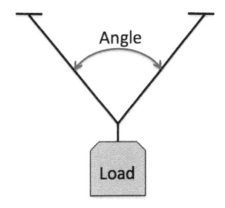

For those of you who are really interested in this question, here is the equation:

$$Angle = \left(Arctangent\ \left(\frac{H1}{V1}\right)\right) + \left(Arctangent\ \left(\frac{H2}{V2}\right)\right)$$

Note: Calculating arctangents was discussed in Lesson 4.

So to find the angle of the bridles above, we do the following:

Angle = [ON/C] 4 [÷] 10 [=] [2ⁿᵈ] [TAN]   Note: Write the result down (21.8)
        [ON/C] 3 [÷] 6 [=] [2ⁿᵈ] [TAN]   Note: Write the result down (26.56)

Angle = 21.8 [+] 26.56

Angle = 48.36 degrees

Why is it important to know the bridle angle? There are at least two reasons. First, it is a good practice to keep the angle of pull on a shackle to 90 degrees or less, unless head room is an issue. Secondly, bridle angles greater than 120 degrees (called a "flat bridle") will put a greater force on the support point/structure than the weight load being supported. In fact, a flat bridle can easily create huge (unsafe) forces. It is a lot easier to see/estimate a 90 degree angle than a 120 angle. Also, you can use the corner of a credit card or a dollar bill to compare it to the bridle to check if the angle is greater or less than 90 degrees.

Sample Problems – Lesson 5

1. Calculate the lengths of both legs of a bridle (L1 and L2) where V1 is 6', H1 is 2', V2 is 6' and H2 is 4'.

2. Calculate the lengths of both legs of a bridle (L1 and L2) where V1 is 12', H1 is 3', V2 is 12' and H2 is 4'.

3. Calculate the lengths of both legs of a bridle (L1 and L2) where V1 is 16', H1 is 6', V2 is 14' and H2 is 5'.

4. Calculate the lengths of both legs of a bridle (L1 and L2) where V1 is 9', H1 is 7', V2 is 9' and H2 is 3'.

5. Calculate the lengths of both legs of a bridle (L1 and L2) where V1 is 11', H1 is 7', V2 is 13' and H2 is 7'.

6. Calculate the angle between the bridles L1 and L2 where V1 is 6', H1 is 2', V2 is 6' and H2 is 4'.

7. Calculate the angle between the bridles L1 and L2 where V1 is 12', H1 is 3', V2 is 12' and H2 is 4'.

8. Calculate the angle between the bridles L1 and L2 where V1 is 16', H1 is 6', V2 is 14' and H2 is 5'.

9. Calculate the angle between the bridles L1 and L2 where V1 is 9', H1 is 7', V2 is 9' and H2 is 3'.

10. Calculate the angle between the bridles L1 and L2 where V1 is 11', H1 is 7', V2 is 13' and H2 is 7'.

Lesson 6:

Tension on Bridle Legs

Now that you know how to compute the lengths of the bridle legs, you can compute the load on each leg. But before we do that, let's discuss the angle between the two legs. We said in the introduction to this unit that bridles are used to create a new anchor point between two existing hanging points, and this is true. It is also true that the two bridle legs share the load being lifted (but not always equally), and bridles can be used to reduce the load on anchor points. You should realize that it is possible to use different combinations of bridle lengths to get the bridle point at the same horizontal position, relative to the existing hanging points, but at different vertical relations to the existing anchor points. In many cases, it is desirable to have the bridle point as high as possible so that it is not seen. But, the higher you place this point, the wider the bridle angle (angle between the two bridle legs) and the greater the forces on the bridle legs. As a general rule, the bridle angle should not exceed 120 degrees. Remember, if the bridle angle is greater than 120 degrees, then the load on at least one of the legs will be greater than the load being lifted. Bridles with very wide angles (flat bridles) can put tremendous loads on their hanging points. Also, some beams are designed to hold force in a particular direction (usually a vertical direction) and may not tolerate horizontal or resultant forces.

To compute the tension on the two bridles, we use the equations

$$Tension\ on\ L1 = Load\ \times\ \frac{L1 \times H2}{(V1 \times H2) + (V2 \times H1)}$$

$$Tension\ on\ L2 = Load\ \times\ \frac{L2 \times H1}{(V1 \times H2) + (V2 \times H1)}$$

Before you start screaming, "I can't remember all of that!" relax and take a deep breath. I will soon teach you a trick that will make it fairly easy to remember. But before we get to that, draw a diagram like the one below.

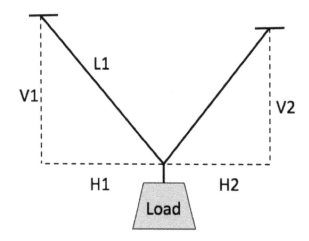

Now, add the following values to your diagram:

L1 = 5'   L2 = 6.7'
V1 = 4'   V2 = 3'
H1 = 3'   H2 = 6'
Load = 500 lb

This will help you to be able to quickly find the values that you need.

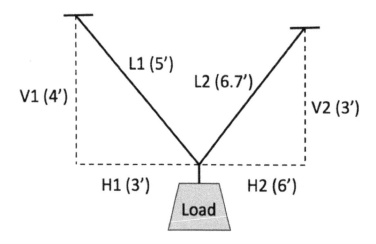

Below is the equation for finding the tension on Leg 1, but I have made the first part of the equation **BOLD**, and I have added an arrow to the diagram so that you can visualize which two numbers are multiplied.

$$\text{Tension on L1} = \text{Load} \times \frac{\text{L1} \times \text{H2}}{(\text{V1} \times \text{H2}) + (\text{V2} \times \text{H1})}$$

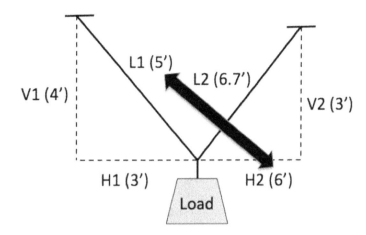

Since you want to find the tension on L1, the "trick" is to begin by multiplying L1 (high) by the "low" side of Leg 2 (which is H2). If you wanted to find the tension on L2, you would multiply L2 (high) by the "low" side of the L1 triangle, which would be H1. Got it? So plugging in these variables in our equation we get:

$$\text{Tension on L1} = \text{Load} \times \frac{\mathbf{5 \times 6}}{(V1 \times H2) + (V2 \times H1)}$$

$$\text{Tension on L1} = \text{Load} \times \frac{\mathbf{30}}{(V1 \times H2) + (V2 \times H1)}$$

Next, we want to figure out what we divide this number by. This is actually very easy to remember. We just need to remember that we multiply V on one side by H on the other, and add the two numbers together. You can also remember that you always multiply one "high" side and one "low" side, if that helps you. So, let's look at the first pair of numbers for this section of the equation:

$$\text{Tension on L1} = \text{Load} \times \frac{30}{(\mathbf{4 \times 6}) + (V2 \times H1)}$$

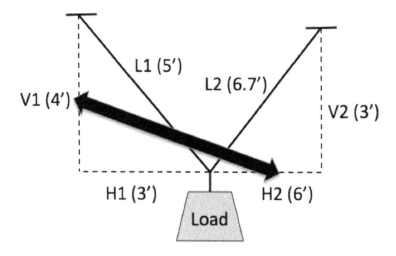

And now the second pair of numbers:

$$\text{Tension on L1} = \text{Load} \times \frac{30}{(4 \times 6) + (3 \times 3)}$$

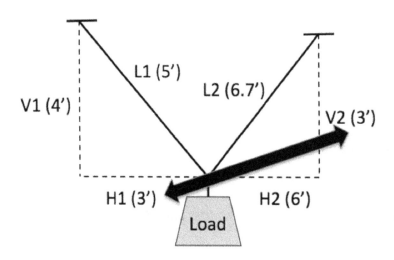

Again, one "high" side and one "low" side. So, now finish solving the equations.

$$\text{Tension on L1} = \text{Load} \times \frac{30}{(4 \times 6) + (3 \times 3)}$$

$$\text{Tension on L1} = \text{Load} \times \frac{30}{24 + 9}$$

$$\text{Tension on L1} = \text{Load} \times \frac{30}{33}$$

$$\text{Tension on L1} = \text{Load} \times .909$$

Finally, we just plug in the Load and multiply.

$$\text{Tension on L1} = \mathbf{500} \times .909$$

Tension on L1 = 454. 5 lb

Let's now calculate the tension on Leg 2.

$$\text{Tension on L2} = \text{Load} \ \times \frac{\text{L2} \times \text{H1}}{(\text{V1} \times \text{H2}) + (\text{V2} \times \text{H1})}$$

Again, we multiply the part that we are trying to find the tension on (now, L2) by the "low" number on the other side of the diagram. Substituting the values we get:

$$\text{Tension on L2} = \text{Load} \ \times \frac{\mathbf{6.7} \times \mathbf{3}}{(\text{V1} \times \text{H2}) + (\text{V2} \times \text{H1})}$$

$$\text{Tension on L2} = \text{Load} \ \times \frac{\mathbf{20.1}}{(\text{V1} \times \text{H2}) + (\text{V2} \times \text{H1})}$$

Did you notice that bottom part of this equation is exactly the same as the equation for finding the tension on Leg 1? Because they are the same, we do not have to re-calculate those numbers. We can plug-in the results from our first equation (33) and we have:

$$\text{Tension on L2} = \text{Load} \ \times \frac{20.1}{33}$$

$$\text{Tension on L2} = \text{Load} \ \times .609$$

$$\text{Tension on L2} = 500 \ \times .609$$

Tension on L2 = 304. 5 lb

This is one of the most difficult problems in this primer. The most common mistake is multiplying when you should divide or dividing when you should multiply, so work on keeping those straight. Work on more problems like this one on the worksheet. After a few problems, you should get the hang of how to do them.

Tension of Bridle Legs when one Anchor Point is Below the Apex

Most bridles will have both anchor points (beams) above the apex, as we have show so far. However, occasionally there will be a situation where one of the beams is actually even with or below the apex. When a bridle leg is even with the apex, it is called a Horizontal Breastline. This will be discussed in Lesson 7. But, for now, let's discuss how to calculate the tension on the legs when one anchor point is below the apex.

The equation is identical to the one discussed earlier

$$Tension\ on\ L1 = Load\ \times \frac{L1 \times H2}{(V1 \times H2) + (V2 \times H1)}$$

$$Tension\ on\ L2 = Load\ \times \frac{L2 \times H1}{(V1 \times H2) + (V2 \times H1)}$$

However, there is one very important twist to the equations - if an anchor point is below the apex, then the Vertical distance for the leg that is below the apex is now a negative number instead of a positive number. For example, the bridle arrangement below, V2 is a negative distance.

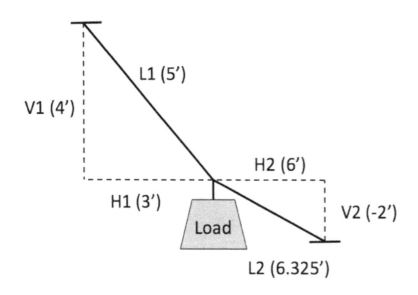

Let's calculate the tension on Leg 1 (Load is 500 lb).

$$\text{Tension on L1} = 500 \times \frac{5 \times 6}{(4 \times 6) + (-2 \times 3)}$$

$$\text{Tension on L1} = 500 \times \frac{30}{(24) + (-6)}$$

$$\text{Tension on L1} = 500 \times \frac{30}{18}$$

$$\text{Tension on L1} = 500 \times 1.66667$$

Tension on L1 = 833.333 lb

So, the first thing we see is that the tension on the bridle leg that is above the apex is greater than the Load. This is very important to realize because it is easy for the tension on this leg to be substantial.

Now, let's calculate the load on L2.

$$\text{Tension on L2} = 500 \times \frac{6.325 \times 3}{(4 \times 6) + (-2 \times 3)}$$

$$\text{Tension on L2} = 500 \times \frac{18.975}{(24) + (-6)}$$

$$\text{Tension on L2} = 500 \times \frac{18.975}{18}$$

$$\text{Tension on L2} = 500 \times 1.054$$

Tension on L2 = 527 lb

Here again the tension is greater than the Load. Whenever you have a beam that is below the apex, you must calculate these tension on these beams to ensure that you are not creating a dangerous situation.

Horizontal and Vertical Tension on Anchor Points

In the Introduction to this unit, you learned that the tension on each bridle leg creates vertical and horizontal forces on anchor points. While it is not usually critical to calculate these forces, it is not difficult to do.

The equations for calculating the vertical force on the anchor points are:

$$VF1 = \frac{V1 \times H2 \times Load}{(V1 \times H2) + (V2 \times H1)}$$

$$VF2 = Load - VF1$$

Because the combined vertical forces on these two anchor points must equal the load, once you have calculated VF1, it is very easy to calculate VF2.

Using the same bridle setup as above, calculate the vertical force on each anchor point.

$$VF1 = \frac{V1 \times H2 \times Load}{(V1 \times H2) + (V2 \times H1)}$$

$$VF1 = \frac{4 \times 6 \times 500}{(4 \times 6) + (3 \times 3)}$$

$$VF1 = \frac{12000}{24 + 9}$$

$$VF1 = \frac{12000}{33}$$

$$\mathbf{VF1 = 363.64\ lb}$$

$$VF2 = Load - VF1$$
$$VF2 = 500 - 363.64$$
$$\mathbf{VF2 = 136.36\ lb}$$

The equations for calculating the horizontal force on the anchor points are:

$$HF1 = VF1 \times \frac{H1}{V1}$$

$$HF2 = VF2 \times \frac{H2}{V2}$$

So…

$$HF1 = VF1 \times \frac{H1}{V1}$$

$$HF1 = 363.64 \times \frac{3}{4}$$

$$HF1 = 363.64 \times .75$$

$$\mathbf{HF1 = 272.73\ lb}$$

$$HF2 = VF2 \times \frac{H2}{V2}$$

$$HF2 = 136.36 \times \frac{6}{2}$$

$$HF2 = 136.36 \times 3$$

$$\mathbf{HF2 = 272.72\ lb}$$

The values for HF1 and HF2 MUST be the same, or nearly the same, depending on the rounding of numbers. In this case, the values are statistically equal. Another formula for calculating the Horizontal Force (on both points) is:

$$HF = \text{Tension on L1} \times \frac{H1}{L1}$$

Pick the formula that works best for you.

Sample Problems – Lesson 6

1. Calculate the tension on the bridles L1 and L2 where V1 is 6', H1 is 2', V2 is 6', H2 is 4', and the load is 500 lb.

2. Calculate the tension on the bridles L1 and L2 where V1 is 12', H1 is 3', V2 is 12', H2 is 4', and the load is 500 lb.

3. Calculate the tension on the bridles L1 and L2 where V1 is 16', H1 is 6', V2 is 14', H2 is 5' and the load is 350 lb.

4. Calculate the tension on the bridles L1 and L2 where V1 is 9', H1 is 7', V2 is 9', H2 is 3' and the load is 400 lb.

5. Calculate the tension on the bridles L1 and L2 where V1 is 11', H1 is 7', V2 is 13', H2 is 7' and the load is 600 lb.

Lesson 7:

Tension on a Horizontal Breastline

A breastline is a unique type of bridle leg. It is a rope or cable that runs horizontally and is used to swing/breast a hanging object out from directly beneath its suspension point(s). For example, you might breast an electric upstage or downstage in order to keep another piece of scenery away from the lighting instruments. Because this line (or lines) runs horizontally, it is not lifting the load, just pulling it out of alignment. There is no vertical force on the bridle attachment point. To compute the tension on a breastline, we use this simple equation:

$$Horizontal\ Force = Load \times \frac{H1}{V1}$$

This equation is very similar to the one that was used in Lesson 6 for finding the Horizontal Force on a hanging point:

$$HF1 = VF1 \times \frac{H1}{V1}$$

Below is a diagram of this configuration.

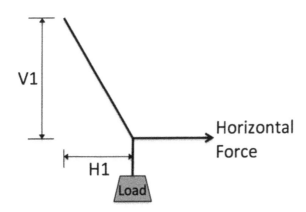

Example: Calculate the horizontal force on a breastline where V1 is 30', H1 is 2', and the Load = 700 pounds.

Before starting, note that in the earlier equations where you wanted to find the tension on the bridle, you took the length of the bridle (L) and divided it by the length of one of the other sides. Since in this problem you want to find the tension on the horizontal line, start with the length of the horizontal distance (H1) and then divide it by the length of the other side (V1). This rule for knowing which side to start your division can help make it easier to learn the equation. So, plugging the numbers into our equation, you get:

$$\text{Horizontal Force} = \text{Load} \times \frac{2}{30}$$

$$\text{Horizontal Force} = \text{Load} \times 0.0666$$

$$\text{Horizontal Force} = 700 \times 0.0666$$

Horizontal Force = 46.62 lb

Tension on the Supporting Leg

When you breast a load out of its normal hanging position, the tension on the supporting line will increase - the tension on the line will be greater than the load. The formula for calculating the tension on this line (or leg) is:

$$Tension\ on\ L1 = Load \times \frac{L1}{V1}$$

This equation is discussed in Lesson 12: Dead-hang Tension on One End of a Truss, and can be used to calculate the tension on a support line in both of these rigging situations.

Sample Problems – Lesson 7

1. Calculate the horizontal force on a breastline where V1 is 25', H1 is 3', and the Load = 500 lb.

2. Calculate the horizontal force on a breastline where V1 is 20', H1 is 10', and the Load = 500 lb.

3. Calculate the horizontal force on a breastline where V1 is 15', H1 is 15', and the Load = 500 lb.

4. Calculate the horizontal force on a breastline where V1 is 40', H1 is 5', and the Load = 500 lb.

5. Calculate the horizontal force on a breastline where V1 is 45', H1 is 7', and the Load = 500 lb.

Lesson 8:

Tension on a Deflecting Line

So far in this unit, we have looked at two methods of hanging a load in a position that is not directly below an existing beam or hanging position. This lesson will look at a third method - a deflecting line. If might be useful to think of a deflecting line as the off-spring of bridle and breastline, because it has characteristics of each.

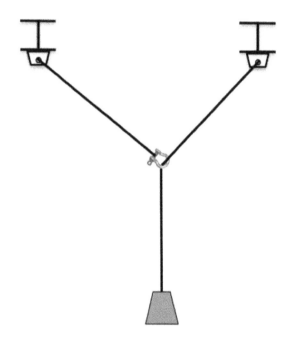

Like a breastline, the entire weight of the load actually hangs on one line (we will call this line the "main line"). This line passes through a shackle, pear ring, carabiner, or other device that is attached to a second line (the deflecting line). This piece of hardware acts as a pulley to change the angle of the main line above the apex. The tension on the main line is always the same as the weight of the load being suspended, but the tension on the deflecting line is what we need to calculate.

Since the piece of hardware at the apex acts as a pulley (in fact it could be a pulley), if you immediately thought of this as a resultant force problem - with the direction of the resultant force being identical to the angle of the deflecting line, give yourself a gold star. If you did not think of this, look at it again and see if that makes sense. We can now use the "Law of Sines" equation that we learned in Lesson 2 to solve this problem.

Before we get to solving this problem, let me introduce two new terms: *Deflected Angle* and *Included Angle*. Look at the diagram below.

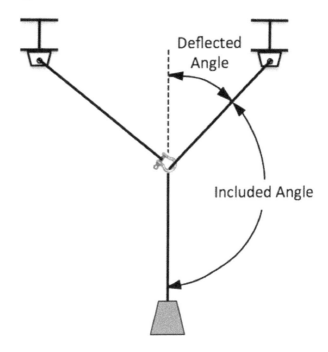

The Deflected Angle is the angle of deviation caused by the pulling of the main line out of its original plumb line. The Included Angle, what I called the "Inside Angle" in Lesson 2, is 180 degrees - the Deflected Angle. In the equation that we will use to find the tension on the deflecting line, we will need to know the Included Angle. But, to find it, we first need to know the Deflected Angle. Luckily, it is pretty easy to calculate it. Here is how.

The equation for finding the Deflected Angle is:

$$Deflected\ Angle\ =\ Arctangent\ \left(\frac{H1}{V1}\right)$$

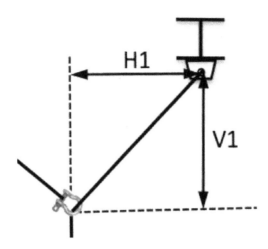

So, if H1 = 3 feet and V1 = 6 feet, then...

$$Deflected\ Angle\ =\ Arctangent\left(\frac{3}{6}\right)$$

$$Deflected\ Angle\ =\ Arctangent\ (0.5)$$

$$Deflected\ Angle\ =\ 26.565\ degrees$$

And if the Deflected Angle is 26.565 degrees, then the Included Angle is 180 - 26.565 or **153.435 degrees**.

Now, we are almost ready to calculate the tension on the Deflecting Line, we just need to know the tension (or Load) on the main line. Lets call this 100 pounds.

When we put these numbers into the Law of Sines equation, we get:

$$Resultant\ Force = Load \times \frac{sine\ of\ angle}{sine\ of\ (angle/2)}$$

$$Resultant\ Force = 100 \times \frac{sine\ (153.435}{sine\ of\ (153.435/2)}$$

$$Resultant\ Force = 100 \times \frac{0.447212797}{sine\ of\ (76.7175)}$$

$$Resultant\ Force = 100 \times \frac{0.447212797}{0.973249092}$$

$$Resultant\ Force = 100 \times 0.459504972$$

$Resultant\ Force = 45.95\ pounds$

By the way, this is not the only equation that can be used to solve this problem. Another equation that works is:

$$Tension = \sqrt{2 \times Load^2 \times COS(Included\ Angle) + 2 \times Load^2}$$

Lets plug in the numbers into this equation and solve it.

$$Tension = \sqrt{2 \times 100^2 \times COS(153.435) + 2 \times 100^2}$$

$$Tension = \sqrt{20000 \times -0.89442759 + 20000}$$

$$Tension = \sqrt{2111.448191}$$

$$Tension = 45.95\ pounds$$

Both equations give you the same answer, so you can pick the one that you can remember easiest. For me, that is the Law of Sines, but you can use either one.

Sample Problems – Lesson 8

Calculate the Resultant Force on the deflecting line when:

1. Load = 300 pounds, H1 = 8 feet, and V1 = 12 feet

2. Load = 200 pounds, H1 = 12 feet, and V1 = 12 feet

3. Load = 500 pounds, H1 = 14 feet, and V1 = 2 feet

4. Load = 300 pounds, H1 = 35 feet, and V1 = 10 feet

5. Load = 700 pounds, H1 =25 feet, and V1 = 35 feet

Lesson 9:

Three-Point Bridle Lengths

A two-point bridle uses two cables (or legs) to create a new hanging point where the two legs join. This junction point (bridle point) is on the same plane as the attachment points for the two legs, just lower and somewhere between the two existing attachment points. A three-point bridle is used when the desired bridle point is not directly between two existing attachment points and must be positioned between three points. This is common in spaces where the existing attachment points are scattered about. When the three legs are the proper length, a new hanging point is created that is in the desired location above the stage.

Calculating Three-point Bridle Lengths

The math for calculating the bridle lengths on a three-point bridle is a little more complicated than calculating the bridle lengths for two-point bridles. With two-point bridles, you have only three-points with which to be concerned; the attachment point for each bridle leg and the bridle point where the two legs meet. Since all three of these points are on a single plane, you only need to know the horizontal and vertical distances of the hanging points from the bridle point in order calculate the two bridle lengths. Therefore, you only need to know four numbers - really simple.

A three-point bridle problem is three-dimensional. You must know the X, Y and Z coordinates of the attachment points for the three bridle legs and the bridle point (12 coordinate numbers). See why it is more complicated?

The first trick to solving this problem is to collect and organize the data. The best way is to complete a coordinate table with the needed data, such as the one below:

P1   X: _____   Y: _____   Z: _____

P2   X: _____   Y: _____   Z: _____

P3   X: _____   Y: _____   Z: _____

P4   X: _____   Y: _____   Z: _____

 Note: P1, P2, and P3 will be the hanging points for our three bridle legs (L1, L2 and L3) and P4 will be the bridle point (where the three legs meet).

    Look at the hanging plot (plan view) below. In this plot you see that the three attachment points are located on two beams, and the bridle point is between them. Each attachment point on the plot, as well as the bridle point, is marked with its X and Y coordinates in parentheses. I called the lower left hanging point on my plot 0,0 so that all of the other coordinates points are positive numbers (since they are in Quadrant I) and relative to this point. You can set up your coordinate system in a way that makes the most sense to you.

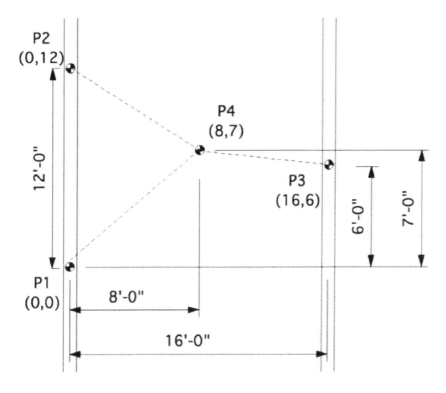

    Now that we have the coordinates, put that data into the table (see below).

P1   X1: ___0___   Y1: ___0_____   Z1: _____

P2   X2: ___0____   Y2: ___12_____   Z2: _____

P3   X3: _16____   Y3: ___6_____   Z3: _____

P4   X4: __8____   Y4: ___7_____   Z4: _____

Next, we need to input the Z coordinates. These are the heights of the points. So, if the bottoms of the two beams are 50 feet above the deck and the bridle point is 35 feet above the deck, the completed coordinate table would look like this:

P1   X1: __0____   Y1: __0_____   Z1: ___50____

P2   X2: __0____   Y2: __12_____   Z2: ___50____

P3   X3: _16____   Y3: ___6_____   Z3: ___50____

P4   X4: __8____   Y4: ___7_____   Z4: ___35____

Note: When the Z height is the same for P1, P2, and P3, some riggers will set these distances as "0" and then make Z4 the distance Z4 is below the three hanging points: -15 in this case. Both method works equally well.

Now that the table is complete, it is time to do some math. The formulas for computing the lengths of the three bridle legs (L1, L2 and L3) are:

$$L1 = \sqrt{(X1 - X4)^2 + (Y1 - Y4)^2 + (Z1 - Z4)^2}$$

$$L2 = \sqrt{(X2 - X4)^2 + (Y2 - Y4)^2 + (Z2 - Z4)^2}$$

$$L3 = \sqrt{(X3 - X4)^2 + (Y3 - Y4)^2 + (Z3 - Z4)^2}$$

This is really just a variation on the Pythagorean Theorem. The big difference is that you must subtract the appropriate axis coordinate for the bridle point (P4) from the same axis coordinate for the three attachment-point coordinates before you square it. If you are taking an exam to become a certified rigger, these formulas may be listed on the formula table that you are given (just be sure you are able to recognize them from the many other formulas on the sheet). After you work a few problems, this is actually a pretty easy equation to remember.

There is one "math thing" that should be noted before we begin, if you square a negative number, the result will be a positive number. In other words, the results of both 5 x 5 and -5 x -5 are 25. Knowing this little tip may help you do some of the math a little faster (and without a calculator).

So, let's plug in the numbers and calculate the lengths of the bridle legs.

$$L1 = \sqrt{(X1 - X4)^2 + (Y1 - Y4)^2 + (Z1 - Z4)^2}$$

$$L1 = \sqrt{(0 - 8)^2 + (0 - 7)^2 + (50 - 35)^2}$$

$$L1 = \sqrt{(-8)^2 + (-7)^2 + (15)^2}$$

$$L1 = \sqrt{64 + 49 + 225}$$

$$L1 = \sqrt{338}$$

$L1 = 18.38$ feet

$$L2 = \sqrt{(X2 - X4)^2 + (Y2 - Y4)^2 + (Z2 - Z4)^2}$$

$$L1 = \sqrt{(0 - 8)^2 + (12 - 7)^2 + (50 - 35)^2}$$

$$L2 = \sqrt{(-8)^2 + (5)^2 + (15)^2}$$

$$L2 = \sqrt{64 + 25 + 225}$$

$$L2 = \sqrt{314}$$

$L2 = 17.72$ feet

$$L3 = \sqrt{(X3 - X4)^2 + (Y3 - Y4)^2 + (Z3 - Z4)^2}$$

$$L3 = \sqrt{(16 - 8)^2 + (6 - 7)^2 + (50 - 35)^2}$$

$$L3 = \sqrt{(-8)^2 + (-1)^2 + (15)^2}$$

$$L3 = \sqrt{64 + 1 + 225}$$

$$L3 = \sqrt{290}$$

$L3 = 17.03$ feet

Another Method

There is another way to calculate three-point bridle lengths, one that uses a variation of the Pythagorean theorem, the same formula used to calculate the lengths of two-point bridles, and is much simpler (in my opinion). Let's look at how this method works.

First, the plan view below is the same as one used earlier, except I have overlaid it with three right triangles (in different shades of grey), one for each of the three bridle legs. Note: the hypotenuse of each of each triangle corresponds to the position of a bridle leg.

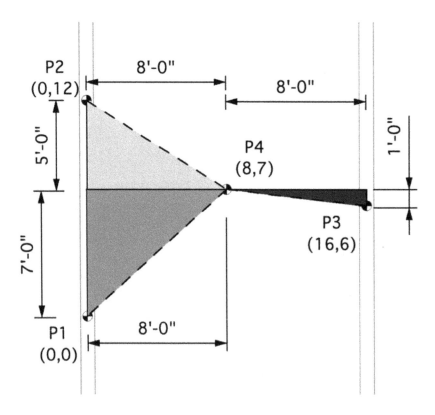

Using this drawing, Let's write down the X and Y lengths for the two non-hypotenuse legs of each triangle.

L1   X: __8__   Y: __7__

L2   X: __8__   Y: __5__

L3   X: __8__   Y: __1__

The next step is to find the Z distance for each leg. If all of these beams are 50 feet above the deck and the Apex is at 35 feet, then the Z distance is 15 feet for each. Let's complete our table.

L1   X: __8__   Y: __7__   Z: __15__

L2   X: __8__   Y: __5__   Z: __15__

L3   X: __8__   Y: __1__   Z: __15__

Now that our table is complete, let's calculate the length of each leg. The equation for doing this is:

$$Leg\ length = \sqrt{X^2 + Y^2 + Z^2}$$

Let's plug in the numbers and calculate the leg lengths.

$Leg\ 1 = \sqrt{8^2 + 7^2 + 15^2}$

$Leg\ 1 = \sqrt{64 + 49 + 225}$

$Leg\ 1 = \sqrt{338}$

$Leg\ 1 = 18.38\ feet$

$Leg\ 2 = \sqrt{8^2 + 5^2 + 15^2}$

$Leg\ 2 = \sqrt{64 + 25 + 225}$

$Leg\ 2 = \sqrt{314}$

$Leg\ 2 = 17.72\ feet$

$Leg\ 3 = \sqrt{8^2 + 1^2 + 15^2}$

$Leg\ 3 = \sqrt{64 + 1 + 225}$

$Leg\ 3 = \sqrt{290}$

$Leg\ 3 = 117.02\ feet$

These are exactly the same lengths as we calculated using the first method. Both methods for calculating the bridle lengths work equally well. I prefer the second method, but you can use the one that fits your way of thinking.

Sample Problems – Lesson 9

Using the coordinates below, calculate the lengths of L1, L2, and L3 (assuming P4 is the bridle point):

1. P1 = (0', 0', 50') P2 = (0', 15', 50') P3 = (15', 5', 50') P4 = (8', 6', 30')

2. P1 = (0', 0', 40') P2 = (0', 10', 40') P3 = (10', 8', 45') P4 = (10', 4', 30')

3. P1 = (0', 0', 45') P2 = (10', 10', 45') P3 = (20', 0', 45') P4 = (10', 4', 30')

4. P1 = (0', 0', 55') P2 = (0', 20', 50') P3 = (20', 12', 60') P4 = (8', 8', 35')

5. P1 = (10', 3', 48') P2 = (10', 25', 48') P3 = (30', 20', 48') P4 = (23', 20', 40')

Lesson 10:
Tension on Three-Point Bridles

Although calculating the lengths of thee-point bridles is relatively simple, calculating the load on each bridle is more involved. While the math is not complicated, there are several steps. Because each step involves numerous operations that use a lot of numbers, it is very easy to get confused and make mistakes. Since just one mistake can throw off everything, calculating the loads on the bridle legs can be a tedious task but not an impossible one.

You will, of course, need the bridle lengths that you computed above, but that is just a start; you will need three more formulas (or sets of formulas). Each formula is a step in calculating the tension on the legs. In the first step you will create a formula matrix, which makes it easy to remember. These formulas calculate nine values that will be needed in steps 2 and 3. Let's get started.

Step 1:
The matrix looks like this:

$$N1X = \left(\frac{X1-X4}{L1}\right) \quad N1Y = \left(\frac{Y1-Y4}{L1}\right) \quad N1Z = \left(\frac{Z1-Z4}{L1}\right)$$

$$N2X = \left(\frac{X2-X4}{L2}\right) \quad N2Y = \left(\frac{Y2-Y4}{L2}\right) \quad N2Z = \left(\frac{Z2-Z4}{L2}\right)$$

$$N3X = \left(\frac{X3-X4}{L3}\right) \quad N3Y = \left(\frac{Y3-Y4}{L3}\right) \quad N3Z = \left(\frac{Z3-Z4}{L3}\right)$$

Write out these formulas, substitute the X, Y and Z values from the coordinate table, and the L dimensions (bridle lengths) that you calculated earlier, and calculate the results. The results of this set of equations are:

$N1X = -0.435 \quad N1Y = -0.381 \quad N1Z = 0.816$
$N2X = -0.451 \quad N2Y = 0.282 \quad N2Z = 0.846$
$N3X = 0.470 \quad N3Y = -0.059 \quad N3Z = 0.881$

These results will be used to compute a divisor number in step 2, below. This divisor, D, will be used in the final set of equations.

Step 2:

$$D = (N1X) \times (N2Y) \times (N3Z) + (N2X) \times (N3Y) \times (NIZ) + (N3X) \times (N1Y) \times (N2Z)$$
$$- (N3X) \times (N2Y) \times (N1Z) - (N1X) \times (N3Y) \times (N2Z) - (N2X) \times (N1Y) \times (N3Z)$$

Wow, what a confusing equation to try to remember. Here is a trick that might help you figure out how to recreate this equation without actually remembering the equation. Work on diagonals. Confused? Look at the revised version of this table below.

N1X = -0.435	N1Y = -0.381	N1Z = 0.816
N2X = -0.451	N2Y = 0.282	N2Z = 0.846
N3X = 0.470	N3Y = -0.059	N3Z = 0.881

and

$$D = (N1X) \times (N2Y) \times (N3Z) + (N2X) \times (N3Y) \times (N1Z) + (N3X) \times (N1Y) \times (N2Z)$$
$$- (N3X) \times (N2Y) \times (N1Z) - (N2X) \times (N1Y) \times (N3Z) - (N1X) \times (N3Y) \times (N2Z)$$

Do you see a pattern with the different shades text in the table? Look at the three sets of numbers with BLACK text. They are arranged in a diagonal line from the upper-left corner to the lower right corner. They are your first set of numbers. Replace the variable names in the equation with their values.

Now, look at the group of numbers with the BLACK background and WHITE text. They also make a diagonal line. (Sure, you have to pick up the stray number at the top of column, but it follows the pattern). They are the second set. Put these values into the equation.

Last, look at the numbers with the GREY background and WHITE text. See the pattern? Put these values into the equation, too.

Now that you have the top line filled in, do the same for the next three groups of numbers - the bottom line. These three diagonal rows move from the bottom-left corner to the top right (opposite of the first three groups). See the pattern here?

N1X = -0.435	N1Y = -0.381	N1Z = 0.816
N2X = -0.451	N2Y = 0.282	N2Z = 0.846
N3X = 0.470	N3Y = -0.059	N3Z = 0.881

and

$$D = (N1X) \times (N2Y) \times (N3Z) + (N2X) \times (N3Y) \times (N1Z) + (N3X) \times (N1Y) \times (N2Z)$$
$$- (N3X) \times (N2Y) \times (N1Z) - \boxed{(N2X) \times (N1Y) \times (N3Z)} - (N1X) \times (N3Y) \times (N2Z)$$

By the way, this equation is not included on some certification formula tables. But, if you remember my "visual trick," you can create the formula without having to remember what may seem like an interrelated mess of an equation.

Replacing the variables in this equation with the values from the matrix, we get:

$$D = (-0.438) \times (0.282) \times (0.881) + (-0.451) \times (-0.059) \times (0.816) + (0.470) \times (-0.381) \times (0.846)$$
$$- (0.470) \times (0.282) \times (0.816) - (-0.451) \times (-0.381) \times (0.881) - (-0.435) \times (-0.059) \times (0.846)$$

Multiplying these six sets of numbers is probably the most tedious step in computing the load on the bridle legs, and where most people make mistakes. I recommend that you ignore the sign of the sets of numbers as you multiply them (treat them as positive numbers) and apply the sign (positive or negative) AFTER you do the multiplication. Here is how you know the sign of the product (result of multiplying the numbers):

- If there is ONE negative number in the group, the product is NEGATIVE
- If there are TWO negative numbers in the group, the product is POSITIVE
- If there are THREE negative numbers in the group, the product is NEGATIVE

So, just multiply the three (positive) numbers in each of the six groups and them apply the sign. The result of multiplying these groups of numbers is:

$$D = (-0.108) + (0.022) + (-0.151) - (0.108) - (0.151) - (0.022)$$
$$D = -0.518$$

That was a lot of work for this one number, but you will need this number in the final step below. You will also need one additional piece of information before you can calculate the load on each bridle leg - the load being supported by the three bridles. For this problem, let's say that the bridles are supporting a 500-pound load. The letter F in the equations below represents this value. We will call the force (tension) on the bridle legs F1, F2 and F3, respectively. So, here is the final set of equations.

Step 3:

$$F1 = \left((N2X \times N3Y) - (N3X \times N2Y)\right) \times \frac{F}{D}$$

$$F2 = \left((N3X \times N1Y) - (N1X \times N3Y)\right) \times \frac{F}{D}$$

$$F3 = \left((N1X \times N2Y) - (N2X \times N1Y)\right) \times \frac{F}{D}$$

Fortunately, these formulas are (or were) on some rigging certification formula tables, so you do not have to memorize them. Let's plug in the values and compute the loads on the three bridle legs.

$$F1 = \left((N2X \times N3Y) - (N3X \times N2Y)\right) \times \frac{F}{D}$$

$$F1 = \left((-0.451 \times -0.059) - (.0470 \times 0.282)\right) \times \frac{500}{-0.519}$$

$$F1 = (0.026 - 0.132) \times -963.39$$

$$F1 = -0.106 \times -963.39$$

F1 = 102.12 lb

$$F2 = \left((N3X \times N1Y) - (N1X \times N3Y)\right) \times \frac{F}{D}$$

$$F1 = \left((0.47 \times -0.381) - (-0.435 \times -0.059)\right) \times \frac{500}{-0.519}$$

$$F1 = (-0.179 - 0.026) \times -963.39$$

$$F2 = -0.205 \times -963.39$$

F2 = 197.49 lb

$$F3 = \big((N1X \times N2Y) - (N2X \times N1Y)\big) \times \frac{F}{D}$$

$$F3 = \big((-0.425 \times 0.282) - (-0.451 \times -0.381)\big) \times \frac{500}{-0.519}$$

$$F3 = (-0.123 - 0.173) \times -963.39$$

$$F3 = -0.295 \times -963.39$$

F3 = 284 lb

The results of your calculations may vary slightly from the ones above (but by less than one pound) based on how many places to the right of the decimal you extend each number, so do not be confused if your results are not exactly as above.

Conclusion

Calculating the lengths of the three bridle legs was pretty easy, but calculating loads on the three bridle legs was a lot of potentially frustrating work. Computing these loads with a rigging app like *RigCalc*, for Android and iPhones, is definitely much easier. Still, there are times when you might have to calculate this by hand.

Practice is the only way to become proficient at doing math problems such as these, so create some problems and work them. Be careful. Most math mistakes are just foolish errors. Use a rigging app to check your answers. Happy calculating.

Sample Problems – Lesson 10

Using the coordinates and leg lengths below, calculate the loads on L1, L2, and L3 (assuming P4 is the bridle point):

1. P1 = (0′, 0′, 50′) P2 = (0′, 15′, 50′) P3 = (15′, 5′, 50′) P4 = (8′, 6′, 30′)
    L1 = 22.4 feet L2 = 23.3 feet L3 = 21.1 feet Load = 500 lb

2. P1 = (0′, 0′, 40′) P2 = (0′, 10′, 40′) P3 = (10′, 8′, 45′) P4 = (5′, 8′, 30′)
    L1 = 13.7 feet L2 = 11.4 feet L3 = 15.8 feet Load = 500 lb

3. P1 = (0′, 0′, 45′) P2 = (10′, 10′, 45′) P3 = (20′, 0′, 45′) P4 = (10′, 4′, 30′)
    L1 = 18.8 feet L2 = 16.2 feet L3 = 18.5 feet Load = 300 lb

4. P1 = (0′, 0′, 55′) P2 = (0′, 20′, 50′) P3 = (20′, 12′, 60′) P4 = (8′, 8′, 35′)
    L1 = 23 feet L2 = 20.8 feet L3 = 28 feet Load = 400 lb

5. P1 = (10′, 3′, 48′) P2 = (10′, 25′, 48′) P3 = (30′, 20′, 48′) P4 = (23′, 20′, 40′)
    L1 = L1 = 22.8 feet L2 = 16.1 feet L3 = 10.6 feet Load = 600 lb

Unit IV:
Truss

Lesson 11:

Center of Gravity for Two Loads on a Beam

It can be handy to know where the center of gravity is when you have two loads on a beam. I use the equations below to calculate the single hanging point on a spreader bar that is used to suspend two loads (performers) of different weights. These equations let me find the point on the spreader bar that will allow it to be "balanced," and hang horizontally. Here is a diagram of the problem.

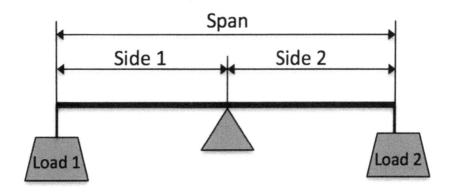

You might want to think of this as a teeter-totter. What is on one side of the fulcrum (lifting point) must balance with the other side. The concept of finding the center of gravity (the lifting point) for two loads on a beam is very simple: Load 1 times the Length of Side 1 must be equal to Load 2 times the Length of Side 2. Since the loads and the distance between them (the "Span") are known, the objective is to determine the lengths of Side 1 and Side 2. The equations to solve this problem are:

$$Length\ of\ Side\ 1 = \frac{Load\ 2 \times Span}{Load\ 1 + Load\ 2}$$

$$Length\ of\ Side\ 2 = \frac{Load\ 1 \times Span}{Load\ 1 + Load\ 2}$$

or

Length of Side 2 = Span – Length of Side 1

Example: If the total span is 10 feet, and Load 1 is 150 lb and Load 2 is 100 lb, where is the center of gravity (what are the lengths of Side 1 and Side 2)?

$$Length\ of\ Side\ 1 = \frac{Load\ 2 \times Span}{Load\ 1 + Load\ 2}$$

$$Length\ of\ Side\ 1 = \frac{100 \times 10}{150 + 100}$$

$$Length\ of\ Side\ 1 = \frac{1000}{250}$$

Length of Side 1 = 4 feet

$$Length\ of\ Side\ 2 = \frac{Load\ 1 \times Span}{Load\ 1 + Load\ 2}$$

$$Length\ of\ Side\ 2 = \frac{150 \times 10}{150 + 100}$$

$$Length\ of\ Side\ 2 = \frac{1500}{250}$$

Length of Side 2 = 6 feet

or

Length of Side 2 = Span – Length of Side 1

Length of Side 2 = 10 – 4

Length of Side 2 = 6 feet

Sample Problems – Lesson 11

1. If the Span is 10', and Load 1 = 500 ls and Load 2 = 100 lb, what are the lengths of Side 1 and Side 2?

2. If the Span is 10', and Load 1 = 500 lb and Load 2 = 300 lb, what are the lengths of Side 1 and Side 2?

3. If the Span is 15', and Load 1 = 300 lb and Load 2 = 175 lb, what are the lengths of Side 1 and Side 2?

4. If the Span is 20', and Load 1 = 400 lb and Load 2 = 500 lb, what are the lengths of Side 1 and Side 2?

5. If the Span is 15', and Load 1 = 400 lb and Load 2 = 100 lb, what are the lengths of Side 1 and Side 2?

Lesson 12:

Uniformly Distributed Loads on a Beam

Sometimes loads are evenly distributed across the entire length of a truss or batten where the supporting lines are equally spaced, such as a curtain hanging on a batten. This is often called a "uniformly distributed load" or UDL. Figuring out how much of the load is on each supporting line is very easy when only two lines support the batten/truss. In this situation, 50 percent of the total load is on each supporting line. It gets more complicated when three or more lines support the truss or batten. Below is a diagram that shows how a uniform load is theoretically distributed when supported by multiple lines.

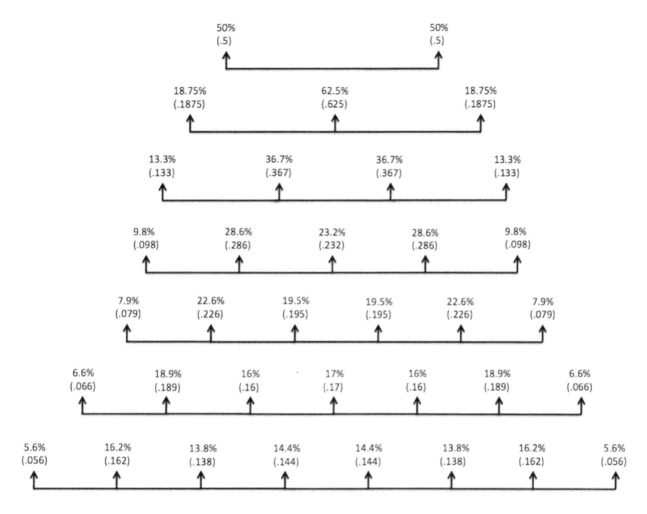

Reprinted with permission from Jay Glerum, *Stage Rigging Handbook* (Carbondale: Southern University Press, 2007), 86.

Note: The term "theoretically" was used in the description above because two conditions **must** exist. The lift lines MUST be equally spaced AND the truss/batten MUST be perfectly horizontal. Since it is nearly impossible to hang a batten/truss perfectly horizontal from more than two lines, especially if chain hoists are involved, these percentages are never achieved in actual practice. Because it is so difficult to distribute the load evenly on a long truss that is supported by many chain hoists, the use of load cells on each point is becoming more commonplace. Still, use of UDL math may be included in some rigging certification exams, so it is covered in this lesson.

To understand how to use this diagram, let's do the following UDL problem.

    If a UDL of 1500 pounds is dead hung from a batten that is supported by three equally spaced lift lines, what is the load on each line?

Look at the diagram above that shows the batten suspended by three lines. The percentage of the total load supported by each line is indicated. In parenthesis is the same value expressed as a decimal number. To find the load on each line, multiply the total load by the number in parenthesis. When we do, we get:

$1500 \times 0.1875 = \mathbf{281.25\ lb}$

$1500 \times 0.625 = \mathbf{937.5\ lb}$

$1500 \times 0.1875 = \mathbf{281.25\ lb}$

You can check your math by adding the loads on all of the lift lines. The sum should be equal to the total load being supported – 1500 pounds in this case.

$281.25 + 937.5 + 281.25 = \mathbf{1500\ lb}$

Looking at the loads on the lines in each UDL situation shows that: a) the outer lines always hold the <u>least</u> load, and b) the next set of lines "on-stage" always holds the <u>most</u> load.

While the diagram above is accurate, it is very difficult to remember and, therefore, not as useful as one that you can remember. Fortunately, there is a simpler (modified distribution load) method for calculating these loads. While the diagram/method below is not as accurate as the one above, it is much easier to remember and is accurate enough for our needs.

Note: For a beam supported by two lift lines, the method of calculating the load supported by each line is identical to the method above – both lines support 50% of the total load. However, for three or more lift lines, the methods differ.

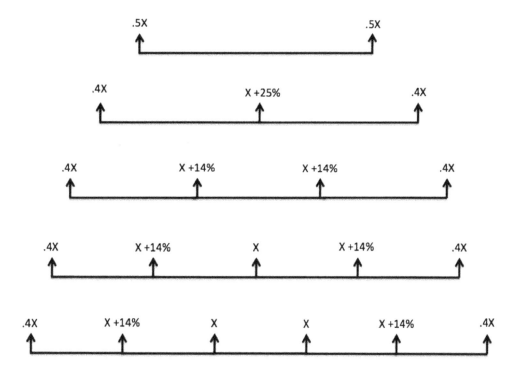

Reprinted with permission from Harry Donovan's, *Entertainment Rigging: A Practical Guide, Chapter 16, Page 14.*

The first thing we need to know is "X." "X" is the total weight of the load, divided by the number of segments of beam. The number of segments is the number of supporting lines minus one. So, for a beam supported by three lines, there are two segments; for a beam supported by four lines, there are three segments; for a beam supported by five lines, there are four segments; etc.

Since the distribution of a load supported by two points is always 50% on each leg, nothing has changed for a two-legged rig from the previous diagram. But for beams supported by three or more evenly spaced lines, there is a difference.

Using the same problem we used above, if a UDL of 1500 pounds is dead hung from a batten that is supported by three equally spaced lift lines, let's find the load on each line.

$X = 1,500 / 2$ (three minus one)

$X = 750$ lb

Now,

$L1 = 750 \times 0.4 = 300$ lb

$L2 = 750 + 25\%$ of $750 \ (187.5) = 937.5$ lb

$L3 = 750 \times 0.4 = 300$ lb

Compare this with the results above.

L1 = 281.25 lb

L2 = 937.5 lb

L3 = 281.25 lb

Pretty close!

If you have a beam supported by four lines, L2 and L3 are X + 14% (not 25%). And for beams supported by five or more lines, all of the "middle" lines are X; only the outer two sets are different (0.4X or X + 14%).

This "modified uniformly distributed load" method is easy to remember and makes it easy to calculate the tension on the lines supporting a uniformly distributed load.

Sample Problems – Lesson 12

Using the "modified distributed load" method, solve the problems below.

1. If a UDL of 1500 lb is dead hung from a batten that is supported by three equally spaced lift lines, what is the load on each line?

2. If a UDL of 1500 lb is dead hung from a batten that is supported by four equally spaced lift lines, what is the load on each line?

3. If a UDL of 2500 lb is dead hung from a batten that is supported by five equally spaced lift lines, what is the load on each line?

4. If a UDL of 1500 lb is dead hung from a batten that is supported by six equally spaced lift lines, what is the load on each line?

5. If a UDL of 2000 lb is dead hung from a batten that is supported by seven equally spaced lift lines, what is the load on each line?

Lesson 13:

Dead-hang Tension on One End of a Beam

The most efficient way to hang anything is to be able to suspend from directly above the object that you want to hang. When that is not possible, you can use bridles to create a point somewhere between two established hanging points. However, when you dead hang a beam/truss, it is possible to hang it so that neither end is directly below a hanging point, yet each end only has one bridle leg. The diagram below illustrates how this can be done.

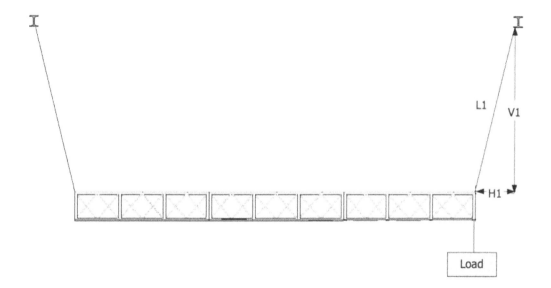

If the hanging point were directly above the load, then the tension on this leg would be equal to the Load. But since the Load is not directly below the hanging point, the tension on the Leg will be greater than the load. So what is the tension on the Leg? The equation to solve this problem is:

$$Tension\ on\ L1 = Load \times \frac{L1}{V1}$$

Note: In this problem we are ignoring the weight of the truss. The weight of the truss will be addressed in Lesson 16.

The way I remember this formula is that the tension on L1 is always greater than the vertical weight of the Load, so the Load must be multiplied by a number that is greater than 1. Since the length of L1 (the hypotenuse of the right triangle) is always greater than the vertical distance (V1), dividing L1 by V1 will always give you a number that is greater than 1. Then, multiply the Load by this multiplying factor.

Example: If H1 = 4', V1 =10', and the Load = 400 lb, what is the tension on L1?

The first thing we need to do is to compute the length of L1 (as we did this in Lesson 5).

$L1 = 10 \ [X^2] \ [+] \ 4 \ [X^2] \ [=] \ [\sqrt{X}]$

L1 = 10.77 feet

Now we put this length into the equation above and get:

$$\text{Tension on L1} = \text{Load} \times \frac{10.77}{10}$$

$$\text{Tension on L1} = 400 \times 1.077$$

Tension on Leg L1 = 430.8 lb

If we have multiple loads on the truss, we would compute the load that would be transferred to each of the two suspension points on the truss. This will be covered in Lessons 14, 15 and 16. Then compute the load on each leg. For now, just work with this single load that is directly below the suspension point on the truss.

Sample Problems – Lesson 13

1. If H1 = 5', V1 =12', and the Load = 500 lb, what is the tension on L1?

2. If H1 = 7', V1 =6', and the Load = 400 lb, what is the tension on L1?

3. If H1 = 4', V1 =4', and the Load = 300 lb, what is the tension on L1?

4. If H1 = 5', V1 =8', and the Load = 500 lb, what is the tension on L1?

5. If H1 = 9', V1 =12', and the Load = 450 lb, what is the tension on L1?

Lesson 14:

Simple Load on a Beam

In Lesson 12, you learned how to compute the load hanging on a single bridle leg at the end of a truss. In reality, that seldom occurs. In most cases the load is somewhere other than directly below the suspension point on the truss. In this lesson, and the two that follow it, you will learn how to compute the vertical force on each end of a truss when the loads are spread out in different locations along the truss. This lesson starts with a single load placed somewhere along the truss. Here is a diagram of the problem.

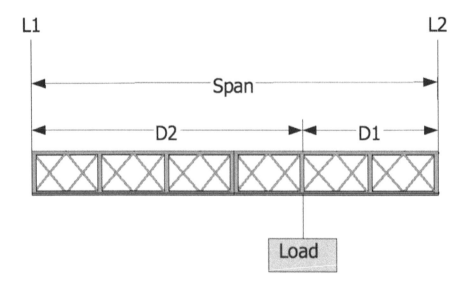

You might have noticed that I use D1 and D2 in the illustration above instead of H1 and H2 as I have used in previous lessons. Why? Maybe it is not a great reason, but it is because this type of problem does not contain a V1 or V2. This will also be true for the problems in Lessons 14, 15 and 16, so I have substituted "D" for "H" in these lessons. I have also switched the numbering of D1 and D2, so do not get confused by this. It does not really make any difference what you label these distances, as long as you understand the concept of which parts you multiply by or divide by to solve the problem.

Our desire is to find the vertical force on the two supporting Legs (L1 and L2). In many cases you can easily determine what percentage of the Span D1 and D2 represents. If so, the load on each end of the truss will correspond inversely to this percentage. For example, if D1 is 25% of the Span, then the load on L2 is 75% of the Load. However, if it is difficult to determine these percentages, then the equations below can be used for solving this type of problem.

$$Tension\ on\ L1 = \frac{Load \times D1}{Span}$$

Note: You can also think of it as L1 = Load x (D1/Span) if that is easier for you to remember.

$$Tension\ on\ L2 = \frac{Load \times D2}{Span}$$

Note: You can also think of it as L2 = Load x (D2/Span) if that is easier for you to remember.

or

$$Tension\ on\ L2 = Load - L1$$

The trick I use to remember the method of solving this problem is to remember that to find the tension on one leg, you multiply the Load by the distance of the Load from the OPPOSITE leg, and then divide by the Span. We used the trick of "multiplying opposites" and then dividing in Lesson 6 on "Tension on Bridle Legs," and the same idea is used with this problem.

So, let's work a problem.

Example: If the Span is 20 feet, D1 is 5 feet and D2 is 15 feet (note: D1 + D2 must equal Span), and the Load 1 is 200 lb, what is the tension on L1 and L2?

$$Tension\ on\ L1 = \frac{Load \times D1}{Span}$$

$$Tension\ on\ L1 = \frac{200 \times 5}{20}$$

$$Tension\ on\ L1 = \frac{1000}{20}$$

Tension on L1 = 50 lb

$$\text{Tension on L2} = \frac{\text{Load} \times \text{D2}}{\text{Span}}$$

$$\text{Tension on L2} = \frac{200 \times 15}{20}$$

$$\text{Tension on L2} = \frac{3000}{20}$$

Tension on L2 = 150 lb

Also, Tension on L1 + L2 must always equal the Load, which is one way to check your work. But, since that is true, once you find L1 you can compute the tension on L2 by using the simple equation Tension on L2 = Load − Tension on L1. Another easy check of your math is to make certain that the leg that is closest to the load has the most tension. Practice these simple problems before going to the next lesson, which puts multiple loads on the truss.

Sample Problems – Lesson 14

1. If the Span is 12', D1 is 5', D2 is 7' and the Load is 300 lb, what is the tension on L1 and L2?

2. If the Span is 20', D1 is 7', D2 is 13' and the Load is 300 lb, what is the tension on L1 and L2?

3. If the Span is 30', D1 is 8', D2 is 22' and the Load is 400 lb, what is the tension on L1 and L2?

4. If the Span is 25', D1 is 8', D2 is 17' and the Load is 350 lb, what is the tension on L1 and L2?

5. If the Span is 20', D1 is 18', D2 is 2' and the Load is 350 lb, what is the tension on L1 and L2?

Lesson 15:

Multiple Loads on a Beam

In Lesson 13, you learned how to compute the tension on L1 and L2 when there was a single load on the beam/truss. In this lesson you will learn how to compute the loads when you have multiple loads that are spread out along the truss. Here is a diagram of the problem.

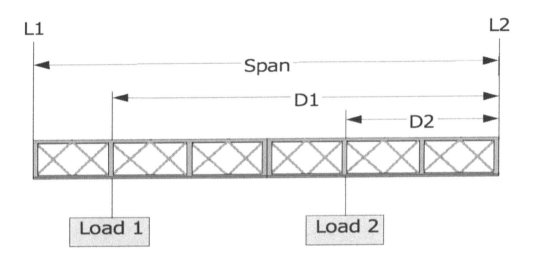

As in Lesson 13, our desire is to find the vertical force on the two supporting Legs (L1 and L2). The equations for solving this problem are:

$$Tension\ on\ L1 = \frac{(Load\ 1 \times D1) + (Load\ 2 \times D2)}{Span}$$

$$Tension\ on\ L2 = (Load\ 1 + Load\ 2) - Tension\ on\ L1$$

Note: Instead of using the equations above, you can use the equations in Lesson 14, and find the tensions on the legs for each load, then add the two tensions for each leg to get the total tension.

Before we begin calculating the tensions, it should be noted that, unlike the problem in Lesson 13, D1 + D2 will NOT equal the Span. The equation for determining the tension on L1 uses L2 as the starting point for D1 and D2. Let me say this again – both D1 and D2 are measured from L2 to their respective loads. This is confusing to some people, but this is correct.

Example: If the Span is 20 feet, D1 is 17.5 feet, D2 is 5 feet, Load 1 is 100 lb and Load 2 is 200 lb, what is the tension on L1 and L2?

$$\text{Tension on L1} = \frac{(100 \times 17.5) + (200 \times 5)}{20}$$

$$\text{Tension on L1} = \frac{1750 + 1000}{20}$$

$$\text{Tension on L1} = \frac{2750}{20}$$

Tension on L1 = 137.5 lb

And because the Tension on L1 + Tension on L2 must equal Load1 + Load 2 we can use the simple equation to determine L2.

Tension on L2 = (Load1 + Load 2) – Tension on L1
Tension on L2= (100 + 200) - 137.5
Tension on L2= 300 - 137.5
Tension on L2 = 162.5 lb

Although this may seem complicated at first, remember that you keep the 1's together (Load1 x D1) and the 2's together (Load2 x D2), then add them and divide the result by the Span. If you have more than two loads, just add "(Load 3 x D3)" and so on to the first part of the equation, and divide the total by the Span. Practice the sample problems before going to the next lesson, which will become even more complex.

Sample Problems – Lesson 15

1. If the Span is 20', D1 is 15', D2 is 5', Load 1 is 300 lb and Load 2 is 400 lb, what is the tension on L1 and L2?

2. If the Span is 20', D1 is 12', D2 is 7', Load 1 is 300 lb and Load 2 is 400 lb, what is the tension on L1 and L2?

3. If the Span is 20', D1 is 20', D2 is 10', Load 1 is 300 lb and Load 2 is 400 lb, what is the tension on L1 and L2?

4. If the Span is 20', D1 is 5', D2 is 0', Load 1 is 300 lb and Load 2 is 400 lb, what is the tension on L1 and L2?

5. If the Span is 25', D1 is 10', D2 is 5', Load 1 is 300 lb and Load 2 is 400 lb, what is the tension on L1 and L2?

Lesson 16:
Cantilevered Load on a Beam

In Lesson 14, you learned how to compute the tensions on L1 and L2 when there were multiple loads on the beam (truss). However, in all of those problems the loads were between L1 and L2. In this lesson you will learn how to compute the loads when one or more of the loads are cantilevered outside of the legs. Here is a diagram of the problem.

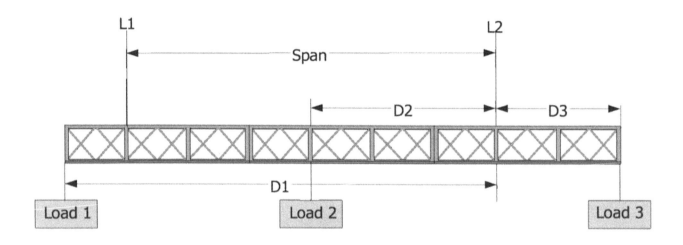

The equations for solving this problem are similar to the ones you learned in Lesson 14, except now we must deal with the Load that is cantilevered outside of the leg that is opposite the leg on which we are computing the tension. This sounds a bit confusing, but will explain shortly. The equations for solving this problem are:

$$Tension\ on\ L1 = \frac{(Load\ 1 \times D1) + (Load\ 2 \times D2) - (Load\ 3 \times D3)}{Span}$$

$$Tension\ on\ L2 = (Load1 + Load\ 2 + Load3) - L1$$

Before we begin, let's note that, as in the previous lesson, the Span has no relevance to D1, D2 or D3. But, as in the previous lesson, all of the distances (D1, D2 and D3) will be measured from L2. I also want to explain the "– (Load 3 x D3)" part of this equation.

Just as in Lesson 10, you need to think of this rig as a teeter-totter or a lever, where the fulcrum is at the point where the Leg attaches to the truss. When we are computing L1, the fulcrum is where L2 attaches to the truss. If Loads 1 and 2 did not exist, the L1 end of the truss would pivot up (at the point where L2 attached to the truss) because Load 3 would not have anything counterbalancing it on the other side (and the L1 cable, chain, or round sling would not provide any resistance).

This would tell you that there is a positive force on L2 but a negative force on L1. (Remember: downward forces are "positive" and upward forces are "negative.") Because this is true, we need to include this negative force when we calculate the load on L1. When all of the loads were between the two Legs, you only had positive forces, so all of the forces were "added." Since we now have a negative force, we need to "subtract" it. That is why we have "– (Load 3 x D3)" in this equation. "– (Load 3 x D3)" is the negative force on L1.

Example: If the Span is 30 feet, Load 1 is 200 lb, D1 is 35 feet, Load 2 is 150 lb, D2 is 15 feet, Load 3 is 100 lb, and D3 is 10 feet, what is the tension on L1 and L2?

$$\text{Tension on L1} = \frac{(\text{Load 1} \times \text{D1}) + (\text{Load 2} \times \text{D2}) - (\text{Load 3} \times \text{D3})}{\text{Span}}$$

$$\text{Tension on L1} = \frac{(200 \times 35) + (150 \times 15) - (100 \times 10)}{30}$$

$$\text{Tension on L1} = \frac{7{,}000 + 2{,}250 - 1{,}000}{30}$$

$$\text{Tension on L1} = \frac{8{,}250}{30}$$

Tension on L1 = 275 lb

Tension on L2 = (Load1 + Load 2 + Load3) – L1
Tension on L2= (200 + 150 + 100) - 275
Tension on L2= 450 - 275
Tension on L2 = 175 lb

The most common mistake in solving these types of problems is adding instead of subtracting for the Load that is cantilevered. With a little practice, you can master these equations.

Although the equations in this lesson are for three Loads on a truss – with two of them cantilevered – in reality, most truss problems will involve many more Loads on the truss. In these cases, you can use variations of these equations to find the tension on the legs. These types of problems will be covered in Lesson 16.

Sample Problems – Lesson 16

1. If the Span is 20', D1 is 25', D2 is 5', D3 is 5', Load 1 is 300 lb, Load 2 is 500 lb and Load 3 is 300 lb, what is the tension on L1 and L2?

2. If the Span is 20', D1 is 30', D2 is 10', D3 is 3', Load 1 is 300 lb, Load 2 is 500 lb and Load 3 is 300 lb, what is the tension on L1 and L2?

3. If the Span is 30', D1 is 35', D2 is 5', D3 is 5', Load 1 is 300 lb, Load 2 is 200 lb and Load 3 is 250 lb, what is the tension on L1 and L2?

4. If the Span is 25', D1 is 30', D2 is 10', D3 is 10', Load 1 is 300 lb, Load 2 is 300 lb and Load 3 is 300 lb, what is the tension on L1 and L2?

5. If the Span is 25', D1 is 30', D2 is 5', D3 is 0', Load 1 is 300 lb, Load 2 is 400 lb and Load 3 is 300 lb, what is the tension on L1 and L2?

Unit V:
Advanced Rigging

Advanced Rigging:
Introduction

Up until now, most of the lessons have been of a theoretical nature. In this section we will look at putting these formulas into practice to solve more real-world problems. As you will see, the practice can involve variations on the formulas that were covered in previous lessons, and often are multi-step processes rather than simple single-step problems. While there is a lot of math in this section, the focus of this section is more on the "process" than the actual math. It some ways this can be even more challenging.

In Lesson 19, you will see that while math is objective (one correct answer), there are subjective decisions that the rigger can make. This means that there may be several equally correct (or at least "acceptable") answers to a problem.

The section begins where Part IV left off, calculating loads on trusses. It will also revisit calculating bridle lengths, and finally discusses tools for doing rigging math, including how to create your own tools.

Lesson 17:

Chain Hoists and Truss and Lights. Oh my!

Lessons 11-15 taught you the mathematics of calculating the loads associated with hanging unspecified types of loads on a truss. However, these lessons ignored the fact that riggers have to hang lights, cable, speakers, and other specific objects on the truss. These lessons also ignored the fact that the truss, the chain hoist, and the chain all have specific weights. In this lesson we will take these facts into consideration and look at real world rigging of truss.

Our objective will be to calculate the load (tensions) on the beams that support the truss and everything else that is suspended. This is a little different than saying that we are calculating the tension on the legs, as you will see.

Note: Appendix 4 contains the weights of specific truss, lighting instruments, hoists, chain and other objects that are typically suspended from structures by rigging. We will use some generic weights in this lesson, just to simplify the process.

We can divide loads that hang on a truss into two categories:

1) **Uniformly Distributed Loads** - loads that are evenly distributed across the truss (or a large segment of the truss)
2) **Point Loads** - loads that are concentrated on one point on the truss but may be distributed on more than one hanging point

Let's look at a rig below and determine the types of load, as well as the load (tension) each puts on the hanging point L1 and L2.

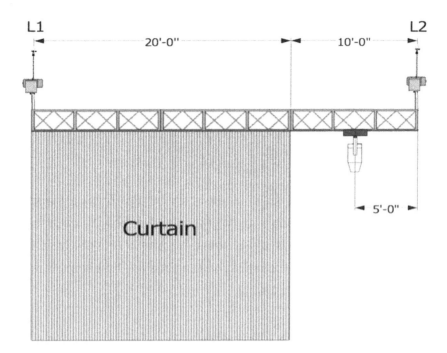

There are two Uniformly Distributed Loads on this rig, the truss itself and the curtain. The truss runs the entire 30-foot span between the lift points, so half of the weight of the truss is on L1 and half on L2. If the truss weighs 10 pounds per linear foot, 300 pounds total, then both L1 and L2 have 150 pounds of tension on them so far.

The curtain is also a Uniformly Distributed Load, but only over 20 feet of the truss, starting with L1. A Uniformly Distributed Load can be converted into a single point load by finding its center of gravity. In this example, the center of gravity (or just the center of the curtain) is 10 feet from L1, or one-third of the span. If the curtain weighs 300 pounds, then 200 pounds of that load is on L1, and 100 pounds is on L2. So now: L1 = 150 + 200 = **350** pounds and L2 = 150 + 100 or **250** pounds**.**

Next, let's look at the Point Loads and calculate the distribution of the weight of one moving light hanging on the truss. This light, weighing 75 pounds, is 5 feet from L2. We can use our basic point load equation to calculate the distribution of this load.

$$Tension\ on\ L1 = Load \times \frac{D1}{Span}$$

$$Tension\ on\ L1 = 75 \times \frac{5}{30}$$

$$Tension\ on\ L1 = 75 \times 0.1666$$

Tension on L1 = 12.5 lb

Tension on L2 = Load – L1
Tension on L2 = 75 – 12.5
Tension on L2 = 62.5 lb

Adding these numbers to our previous totals for L1 and L2, we get: L1 = 350 + 12.5 = 362.5 pounds and L2 = 250 + 62.5 = 312.5 pounds.

The last thing to add is the weight of the chain hoist and chain. These are also Point Loads, but since they are a part of the "leg" itself, their weight gets added directly to each leg. If a chain hoist weighs 120 pounds and there are 50 feet of chain, weighing one pound per foot, that form each "leg," then we add 170 pounds to both L1 and L2. The tensions on the beams that support L1 and L2 are **532.5 pounds** and **482.5 pounds** respectively.

If you do not understand how to solve this problem, go through it until you do. The next problem is more complicated, and you will be completely lost unless you have mastered the problem above.

Let's now look at a more complicated rig – one with three supporting legs and part of the truss being cantilevered.

There are several ways to calculate the loads hanging from three or more points on a truss, and this lesson will only cover one method. It is important to realize that other methods will give slightly different results. Which method gives you the "correct" answer? Probably none of them. Remember, whenever you hang a truss by three or more points, you cannot accurately calculate the load on the points because you are assuming that the truss is PERFECTLY level. A tiny discrepancy can cause the tension to shift and <u>greatly</u> increase or decrease the load on two or more points. Therefore, always plan for the load on the points to be greater than the calculated load, no matter what method you use.

Note: The difficulty with using three or more points to suspend a truss cannot be over emphasized. Even if the truss is perfectly balanced at working height, it will be out-of balance when you get it up in the air. For this reason, more and more tours are using load cells on all points so that they can monitor the loads and adjust the trim of each point to balance the loads properly. With shows suspending much heavier loads each year, this is becoming an important safety procedure.

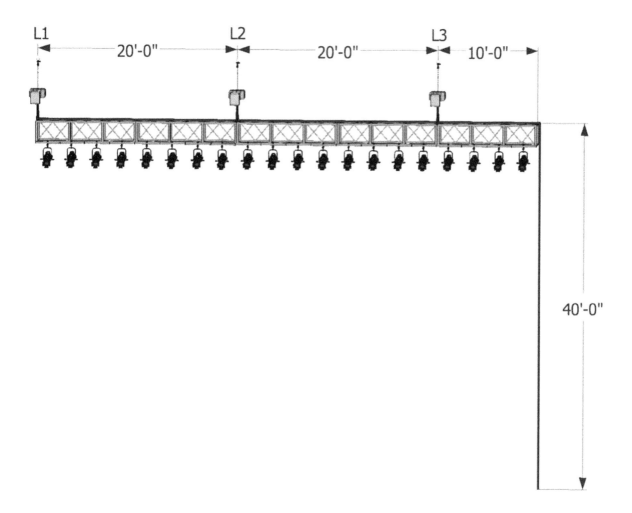

This rig has three uniformly distributed loads: the 50 feet of truss (10 pounds per foot), 20 Lekos (15 pounds each or 6 pounds per foot) and 50 feet of electrical cable (3 pounds per foot). There are also two point loads, each chain hoist and its 70 feet of chain (100 pounds per hoist and 1 pound per foot of chain), and the 40 feet of electrical cable that drops from the top of the truss to the floor (3 pounds per foot or 120 pounds of total weight). As before, we will keep a "running total" of the force on the three hanging points as we calculate them.

Both sections L1-L2 and L2-L3 have:

20 feet of truss at 10 pounds per foot	=	200 pounds
8 Lekos at 15 pounds each	=	120 pounds
20 feet of electrical cable at 3 pounds per foot	=	60 pounds
	Total	380 pounds

Since we know that L1 and L3 are only supporting half of that load, Tension on L1 = 190 pounds, Tension on L2 = 380 pounds, and Tension on L3 = 190 pounds.

Let's go ahead and add the 170 pounds of each chain hoist and chain to these points. We now have: Tension on L1 = 190 + 170 = 360 pounds, Tension on L2 = 380 + 170 = 550 pounds and Tension on L3 = 190 + 170 = 360 pounds.

Now, we just have to deal with the weight that is cantilevered beyond H3. Since we know that this 10-foot of section of truss, lights, and cables weigh half of our 20-foot long sections. It weighs 190 pounds. And because the load is uniformly distributed across those 10 feet, it is the same as 190 pounds being suspended at 5 feet from L3. So, doing the math, we get:

$$\text{Tension on L2} = -\text{Load} \times \frac{D1}{\text{Span}}$$

$$\text{Tension on L2} = -190 \times \frac{5}{20}$$

$$\text{Tension on L2} = -190 \times .25$$

Tension on L2 = -47.5 lb

$$\text{Tension on L3} = \text{Load} - \text{L2}$$
$$\text{Tension on L3} = 190 - -47.5$$
Tension on L3 = 237.5 lb

So now, Tension on L1 = 360 pounds, Tension on L2 = 550 − 47.5 = 502.5 pounds and Tension on L3 = 360 + 237.5 = 597.5 pounds.

The last thing we need to calculate is the 120 pounds of cable hanging off the end of the truss, so,

$$\text{Tension on L2} = -\text{Load} \times \frac{D1}{\text{Span}}$$

$$\text{Tension on L2} = -120 \times \frac{10}{20}$$

$$\text{Tension on L2} = -120 \times .5$$

Tension on L2 = -60 lb
$$\text{Tension on L3} = \text{Load} - \text{L2}$$
$$\text{Tension on L3} = 120 - (-60)$$
Tension on L3 = 180 lb

So, adding these numbers to our previous totals, we get:

Tension on L1 = 360 lb
Tension on L2 = 502.5 – 60 = 442.5 lb
Tension on L3 = 597.5 + 180 = 777.5 lb

Also important is the fact that up until now we have only calculated the static load being suspended, not the dynamic load. When a truss is raised or lowered, the starting and stopping of that truss produces a shock load. The faster the starting or stopping, the greater the shock load. The starting and stopping of chain hoist can produce shock loads of 20 to 200 percent of the static load. Although shock loads are often very short in duration, the increase in the load on the hanging points and all other parts of the truss can be significant and must be taken into account.

Remember, a failure at one point on a rig will cause increased load on other points and will often result in a chain reaction of failures across the rig, causing catastrophic results. Shock loads are covered in greater detail Lesson 24.

Sample Problems – Lesson 17

Calculate the approximate load on each hanging point based on the drawing and information below. The truss weighs 10 pounds per linear foot, Lekos weigh 15 pounds each, moving lights weigh 75 pounds each, chain hoists weigh 100 pounds each, and each hoist has 80 feet of chain weighing 1 pound per foot.

1.

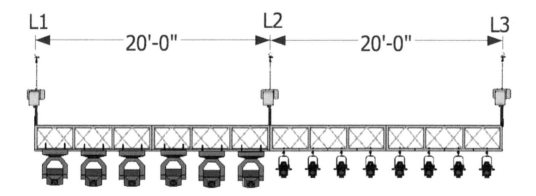

2.

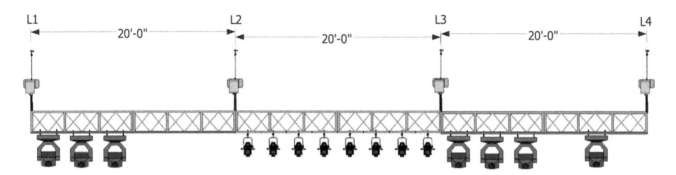

3.

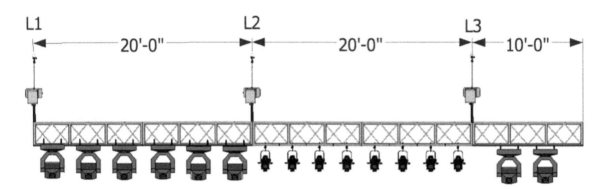

Lesson 18:

Ground-Supported Systems

There seems to have been a growing number of accidents in recent years involving ground-supported rigging, some very high profile. Because there have been numerous causes of these accidents, ground supported rigging, primarily used outdoors, is a subject that deserves some coverage in this book. It should be noted that *ANSI E1. 2006, Temporary Ground-Supported Overhead Structures Used To Cover Stage Areas and Support Equipment in the Production of Outdoor Entertainment Events* provides guidelines to rigging these structures. Appendix 7 explains how you can obtain this and other ANSI Standards related to entertainment rigging free of charge.

Ground-supported systems are different from overhung rigs in several ways, but most importantly, a LOT of weight is supported by a very few number of points, compared to overhung truss rigs. An entire ground-supported rig may be supported by as few as four points. The second big difference is that overhung rigs are supported by beams that have engineered load limits, whereas ground-supported rigs sit on the ... well, the ground, which has usually not been engineered for supporting specific loads. *ANSI E1. 2006* includes detailed information on this subject. A third difference is that ground-based rig are typically used outdoors, where they are subject to wind, snow and rain.

A typical ground-supported system is not a single length of truss, but is actually a grid-work of truss. This truss grid-work may support a roof as well as lights and speakers used for an event. To understand how all of this gets into the air, let's begin our discussion by looking at the towers that typically sit on the corners of the rig and support the truss that makes up the rig. There are many different ways to configure a ground-supported rig, but we will look a simple rig with four towers, one on each corner.

Below is a drawing of the basic parts of a ground-supported truss. (Note: I will be describing a 15" Tower System by James Thomas Engineering. Other tower systems may differ slightly in their design.) Four legs give it a wide base for stability and the leg braces help support the tower. Guy lines, not shown, help stabilize the tower stable. The sleeve block has 16 roller guides and encircles the tower. James Thomas Engineering recommends that the chain hoists be attached to either the outside or downstage side of the sleeve block although I have seen it mounted over the stage for many installations. The chain runs up over the head block and back down to truss attached to the other side of the sleeve block. This configuration creates a double-fall rig and results in:

- the motor only lifting half of the weight on the truss (a 1-ton capacity chain hoist can lift two tons of load)
- the hoist and the truss ascending at a rate of half the speed of the hoist
- the downward force on the truss is equal to the distributed load for the end of the truss (it would have been double that amount if the hoist had been mounted at the base of the tower). As you can see, math has already played an important part in our rigging.

Notes:

1) Different sleeve blocks are required depending on the size of truss needing to be used.

2) Detailed information on Thomas Tower Systems and Truss, including instructions on tower assembly, can be downloaded from http://jthomaseng.com/

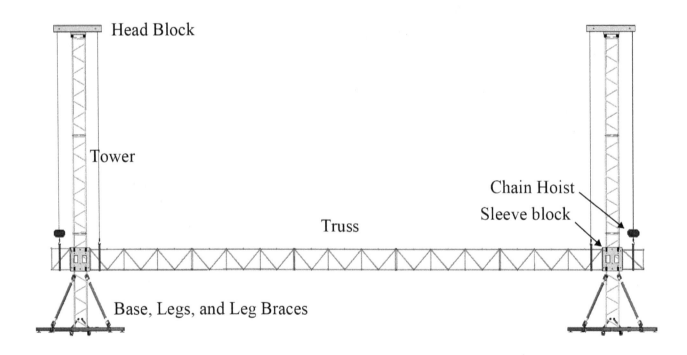

Now, let's look at the truss grid that we will be discussing. Looking at the rig from above, the truss grid is a simple rectangle with three horizontal truss members (Truss 1, Truss 2, and Truss 3) and two vertical members (Truss 4 and Truss 5). The towers are in the corners.

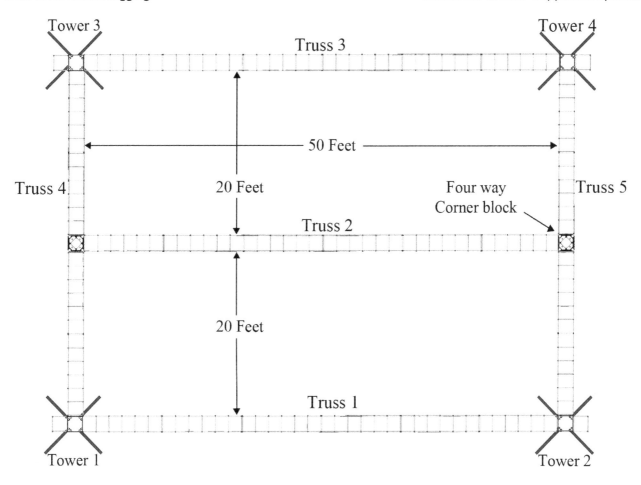

Now, let's put some loads on these trusses. To make things simple, Truss 1, Truss 2, and Truss 3 will have identical loads, except Truss 2 will not have sleeve blocks on the ends. Here is the position of the lights, and the three cable runs.

Where:

20.5" x 2.5" Truss = 8.8 lb per foot

Sleeve block = 75 lb

4-way Block = 37 lb

Conventional fixtures = 25 lb per instrument

Moving Lights = 75 lb per instruments

Cables = 3 lb per foot per cable

Note: Three cables lay on top of each truss, running from SR: Cable 1 is 7.5 feet long, Cable 2 is 25 feet long, and Cable 3 is 42.5 feet long. The cables will run off the SR end of the truss and drop 30 feet to the ground.

Let's now calculate the distribution of the load, as we did in Lesson 16.

The weight of the truss, the moving lights and the conventional fixtures are uniformly distributed across the entire length of the truss. We can total their weights and half of that amount will be distributed to each end of the truss. So,

Truss – 8.8 x 50 = 440 or **220 pounds** per point

Moving lights – 75 x 10 = 750 or **375 pounds** per point

Conventional fixtures = 11 x 25 = 275 or **137.5 pounds** per point

At present we have 712.5 pounds of load distributed to SR and SL ends of the truss. Now, let's calculate the distribution of loads for the cables.

We need to calculate four cable runs; the three that run from the SR end of the truss to their various termination points, and the cable drop - the three cables that run from the top of the truss to the ground. So,

Cable 1 (SR point) = ((3 x 7.5) x (50 – (7.5/2))) / 50

Cable 1 (SR point) = (22.5 x (50 – 3.75)) / 50

Cable 1 (SR point) = (22.5 x 46.25) / 50

Cable 1 (SR point) = (1040.625) / 50

Cable 1 (SR point) = 20.8125 lb

Cable 1 (SL point) = 22.5 – 20.8125

Cable 1 (SL point) = 1.6875 lb

Cable 2 (SR point) = ((3 x 25) x (50 – (25/2))) / 50

Cable 2 (SR point) = (75 x (50 – 12.5)) / 50

Cable 2 (SR point) = (75 x 37.5) / 50

Cable 2 (SR point) = (2812.5) / 50

Cable 2 (SR point) = 56.25 lb

Cable 2 (SL point) = 75 – 56.25

Cable 2 (SL point) = 18.75 lb

Cable 3 (SR point) = ((3 x 42.5) x (50 – (42.5/2))) / 50

Cable 3 (SR point) = (127.5 x (50 – 21.25)) / 50

Cable 3 (SR point) = (127.5 x 28.75) / 50

Cable 3 (SR point) = (3665.625) / 50

Cable 3 (SR point) = 73.313 lb

Cable 3 (SL point) = 127.5 – 73.3125

Cable 3 (SL point) = 54.188 lb

Cable Drop (SR) = 3 x 3 x 30

Cable Drop (SR) = 270 lb

So, the total is:

	SR End	**SL End**
Truss	220.00	220.00
Moving Lights	375.00	375.00
Conventional fixtures	137.50	137.50
Cable 1	20.81	1.69
Cable 2	56.25	18.75
Cable 3	73.31	54.19
Cable Drop	270.00	0.00
TOTAL	**1,152.87**	**807.13**

And the total load per truss is **1,960 pounds.**

This is the total weight, so far, for all three trusses running SR/SL. But before we continue on, we need to check two things: the Maximum Allowable Uniform Load and the Maximum Allowable Center Point Load for the GP 20.5 x 20. 5 truss.

The Maximum Allowable Uniform Load for a 50-foot span using GP 20.5 x 20.5 truss (see http://jthomaseng.com/general-purpose-truss.html) is 1,960 pounds. While our 1,960-pound load is not uniform, it is at the max limit, so we need to be a little concerned.

The SR and SL ends of Truss 2 connect to the 42' truss (Truss 4 and Truss 5) and the middle of their spans. The Maximum Allowable Center Point Load for a 40-foot span is 1,322 pounds. We are fine on SL but kind of close on SR.

This is the point where you should pick up the phone and call the truss manufacturer to check to see if "all is well." Truss manufacturers deal with these questions on a daily basis and they are there to help you, so call them if you are not absolutely certain that your truss is strong enough for the load you intend to hang on it.

In this case, let's assume that the truss manufacturer gives you the "OK" to proceed without changing the size of the truss. So, the next step is to calculate the loads on the four towers. But, before you do, you need to add the weight of the sleeve block, the chain hoist and the chain, as well as half of the weight of Truss 4 and Truss 5 to each tower's load. So, let's add up the loads on the towers.

	Tower 1	Tower 2	Tower 3	Tower 4
Truss 1	1153.0	807.0	0.0	0.0
Truss 2	576.0	404.0	576.0	404.0
Truss 3	0.0	0.0	1153.0	807.0
Truss 4	194.5	0.0	194.5	0.0
Truss 5	0.0	194.5	0.0	194.5
Sleeve Block	75.0	75.0	75.0	75.0
Chain Hoist	114.0	114.0	114.0	114.0
Chain (70 feet)	70.0	70.0	70.0	70.0
TOTALS	**2,182.5**	**1,664.5**	**2,182.5**	**1,664.5**

Note: These weights are rounded and do not include the weight of the tower, head block (roller beam), the base, legs or leg braces. A 35-foot tower, with base, will add approximately 500 pounds to each tower. When the tower is placed on the deck of a stage, be certain that the deck can support the weight. Also, guy wires must to used to stabilize each tower.

Remember, because the truss is rigged as a double-fall, a 1-ton chain hoist can lift 4,000 pounds.

Finally, it is extremely important that the truss-grid is absolutely level before it is raised and that the grid is raised evenly so that it remains level at all times. Should one corner of the truss-grid get too high or too low, the entire weight of the grid becomes supported by only two points, which could be EXTREMELY dangerous. This could cause the truss to torque, bend, break and fall. Also, if the rig is outdoors, it will be subject to wind and other atmospheric factors that WILL increase the load.

This lesson only covered some of the basics of ground-supported rigging. Truss and hoist manufacturers offer specialized seminars on ground-support rigging systems, and these seminars are highly recommended for anyone doing this type of rigging.

Lesson 22 covers more truss calculations.

Lesson 19:
Effective Length of Hitch

The most common way to attach a bridle line to a beam is by making a basket hitch around the beam with a sling. A basket hitch is not only simple to make, but it is the strongest way to attach the bridle line to the beam. However, when a basket hitch is made, the basket itself becomes part of the total length of the bridle, and that must be calculated.

The "Effective Length of Hitch" (ELOH) is the distance from the center of a beam to the end of the basket – including hardware. The factors that determine the ELOH are height and width of the beam, the length and diameter of the sling used to make the bridle and the size of the shackles.

Before we begin, it is important to note that the method described in this lesson ONLY works for "I", "H", "C", square and rectangular beams. This method does not work for T, inverted T or angle iron beams.

In *Entertainment Rigging*, Harry Donovan uses the circumference of the beam to determine the ELOH, but he does not say how he uses it. While it may seem obvious that you need to know the height and width of the beam to calculate the ELOH, what might not be obvious is that you really need to know both the height and width of the beam, plus the diameter of the steel wire rope sling. Why? Because you need to know the segment lengths of the *center* of the slings, as it passes around the beam. Because the circumference of a 5' x 3/8" sling passing around a 12" x 12" beam is shorter than the circumference of a 5' x 1/2" sling passing around a 12" x 12" beam, its ELOH will be longer. This will be made clearer shortly.

The second variable is the length of the sling used to create the basket. Most rigging companies have 5', 10', 20', 30',and 50' wire rope slings, sometimes just referred to as "Steel," for making bridles. Some rigging companies also have 2' and 2.5' slings, called "dog bones." The head rigger will typically choose the shortest sling that wraps around the beam and provide enough extra length to make it easy to create the basket.

The last thing we need to know is the size of shackles being used, or more precisely, we need to know distance from the inside of the bell of the shackle to the pin. For 3/8" diameter slings, 5/8" shackles are commonly used. The distance we need to know for these shackles is 2-3/8". For 1/2" diameter slings, 3/4" shackles are commonly used. Here, the distance we need to know for these shackles is 3".

They are several ways to hitch a sling to a beam, but we will calculate for two of the most common methods - the basket hitch and the split basket hitch.

Since shackles are used to make these basket hitches, we need to know the size and number of shackles needed, so we can add these lengths to the length of our wire rope sling, to calculate the total length of the basket. A regular basket is typically made using two shackles while a split basket is typically made using three shackles. Again, this will all be explained in greater detail shortly, so just be patient.

Finally, when the basket is made around the beam, the two ends form a bridle. And like all bridles, the bridle angle here needs to be 90 degrees or less. A good "rule of thumb" that is easy to remember for calculating the minimum length sling that will form the basket, where the bridle angle of the basket is never greater than 90 degrees (the MBL) is to add the height of the beam to the circumference. For example: if the beam is 12" high and 9" wide, the circumference is 3.5 feet and the MBL is 4.5 feet. The closest standard length sling that is at least 4.5 feet long is 5 feet, so that is probably the best choice. Of course, making the basket longer than the minimum length is not going to hurt anything, so our "rule of thumb" method works just fine.

Effective Length of the Hitch (ELOH) – Quick method (for a standard basket)

There is a simple formula that will get you pretty close to an accurate ELOH measurement:

ELOH = ((Length of sling + (1.5 × $shackle\ length$)) – (Height of beam + width of beam)) / 2

Let's test this on a 12" x 9" beam and a 5-foot basket.

ELOH = ((60 + (1.5 × 2.375) – (12+9)) / 2

ELOH = ((60 + 3.5625) – 21) / 2

ELOH = (63.5625 – 21) / 2

ELOH = 42.5625 / 2

ELOH = 21.28125 inches

We will check this later against our "more accurate" method, so let's get started on it.

Effective Length of the Hitch (ELOH) – Accurate method (for a standard basket)

The first thing we need to do is to calculate the total basket length. This is done by adding the shackle length times the number of shackles needed to the sling length, minus one. Since a regular basket uses two shackles, we add the length of one shackle to the length of the sling. So, to make with a 5' x 3/8" sling, the formula would be:

Basket Length = (5 × 12) + 2.375

Basket Length = 60 + 2.375

Basket Length = 62.375 inches

Notes: 1) If this were a split basket, we would have added the length of two shackles, 2) Don't worry, the missing shackle will come back into the equations later on.

The next step is to subtract the "adjusted" beam width plus the "adjusted" beam height from the Basket length, and then divide that result by 2. By "adjusted," I mean that we add the sling diameter to the actual height and width of the beam. So...

$$B = \frac{\text{Sling length} - ((\text{Beam width} + \text{sling dia.}) + (\text{Beam height} + \text{sling dia.}))}{2}$$

So what the heck did this do? Quite simply, it tells us the (equal) lengths of the "legs" of the sling that remains after it wraps around the beam.

$$B = \frac{62.375 - ((9 + 0.375) + (12 + 0.375))}{2}$$

$$B = \frac{62.375 - (9.375 + 12.375)}{2}$$

$$B = \frac{62.375 - 21.75}{2}$$

$$B = \frac{40.625}{2}$$

B = 20.3125 inches

Next, we need to calculate the distance from the center point of the beam to the center of the sling at the bend point. We do this by using the Pythagorean Theorem. I will call this length "A."

So, for a 9" x 12" beam, and a 3/8" diameter sling ...

$$A = \sqrt{\left(\left(\frac{9.375}{2}\right) \times \left(\frac{9.375}{2}\right)\right) + \left(\left(\frac{12.375}{2}\right) \times \left(\frac{12.375}{2}\right)\right)}$$

$$A = \sqrt{(4.6875 \times 4.6875) + (6.1875 \times 6.1875)}$$

$$A = \sqrt{21.97265625 + 38.28515625}$$

$$A = \sqrt{60.2578125}$$

A = 7.762590579 inches

The drawing below shows the location of "A," that we just calculated. The two ends of the sling "B" are shown, as well as "X," the direction of the bridle leg. We now need to determine where the two ends will join on line "X." The distance from this point to the intersection of "A" and "X" is the "Effective Length of Hitch."

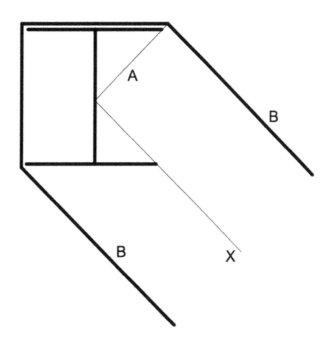

Since the intersection of "A" and "X" is a right angle, we can use a variation of the Pythagorean Theorem to calculate this distance using the equation:

$$ELOH = \sqrt{(B \times B) - (A \times A)}$$

So, plugging in the numbers we have already calculated, we get:

$$ELOH = \sqrt{(20.3125 \times 20.3125) - (7.762584541 \times 7.762584541)}$$

$$ELOH = \sqrt{412.5976563 - 60.25771876}$$

$$ELOH = \sqrt{352.3399375}$$

ELOH = 18.77072022 inches

The final step is to add the length of the missing shackle from earlier. So...

ELOH = 18.77072022 + 2.375

ELOH = 21.14572022 inches

Let's compare this result to our quick calculation at the beginning of this lesson.

Quick ELOH = 21.28125 inches

Accurate ELOH = 21.14572022 inches

This is about 13/100" of an inch difference. Very close.

Note: If you measure the distance between the eyes of a cable sling, you are unlikely to get the measurement that you expect. For example, some cable slings are 1/2" or more shorter than the described length. For this reason, calculating exact ELOHs and bridle lengths is not a reasonable expectation.

Sample Problems – Lesson 19

1. Calculate the ELOH of a basket made around an 18" x 12" I-Beam using a 10' Steel.

2. Calculate the ELOH of a basket made around an 12" x 12" I-Beam using a 15' Steel.

3. Calculate the ELOH of a basket made around an 24" x 12" I-Beam using a 15' Steel.

4. Calculate the ELOH of a split basket made around an 12" x 6" I-Beam using a 5' Steel and a 2.5' Steel.

5. Calculate the ELOH of a split basket made around an 30" x 12" I-Beam using a 5' Steel and a 10' Steel.

Lesson 20:
Two-Point Bridles in an Arena

In Lesson 5 we discussed how to calculate the length of a bridle based on knowing the Horizontal and Vertical distance the Bridle Point would be from the Hanging points. In other words, the head rigger needs to determine the exact position of the Bridle Point and then calculate the lengths of the bridle legs that would create this position. While this will work, it is not always the way it is done.

For example, the head rigger will need the Bridle Point at a specific location in plan view, but instead of needing to put the Bridle Point at an <u>exact</u> height, the head rigger may want it at a <u>minimum</u> height above the deck (high enough to get the truss at the needed height). There is also a <u>maximum</u> height above the deck for the Bridle Point, which is determined by the point where the bridle angle reaches 120 degrees (90 degrees is preferred). As long as the Bridle Point is between the minimum and maximum heights, all is well because the chain hoist will control the height of the truss. To understand why the head rigger does not just choose an arbitrary point between the minimum and maximum heights, we need to understand the resources for making bridle leg.

As discussed in Lesson 18, common lengths of steel slings that rigging companies have include 2', 2.5', 5', 10', 20,' 30' and 50' lengths. Baskets and bridle legs will be made from a combination of these standard length slings. When a bridle leg is an "odd length," one that cannot just be made from the standard lengths listed above, links of STAC chain (aka Deck chain) are added to make the desired length bridle leg.

Note: Actual deck chain is very seldom used anymore - it has been replaced by Special Theatrical Alloy Chain (sometimes called Special Theatrical Adjusting Chain) or STAC chain. Many riggers use the term "Deck chain" when referring to "STAC chain."

STAC chain, which can be purchased in 3-foot and 5-foot lengths, is VERY expensive, especially when compared to the price of cable slings, so rigging companies typically carry only a minimum amount of this chain for rigging. The fewer components in the rig, the fewer chances for mistakes. Because of this, it is usually necessary that at least one bridle leg be able to be made by using ONLY the standard length steel slings. Not using any STAC chain in a bridle is even better.

In the drawing below, we have a bridle where the Bridle Point (also called the "apex") needs to be 10 feet from one I-beam and 15 feet from the second I-beam. This establishes a vertical line on which the Bridle Point must be placed, but where on that line? We see that the I-beams are 80 feet above the deck, and have determined that the minimum height of the bridle point needs to be 40 feet above the deck, and the maximum height of the bridle point is 65 feet above the deck. So, the Bridle Point can be anywhere along the 25-foot long space between these points.

As you see, I have indicated that the first bridle leg is 25 feet long. You might be asking how did I come to choose this length? First, it is a bridle length that I could make with standard length slings (a 20-footer and a 5-footer); and second, it is a distance that I knew from experience would reach from the I-beam to "somewhere" on the line, between the minimum and maximum height points. Of course, if you are not sure if a certain length will work, make a quick, scaled drawing and measure. I will give you more hints on estimating this length shortly, but first let's use this length.

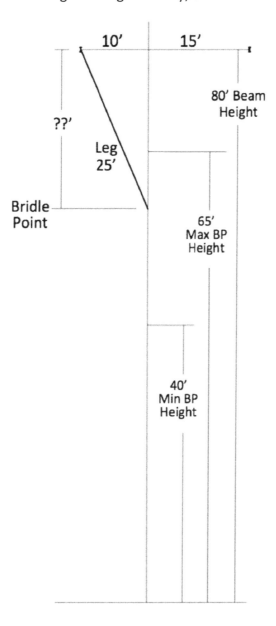

It is important to note now that this leg will be longer than 25 feet. Why? Because I have not added in the Effective Length of Hitch (ELOH) for the basket, and because I have not added in the additional length of the shackle that connects the two sings needed to make 25'. Assuming we use a basket make with a 5-foot sling that is going around a 12" x 9" I-Beam (the example in Lesson 18), we get:

Leg 1 = 25 (the sling) + 1.698661968 (the ELOH in feet) + 0.197916667 (the length of a shackle in feet)

Leg 1 = 26.89657864 feet

Remember, this bridle leg, as calculated, is made without any STAC Chain.

Not only do we know the length of the leg, but also we now have two of the three lengths that make up the bridle triangle. The bridle leg (the hypotenuse) is 27.01 feet long and one leg (the Horizontal distance) is 10 feet long. With this information we can calculate the third leg of the triangle (the Vertical distance). Why this distance is important will become clear soon.

So, using the following variation of the Pythagorean Theorem to calculate this distance using the equation:

$$V = \sqrt{(Leg \times Leg) - (H \times H)}$$

So, plugging in the numbers, we get...

$$V = \sqrt{(26.89657864 \times 26.89657864) - (10 \times 10)}$$

$$V = \sqrt{723.4259423 - 100}$$

$$V = \sqrt{623.4259423}$$

$$V = 24.968499$$

or

V = 25 feet

Before we go on the next step, as promised, here are a couple of suggestions that might help you in estimating the length of the first bridle leg, if you choose not to make a drawing and measure.

Option 1: After you estimate the bridle length and calculate the height of the Bridle Point from the beams, subtract that number from the height of the beam and compare it to the minimum and maximum Bridle Point heights. Using the problem above:

Bridle Point Height = 80 – 22.9

Bridle Point Height = 57.1 feet

Since this measure is greater that the minimum Bridle Point height (40 feet) and less than the maximum Bridle Point Height (65 feet), it is "Good."

Option 2: Take the beam height and subtract the minimum Bridle Point height (80 – 40 = 40 feet). This is going to the somewhere near the maximum length of the bridle. We also know that the bridle length must be greater than the distance from the beam to the maximum Bridle Point height (80-65 = 15 feet). A good compromise length is often somewhere in between, so 40 – 15 = 25 feet.

As we now are beginning to see, several standard bridle lengths would have put the Bridle Point between the minimum and maximum Bridle Point heights.

Option 3: The Bridle Point must falls between the minimum and maximum Bridle Points heights. We can see the range of lengths that would work by calculating the bridle lengths for both these heights.

Leg Length (Min) = $\sqrt{(15 \times 15) + (10 \times 10)}$

Leg Length (Min) = $\sqrt{225 + 100}$

Leg Length (Min) = $\sqrt{325}$

Leg Length (Min) = **18 feet**

Leg Length (Max) = $\sqrt{(40 \times 40) + (10 \times 10)}$

Leg Length (Max) = $\sqrt{1600 + 100}$

Leg Length (Max) = $\sqrt{1700}$

Leg Length (Max) = **41.23 feet**

Based on this range, the following bridle lengths would all work: 20', 25', 30', 35' and 40 feet. Whichever one you choose, you will need to calculate the distance from the beam to the bridle point.

So, why is the 25.08 foot distance so important? It is because we need to know this distance in order to find the length of the <u>other</u> bridle leg. We now know the Horizontal distance (15 feet) and the

Vertical distance (25.08 feet), so we can plug them into the Pythagorean Theorem and find the length of the leg. (This assumes both beams are at the same height above the deck).

Leg = $\sqrt{(15 \times 15) + (25 \times 25)}$

Leg = $\sqrt{225 + 625}$

Leg = $\sqrt{850}$

Leg = 29.155 feet

Finally, we need to figure out how to make a bridle leg that is 29.223 feet long.

Figuring out how to create this bridle will take a bit of trial and error. However, before you begin you should know that there is no one correct answer, and how you do it will be based on what lengths of Steel and STAC Chain are available to you. But, let's look at you might approach this problem.

By using one 20-foot, one 5-foot pieces of Steel (and the lengths of one shackle). So,

L2 = 20 + 5 + 0.1979

L2 = 25.1979 feet

We still need 4.0247 feet of leg.

We know we need a basket, so let's add 1.6093 feet to our leg for a 5' basket.

L2= 25.1979 + 1.781995096

L2 = 26.9802951 feet

That still leaves us 2.242704904 feet short. The big question now is "how do we create this length?"

The answer depends on what we have to use. STAC chain is a common material, but if we have a 2-foot long piece of Steel, that could be used as well. No matter what we use, we need to remember that each new piece of hardware will require an additional shackle (and we can also use shackles to add length). Let's look at two ways two ways to create that additional length of the leg.

Since we know that we will need a shackle, subtract the length of the shackle (0.1979 feet) from desired length (2.242704904 feet). We get 2.044404904 feet. If you added a 2-foot Steel here, the remainder would be a mere 0.0444 feet, or 0.5328 inches. That is REALLY close.

    If we do not have a 2-foot Steel, or if we just want to check another option, we can make this length entirely from STAC chain. Again, we subtract the length of the shackle (0.1979 feet) from desired length (2.242704904 feet to get 2.044404904 feet. Now, to determine the number of needed links of chain, we divide this length by the internal measurement of one link of STAC chain. One common size of STAC chain had 3.174 inches (or 0.2645 feet) links, so we will use this measurement.

Number of links = 2.044404904 /0.2645

Number of links = 7.72797

    Since you cannot add a fraction of a link, you have round to the closest number, in this case it is eight links. This is only 0.8634 inches from the desired length - which is also REALLY close.

    As stated earlier, there is more than one possible solution to this problem. Had we selected to use a longer basket, the ELOH would have been greater, which would have resulted in different lengths of Steel and STAC chain needed. It would be extremely time consuming to manually calculate every single configuration for making up a bridle legs. In Lesson 21, we will look at tools that can help you look at lots of options very quickly.

Lesson 21:
Math Tools of the Trade

While being able to do a rigging math problem from memory is good, in the real world, calculating loads, bridle lengths, etc. is not a "hand operation." The job is too serious and the result of a mistake can be far too costly. There are several tools that help make your calculations faster and help ensure accuracy. Remember, these are tools for riggers, and not tools that make you a rigger.

Apps

There are several good rigging apps riggers can keep on their smart phones and use in the field. Below are some of the best.

PocketRigger by Delbert Hall: *PocketRigger* has more than 47 calculators and reference charts to help you solve rigging problems of all types. This is a web app, which means in can run on any device (computer, tablet, or smartphone, with a web browser.

RigCalc by Alex French (originally created by Delbert Hall): This app has numerous calculators to help solve many different types of rigging math problems, both for arena and stage rigging.

Bridle by Production Innovators: This app quickly calculates the lengths of bridles (including the number of links of deck chain) needed for any bridle setup. This would be a great app if it were not for errors in reporting the number of chain links needed.

iBridle by iBridle: This app does a good job of calculating basic lengths of bridle legs.

Rigging Solutions by Dan Hoffman Productivity: Another app for doing basic bridle calculations.

iRigging by J.R. Clancy: This is a good free app for stage riggers with information on fleet angles, wire rope, arbor and counterweight data, blocks, rope, curtains and more.

RigRite by AppEnginz: This app lets you photograph bridles, and then using the photo as your reference, you draw the bridle and set the load. *RigRite* then tells you the angles and the tension on each leg. This is a very slick and easy-to-use app that is very useful for any rigger.

Angle Meter by Jin Jeon: Of the many angle finding apps available, *Angle Meter* is my favorite. This is free, simple to use app that quickly lets you find the angle of any surface.

Stretch Calculator by Loos & Co.: This free app calculates the stretch of wire rope under a load.

Software (for Windows)

Need a serious rigging program? If so, then Harry Donovan's RigRight 1.0 software may be what you need. At $340, it is not cheap, but it has a lot of features. According to the website, http://www.riggingbooksandprograms.com/Products/RigRight_1.0:

> RigRight is a program that computes and adjusts rigging geometry and forces. It calculates positions, lengths, and forces for bridles, breastlines (taglines), and deadhangs. It manages any number of loads simultaneously, of any weight and at any location, rigged from beams at any location. It does solutions in both 2 and 3 dimensions. Individual solutions can be adjusted to fit a particular situation. It supports files of beams and show rigging points. Solutions can be viewed individually, printed, recorded, and exported in spreadsheet form singly or as part of a group.

> It calculates the forces on rigging equipment and beams exactly, so you know whether they are within safe load limits. Locations are accurate to the inch. Practical solutions can be optimized quicker and better than by any other method. It can cut rigging time and cost in half. It imports and exports files of beams and show rigging points. It is comprehensive, practical, and proven, having been developed and used for 10 years by one of the world's most experienced riggers.

Creating Your Own Rigging Tools

Creating your rigging math tools is not as difficult as it may sound. Plus, they can be a simple or as complex as you want them to be. And, because YOU are creating them, they can be organized in a way that makes the most sense to you. So how can you create these tools? Use Excel or another spreadsheet program to create them.

Long before *RigCalc* was an app, it was a collection of spreadsheets, or "worksheets" as Microsoft calls them, in an Excel workbook. Some of these spreadsheets were very simple, others more complex, but they all solved rigging math problems. One nice thing about a spreadsheet is that it allows the user to enter numbers into cells that contain formulas and quickly see "what if." This is a great tool for rigging problems like the ones covered in Lesson 18, where we are trying to decide between several options.

If you do not know how to create a spreadsheet, I strongly suggest you start learning. Excel and other spreadsheet programs are not hard to learn and you will find scores of ways that they are useful - and not just for rigging math. Appendix 6 is a short introduction to Excel, for those with no experience creating spreadsheets.

Downloads

The remainder of this lesson discusses three Excel workbooks: The Bridle Calculator, the Truss Load Workbook, and Bridle Calculator Pro. You can download these workbooks for free from: www.SpringKnollPress.com/RiggingMath/downloads.

The Bridle Calculator

The Bridle Calculator helps you figure out how to create the bridles needed for any bridle rig (lengths of steel slings and number of links of STAC chain for each leg). The sheet is divided in six parts, each part having its own purpose in the process of solving bridle length problems. Some of these sections are optional, while others must be fully completed. I like to "color code" cells so that I know if a cell is for data entry, displaying a calculated result, or for another purpose. Below is an explanation of the color fills in the workbook.

White – Text cells
Blue – Data entry cells
Yellow or Red – Calculated result cells the ARE critical to the user
Grey – Calculated result cells that are used by other formulas and are not an "end result" calculation

Now, begin your spreadsheet by starting Excel and opening a New Workbook.

Beam Info Section
The Beam Info section is short but critically important. This is where you enter the information about the two beams to which your bridle legs will be attached. You must fill-in data for ALL of the Blue cells.

Beam Info	Beam 1		Beam 2
Height of Beam (in)	12		12
Width of Beam (in)	9		9
Circumference of Beam	3.5		3.5
Height above Deck (ft)	80		80
H Distance (ft)	10.0		15.0
Span (ft)		25.0	

Do not worry about the calculated results at this point – you do not need to deal with them directly. However, they will be used by other formulas elsewhere in this spreadsheet, so enter them first thing.

The Minimum and Maximum Bridle Point Heights

These are "optional" sections. Their purpose is to help you figure out the minimum and maximum heights that the Bridle Point is above the deck. As discussed in Lesson 18, you probably know, or can calculate in your head, the minimum height that this bridle point need to be above the deck. When you enter this height into the appropriate cell in the MIN Bridle Height section, the Vertical Distance from the beam and the Length of the both bridle legs are calculated, as well as the angle between the legs.

MIN Bridle Point Height (ft)		40.0	
V Distance (ft)	40.0		40.0
Bridle Leg Length (ft)	41.2		42.7
		Bridle Angle (Degrees)	
		34.6	

Exactly the same thing happens in the MAX Bridle Height section. However, since we probably do not know the Max height, this section can help us find it.

Enter a number that is greater that the MIN. height and less than the height of the beam into the Data Entry cell in this section. Then check the angle. The goal is to get the angle as close to 90 degrees as possible. Keep changing the height until the angle is 90 degrees (or very close). Now you know the Max height.

MAX Bridle Point Height (ft)		67.0	
V Distance (ft)	13.0		13.0
Bridle Leg Length (ft)	16.4		19.8
		Bridle Angle (Degrees)	
		86.7	

Effective Length of Basket Hitch

The purpose of the Effective Length of Basket Hitch is to calculate the ELOHs, based on the sizes of the beams entered in the Beam info section and the Steel Length (for the basket) entered in this section. Also taken into consideration is whether the basket is made from a single piece of Steel or is a split basket. You MUST do this, since every bridle has a basket.

To help you in choosing what length of Steel to use, the Minimum Basket Lengths (MBL) based on the size of the I-Beams, are displayed next to the calls where the user enters the length of the Steel. The user also enters "Y" or "N" to indicate if this is a split basket or not.

There are six calculated results that are "steps" in finding the ELOHs. These cells have a dark grey background and white text. Remember, these are not results that you need to be concerned about.

Effective Length of Basket Hitch

Leg 1

Steel Length (ft)	MBL (ft)	ELOH (ft)	Split Y/N	(Steel - (H+W))/2	A	
10.0	3.91	4.1786	N	4.22415	0.618718434	0.1983

Leg 2

Steel Length (ft)	MBL (ft)	ELOH (ft)	Split Y/N	(Steel - (H+W))/2	A	
10.0	3.91	4.1786	N	4.22415	0.618718434	0.1983

STAC/Deck Chain Length

This section only asks one question, how long is the internal length of the STAC chain you are using? Different manufactures of STAC chain make links of different lengths. My STAC chain has links with and internal length of 3.125 inches (although 3 inches is close enough). You MUST have a length entered here or the next section will not know how to calculate the number of chain links needed.

STAC/Deck Chain Length

Inside Length of Chain Link	3.125	inches

Bridle Length Workspace

The Effective Length of Basket Hitch is where everything comes together and the user determines the components that will make each bridle leg. Remember, there is more than one way to make a set of bridles that meets your needs, so you could think of this section as doing the math behind the "art" of making brides.

Bridle Length Workspace

	Basic Length	25.0	feet		Bridle Angle	48.1	degrees		Bridle Point 27.83	feet below beam		Bridle Point 52.17	feet above floor

Leg 1*

Total Length	Remaining	Basket	2' Steel	2.5' Steel	5' Steel	10' Steel	20' Steel	30' Steel	50' Steel		# of Shackles	
29.58	0.0	10.0	0		1	0	1	0	0		2	0.3966
			0.0	0	5	0	20	0	0			29.575191955

Leg 2

Total Length	Remaining	Basket	2' Steel	2.5' Steel	5' Steel	10' Steel	20' Steel	30' Steel	50' Steel	Links of STAC Chain	# of Shackles	
31.62	0.0738	10.0	0	0	1	0	1	0		7	3	0.5949
			0	0	5	0	20	0	0		2	29.77349195
												1.8444

* Leg that is calculated first and will have NO STAC/Deck Chain

The first BIG decision is to indicate the "Basic Length" of the bridle leg for Leg 1. This should be either a standard Steel length, of one that can be made for combining two or more standard length cables. This length should be greater than (or equal to) the MAX Bridle Length and less than the MIN Bridle Length that you determined in the sections above (if you used them). Having a range to choose from is the reason those sections are important.

Once you enter a length into the cell for the "Basic length," a "Total Length" will be calculated for Leg 1 and the "Remaining" length is displayed next to it. These are important numbers. Now choose lengths of Steel that equal the "Total Length." As you enter Steel, the "Remaining" length decreases. Once "Remaining" is "0.0" you see all the components needed to make this leg. Remember, this leg will not use any Deck Chain.

Next, you pick the components that make Leg 2. Again, the "Total Length" is displayed, but the "Remaining" length is probably a relatively low number (possibly even 0.0). Why? Look to the right and see the number of "Links of Deck Chain" that are needed. This section adds up the lengths of Steel that has been selected and completes the "Total Length," as close as possible with links of Deck Chain. The "Remaining" cell shows you how close the components are to the desired length. A positive number means the total length of the chosen components are shorter than the "Total Length" and a negative number means the leg is longer than the "Total Length."

The goal now is to add lengths of Steel and bring the number of "Links of Deck Chain" as close to "0" as possible. Remember, in addition to adding Steel to the leg, increasing the basket size (ELOH) can also reduce the number of "Links of Deck Chain."

There you have it. With a little practice you can get the hang of how to use this spreadsheet efficiently. It can save you a lot of work over doing the calculations manually.

The Truss Load Distribution Worksheets

The Truss Load Distribution Worksheet is a collection of spreadsheets (or "worksheets" as Microsoft likes to call them) that can be used to calculate the loads on "points" used to suspend a truss. There are separate spreadsheets of truss suspended by two, three, four, five and six points. The spreadsheets calculate both the static and dynamic loads on each point supporting the truss. Below is a more detailed description of the workbook and how to use it.

The Setup Spreadsheet

Begin by opening the workbook and clicking on the "Setup" tab at the bottom of the screen. The Setup spreadsheet contains two tables - one for truss and a second for chain hoists. Setting up these tables is important because the data from them will be used by all of the other spreadsheets in this workbook. While there is some data already in each table, the tables can be edited by the user to include information about truss or hoists from any manufacturer. As with all the spreadsheets in this workbook, BLUE cells are intended for data input from the user. Most of the other cells are "locked" to prevent accidentally changing a formula or the width of columns.

The truss table has spaces for 8 different trusses and the hoist table has spaces for 12 different hoists. Technical data on several types of truss and hoists can be found in Appendix 4, or taken from information supplied by the manufacturers. The first column in each table is for the Truss Number (1 through 8) or the Hoist Number (1 through 12). These numbers, called "Ref. #" in the load distribution spreadsheets, are very important because they are used to specify the specific truss or hoist used in each rig.

Truss No	Description	Weight /foot
1	12" x 12" Box	6
2	20.5" x 20.5" Box	8.8
3	30" x 20.5" Box	8.8
4	26" x 15" Box	7.5
5	Generic truss	10
6		
7		
8	None	0

The hoist table has a special column titled "Dynamic Load Factor." The cells in this column, like all Red cells in this workbook, are calculated results related to Dynamic Loads. The formula used to calculate these factors is discussed in Lesson 24: Shock Loads. That is all there really is to this sheet. Once you have entered the data for the truss and hoists, you are done with this sheet and can move on to actually calculating loads on points.

Hoist No	Description	Weight	Capacity	Chain Weight	Speed	Dyn. Load Factor
1	CM Loadstar - Model F	74	1/2 Ton	0.5	16	0.266666667
2	CM Loadstar - Model L	114	1 Ton	1	16	0.266666667
3	CM Loadstar - Model RR	112	2 Ton	1	16	0.266666667
4	CM Loadstar - Model F	74	1/2 Ton	0.5	32	0.533333333
5	CM Loadstar - Model L	114	1 Ton	1	32	0.533333333
6	CM Loadstar - Model RR	112	2 Ton	1	32	0.533333333
7	Generic Hoist	120	1 Ton	1	16	0.266666667
8						0
9						0
10						0
11						0
12	None			0		0

Load Distributions Spreadsheets

The load distribution spreadsheets are setup in an identical fashion, so once you have been through the process of entering data in one spreadsheet, you can enter data in any sheet. So, click on the "Two Point" tab to display the spreadsheet for calculating the load distributed on a truss supported by two points.

Column B contains two lists, one for truss and one for hoist. These lists are a type of "cheat sheet" to help users know the reference numbers for the truss and hoists in the tables in the Setup spreadsheet. So, edit the list to accurately reflect the information entered in the Setup spreadsheet. These are only reference lists for the user - they are not used for any actual calculations.

Hoist Ref. Index
1 = 1/2 Ton, 16 fps
2 = 1 Ton, 16 fps
3 = 2 Ton, 16 fps
4 = 1/2 Ton, 32 fps
5 = 1 Ton, 32 fps
6 = 2 Ton, 32 fps
7 = Generic
8 =
9 =
10=
11=
12=

Truss Ref. Index
1 = 12" x 12"
2 = 20.5" x 20.5"
3 = 30" x 20.5"
4 = 20" x 15"
5 = Generic
6 =
7 =
8 =

The rest of the page is divided into two parts, both with BLUE cells for entering data. The BLUE cells in the top portion relate to the truss and hoists and ALL must have a number in them, even if the number is "0." The bottom portion is where the information about the loads that are hung on the truss is entered. There are 30 load rows, and you can use as many or as few of them as needed. This section will be discussed later, for now let's look at the top portion – the Rig Setup Space.

Rig Setup Space

The two YELLOW and RED cells at the top of the page are where the calculated static and dynamic loads for each "point" will be displayed, and the ORANGE and VIOLET cells on the upper right are the Total Static and Total Dynamic Loads for the entire rig. These numbers are the entire point of this workbook, they are the results of all the calculations in the worksheet, so they are at the top of the page. The rest of the space is dedicated to data entry and a graphical representation of the truss.

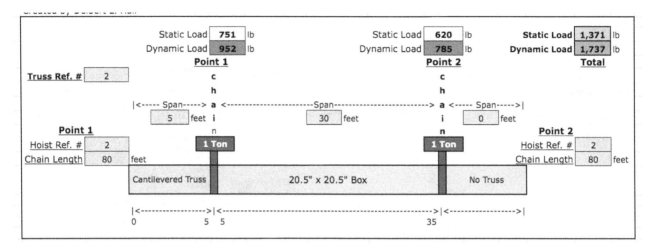

Begin by entering the Ref. # for the truss. When you do, the "Description" of the truss from the Setup sheet will appear in the truss. Next, you will see a row with three Blue cells with "Span" over them. Enter the lengths of the spans (in feet). Your truss may or may not have cantilevered ends. If the end of the truss is not cantilevered, enter "0." (Do not enter negative numbers). When you enter the spans, three things will happen:

- Either "No Truss" or "Cantilevered Truss" will be displayed in the graphical representation of the "end" portions of the truss to best describe these portions.
- The measurements for the truss will change to show "0" at the left end and the measurement at key points on the truss.
- The static and dynamic loads will be displayed at the top of the space, changed. This is not really important right now, but it did happen and you should be aware of it. The point loads are recalculated every time you change the data in a cell.

The last thing to do in this section is to enter the Ref. # and the length of the chain for each hoist. When you do, the description of each hoist will be displayed inside its graphical representation, and the static and dynamic loads will change again. At this time, the point loads for an empty truss have been calculated and displayed at the top of the page, and it is time to add the loads to the truss.

The Load Entry Space

There are four columns in this section. The first column is just the load numbers. No big deal. But, the next three columns are where the information about your loads (lights, speakers, curtains, etc.) is entered, and that is a big deal. Enter the location (in feet) in the "Loc" column and the weight of the item in the "Weight" column. You can, and probably should, enter a short description of the item in the "Notes" column to help remind you what this load is.

Load #	Location	Weight	Notes
1	2.5	75	Moving Light
2	20	600	8 Moving Light (UD)
3			
4			
5			
6			
7			
8			
9			
10			
11			
13			
14			
15			
16			
17			
18			
19			
20			
21			
22			
23			
24			
25			
26			
27			
28			
29			
30			

If you specify the location of a load that is less than zero (a negative number), or greater than the total length of the truss, a warning message will be displayed. If this happens, first check the load location and then the span lengths. Correct the problems and then enter the next load.

While you may initially think of a "Load" as a single item, and it can be, it can also be a group of items. For example, if you have 8 conventional lighting fixtures, each weighing 25 pounds, that are equally spaced over the span between Point 1 and Point 2, then it is the same as a 200-pound load located in the middle of the span. You can save time by making the instruments a single large load instead of eight smaller loads. As long as you can find the center point of a group of identical items, you can use that point and their combined weight to simplify data entry. As before, as you entered loads, the static and dynamic loads on each point are recalculated.

If you have a uniformly distributed load that runs the entire length of the truss, such as a large number of lighting instruments, you can really simplify and speed-up your data entry by creating a "truss" in the Setup spreadsheet (call it "Truss and Lights" or some descriptive name). List the weight per foot as the combined weight of the truss AND the lights (per foot). Now, when you select item as your truss, the distribution of loads for both the truss and the lights are calculated at one time.

Completion

Once all the loads have been entered, you are probably done. However, if after looking at the point loads you decide you either need a larger or a smaller capacity chain hoist, no problem. Just specify a different hoist reference number. When you do, if the hoist weight is different, the new point loads are instantly recalculated.

All of the load distribution spreadsheets in this workbook are organized in the same fashion, just the number of hoists and spans change. Click on one of the other Load Distribution tabs and see for yourself.

One Last Important Thing

As accurate as these calculations may seem, it is important to remember that point load calculations for a truss suspended by more than two points is only a rough estimate. A truss that is out of level, by even a single link in a leg, will significantly affect the loads on all supporting legs. Since the hoists are not synchronous, they will travel at different speeds, the loads will vary and the dynamic loads on the points will fluctuate.

Using load cells on truss is the best way to know the actual loads and how they fluctuate, but they are expensive. Some shows use load cells on the truss for the initial setup. By monitoring the loads the head rigger has a good idea of the loads during future load-ins. The insertion of a load cell in a bridle leg will alter the bridle leg length and must be accounted for in calculations.

Point loads of truss suspended by more than two points are complex, but it is important to know what the approximate load should be and allow enough leeway for all of the variants that routinely occur.

Bridle Calculator Pro

Bridle Calculator Pro (BC-Pro1.xlsx) is an advanced version of the Bridle Calculator discussed earlier. It has a number of features not included in the other bridle workbook. Once you know how to use the Bridle Calculator, learning to use Bridle Calculator Pro should not be difficult. However, there are a few things that you really need to know in order to use it.

The biggest thing that users must know is that Bridle Calculator Pro makes use of an "add-in" called InchCalc. InchCalc is a separate program that must be downloaded to your computer, and then you must link it to the Bridle Calculator Pro worksheet in order for the InchCalc functions that are in this workbook to work. InchCalc.xla can be downloaded from www.SpringKnollPress.com/ RiggingMath/downloads. Appendix 7 explains how to install and link this file to Bridle Calculator Pro.

So, what does this add-in do? In short, it lets measurements be input and output in traditional feet and inches format - for example: 32'-8 1/2" (instead or 32.70733333 feet). Measurements can be entered as feet, inches or both. For example 3', 36" and 3'-0" all work fine. Because the dash symbol is optional - 3' 0" is also OK. However, if you forget to use the either a foot or inch symbol (and you will most likely make this mistake at some point), you will get a "#VALUE!" error wherever this value is referenced. So, when you see this error, just look for the place you left off the measurement symbol and put it in.

Other features of Bridle Calculator Pro include a listing of slings needed to make up each leg and a graphical representation of the bridle.

Conclusion

Worksheets (spreadsheets) can be very powerful and very useful. I use them almost daily for making calculations of all types. In fact, both *Pocket Rigger* and *RigCalc* app started as a collection of worksheets in an Excel workbook. The workbooks discussed in this lesson are free for you to download and use as you wish. However, their proper use is YOUR responsibility and liability for their improper use lies with you.

Finally, I am not the only rigger who creates workbooks. Download Ben Kilmer's Roof Load Calculator from www.RigWorld.org. And if you develop a cool rigging worksheet, I hope you will share it with me and others.

Lesson 22:

Calculating Bridle Lengths Using Little or No Math

The last two lessons have been very math intensive - hardly "simple" math at all. This lesson does a great deal of what was covered those lessons but without the need for quite as much math. You might be wondering "why didn't you just cover this and forget about that complicated stuff?" There are two reasons: 1) much of what is covered it this lesson are "shortcuts" to what you learned earlier, and before you learn to "cut corners" you need to know as much as possible about the task; and 2) some of the methods in this lesson "round-off" or "estimate" certain things, so it is not as accurate as the methods you learned earlier. If this lesson had a subtitle, it might be "close is close enough." This will make sense as we get into the lesson.

Much of this lesson is a summary of Fred Breitfelder's book, *Bridle Dynamics for Production Riggers*. This book is available as an eBook (PDF file) that can be purchased from Fred's website http://www.bridledynamics.com. The entire premise of Fred's book is to teach riggers how to calculate bridle lengths quickly and without the need of a calculator. If you like these "old school" rigging techniques, I highly recommend that you purchase Fred's book.

ELOH

Lesson 19 was devoted to leaning how to calculate the Effective Length of a Hitch (ELOH), or what Fred calls the "push." Much of what I covered in that lesson Fred shortens to: ELOH of a 5-foot basket is 2 feet and the ELOH of a 10-foot basket is 3 feet - period. There is no accounting for the size of the beam, you only have to remember these two lengths.

As you can see, the math just got <u>much</u> simpler; in fact there is no math at all here. However, the numbers are not as accurate - see what I meant in the first paragraph above? While this may seem like a gross simplification, it is often "close enough" to the actual ELOH for many rigging situations, and it makes determining the bridle lengths much faster and easier. We will use these ELOHs throughout this lesson, so keep keep these numbers in mind.

The Give-and-Take Method of Calculating Bridle Lengths (for beams at the same height)

This method, like many of the methods discussed in this lesson, require that you compare the "desired bridle" to a "reference bridle." This reference bridle has legs that are equal length, so the apex is centered between the beams. The length of the legs is proportional to the Span distance, and are either 100% of the Span distance, 70% of the Span distance (Span distance times 0.7), or 60% of the Span distance (Span distance times 0.6). Which length you choose is dependent on the height of the steel and the minimum hook height required. However, the smaller the percentage, the flatter the bridle, and the greater the force on the beams. So, when possible, use the steepest (longest) bridle possible.

The table below shows the approximate bridle angle using the percentages of the Span discussed above. Remember, the bridle angle should NEVER exceed 120 degrees.

Leg Length compared to Span	Approximate Bridle Angle
100%	60 degrees
70%	90 degrees
60%	120 degrees

We really care about calculating the depth (vertical distance) of the bridle. It is just whatever it is. What we are concerned about is the Span and the Leg Length.

Now that you understand the reference bridles, we need to look at how we use them to calculate the Leg Lengths that will put the apex at the desired horizontal location. This method is called Give-and-Take because we will add length to one bridle leg, and take away the same distance from the other leg. What we need to calculate is the length to add and subtract. To do this we have to know the horizontal distance that the apex is from the center of the Span (where it is in our reference bridle).

Let's work out an example where the Span is 24 feet and the apex needs to be 18 feet from one beam and 6 feet from the other. What we really need to see is that the apex is 6 feet from the center of the Span. Now that we have this number (let's call it the "Off-center Distance"), we can plug it into our formula.

The formulas to calculate the leg lengths are slightly different depending on which of the three reference bridles you use. The easiest one is the reference bridle whose legs are 100% of the Span.

Long Leg Length = Span + (Off-center Distance /2)

Short Leg Length = Span - (Off-center Distance /2)

So, plugging the numbers from our example into the formulas, we get:

Long Leg Length = 24 + (6/2)

Long Leg Length = 24 + 3
Long Leg Length = 27 feet

Short Leg Length = 24 - (6 /2)
Short Leg Length = 24 - 3
Short Leg Length = 21 feet

Now, to make these bridle legs we need to subtract the ELOH for the basket lengths. So if we are using 5-foot baskets, we get:

Long Leg Length = 5B/19
Short Leg Length = 5B/25

If the apex is too low when using the 100% reference bridle, then you may have to use either the 70% or 60% reference bridles. When you use these reference bridles, the formulas are:

Long Leg Length = (Span x 0.7) + (Off-center Distance x 0.7)
Short Leg Length = (Span x 0.7) - (Off-center Distance x 0.7)

and

Long Leg Length = (Span x 0.6) + (Off-center Distance x 0.6)
Short Leg Length = (Span x 0.6) - (Off-center Distance x 0.6)

respectively. So, using the same example with a 70% Reference Bridle, we get:

Long Leg Length = (24 x 0.7) + (6 x 0.7)
Long Leg Length = 16.8 + 4.2
Long Leg Length = 21 feet

Short Leg Length = (24 x 0.7) - (6 x 0.7)
Short Leg Length = 16.8 - 4.2
Short Leg Length = 12.6 feet

When we specify the bridle make up, we will probably do more rounding so that we can make them with standard length slings. Doing so, we might get:

Long Leg Length = 5B/20   Note: Remember, a 5-foot bridle gives and ELOH of 2 feet
Short Leg Length = 10B/10   Note: Remember, a 10-foot bridle gives and ELOH of 3 feet

One-Leg-Adjustment Method (for beams at the same height)

The Give-and-Take Method allows us to calculate the lengths of the bridle legs very accurately, but we have to calculate changes to both legs. The One-Leg-Adjustment Method allows us to keep one leg the same length as the Span and only adjust one leg length. While this method has half the math, it is not as accurate as the Give-and-Take Method. Plus, the more you need to move the apex from the center of the Span, the less accurate it becomes. For this reason, this method is best when you need to move the apex 30% or less of the Span distance.

This method can be used two ways:

1) Add length to one leg, or 2) Subtract length from one leg

This method is based on adding or removing a percentage of the Span to or from one leg. To understand both how this works, and the distortion that occurs, look at the tables below. In this example, will will be using a Span of 20 feet, so we start with a reference bridle that has two 20-foot long legs and show changes of one leg in 12" increments (5% changes).

Adding length to one leg

Leg length	Add Length	% of Span	Off-center Distance
20'	0"	100%	0"
21'	12"	105%	12"
22'	12"	110%	12.6"
23'	12"	115%	13.2"
24'	12"	120%	13.8"
25'	12"	125%	14.4"
Total	**60"**		**66"**

Note: Each Off-center Distance change is 5% greater than the one above it.

Subtracting length from one leg

Leg length	Add Length	% of Span	Off-center Distance
20'	0"	100%	0"
19'	12"	95%	12"
18'	12"	90%	11.4"
17'	12"	85%	10.8"
16'	12"	80%	10.2"
15'	12"	75%	9.6"
Total	**60"**		**54"**

Note: Each Off-center Distance change is 5% less than the one above it.

As you can see, this cumulative effect causes the distortion to increase as you move away from the center. In this case it is 6 inches, either long or short, depending on which method you use. Many riggers use this method as follows:

- They begin by making each leg of the bridle the same length as the Span distance. This creates an equilateral triangle with the Span and the two bridle legs.
- Then, whatever distance the apex needs to be offset from center, they add that length of Deck Chain to one leg. Example: adding 1 foot of chain to one leg moves the apex 1 foot away from the center (away from the long leg).

While this method may not always be as accurate as other methods, for short offsets it is usually accurate enough. Plus, it is a very quick and easy way to calculate bridle lengths.

The One-Eighth Bridle Trick

This is a quick and easy way to calculate the legs of a bridle that will put the apex 1/8 of the span distance from one beams and 7/8 of the span distance from the other beam, no matter the length of the Span.

Long Leg = 100% of Span
Short leg = 50% of Span

Beams at Different Heights

Up until now, we have been working with beams at the same height. While this is the most common situation, it is certainly not unusual to have beams at different heights. In this section we will look at how to calculate the lengths of legs when the apex is centered between two beams of different heights.

Let me lay out the two formulas/rules that you use for these calculations, then I will explain when to use each one. Before I do this I need to define one term - "Rise." Rise is the difference in heights of the low and high beams. If the low beam is 80 feet above the deck and the high beam is 100 feet above the deck, the Rise is 20 feet. Got it?

The 90% Rule
Short Leg Length = Span
Long Leg Length = Span + (Rise x 0.9)

The 80% Rule
Short Leg Length = Span
Long Leg Length = Span - (Rise x 0.8)

Knowing when do you use each is important.

Use the 90% Rule if: Rise is greater than 40% of the Span
Use the 90% Rule if: Rise is 40% of the Span or less

Of course, the minimum required height of the hook (apex) is also a consideration in choosing a one rule/formula over the other.

Let's do an example. If the low beam is 80 feet above the deck and the high beam is 90 feet above the deck, the Rise is 10 feet. If the Span is 20 feet, then the Rise is 50% of the Span, so use the 90% Rule. So, the lengths of the legs will be:

Short Leg Length = 20 feet

Long Leg Length = 20 + (10 x 0.9)
Long Leg Length = 20 + 9
Long Leg Length = 29 feet

Bridle Length Cheat Sheets

Whether the beams are at the same height or at different heights, one way to eliminate the need for doing math in the field is to create Bridle Reference Guides (aka "cheat sheets").

There are many ways to create these cheat sheets, but they sometimes involve one bridle leg that can be made from common steel sling lengths (what I call the "Fixed Length Leg"), and another leg that compliments the first and horizontally positions the apex at the desired location. Both of my cheat sheets below use this practice.

I created my cheat sheets with Microsoft Excel. This makes it is easy to edit things like the Span, the Fixed Leg Length, and the Basket length to create other cheat sheets. By printing cheat sheets and taking them to the arena, you can determine the bridle lengths for many different situations without needing to do any math in the field.

Note: You can download these files from www.SpringknollPress.com\RiggingMath\downloads. Please feel free to edit these files to make them suit your purposes, and to improve them.

The first cheat sheet below is for determining the lengths of the legs for bridles hung from beams at different heights, while the second cheat sheet is for beams at the same height. Both provide the user with a great amount of information about the bridles.

Uneven Beam Height - Bridle Leg Cheat Sheet

High Beam Height:	90	feet
Low Beam Height:	80	feet
Rise:	10	feet
Fixed Leg length:	**32**	**feet**
Span:	24	feet
Basket Length:	5	feet
ELOB:	2	feet

5B/30   32-foot leg is attached to HIGH BEAM

High Beam / **Low Beam**

Offset (feet)	Depth (feet)	Low Beam Leg Length	Bridle Makeup	Bridle Angle
12 (High)	11.2	11.2 feet	5B/9.2	65
11	12.2	12.3 feet	5B/10.3	65
10	13.2	13.4 feet	5B/11.4	64
9	14.1	14.5 feet	5B/12.5	63
8	15.0	15.5 feet	5B/13.5	62
7	15.7	16.5 feet	5B/14.5	61
6	16.5	17.5 feet	5B/15.5	60
5	17.1	18.5 feet	5B/16.5	59
4	17.7	19.4 feet	5B/17.4	58
3	18.3	20.4 feet	5B/18.4	57
2	18.8	21.3 feet	5B/19.3	56
1	19.2	22.2 feet	5B/20.2	55
0 (CL)	19.7	23.0 feet	5B/21	53
1	19.2	22.2 feet	5B/20.2	54
2	18.8	21.3 feet	5B/19.3	54
3	18.3	20.4 feet	5B/18.4	54
4	17.7	19.4 feet	5B/17.4	54
5	17.1	18.5 feet	5B/16.5	54
6	16.5	17.5 feet	5B/15.5	54
7	15.7	16.5 feet	5B/14.5	54
8	15.0	15.5 feet	5B/13.5	54
9	14.1	14.5 feet	5B/12.5	53
10	13.2	13.4 feet	5B/11.4	52
11	12.2	12.3 feet	5B/10.3	51
12 (Low)	11.2	11.2 feet	5B/9.2	49

Bridle Leg Cheat Sheet

Fixed Leg length:	22	feet		5B/20
Span:	30	feet		
Basket Length:	5	feet		
ELOB:	2	feet		

Off-center Distance (feet):	15	14	13	12	11	10	9	8	7	6	5	4	3	2	1	0
Depth (feet):	22.0	22.0	21.9	21.8	21.6	21.4	21.2	20.9	20.5	20.1	19.6	19.1	18.4	17.7	17.0	16.1
Length of Leg:	37.2 feet	36.4 feet	35.6 feet	34.7 feet	33.8 feet	32.9 feet	32.0 feet	31.0 feet	30.1 feet	29.1 feet	28.0 feet	26.9 feet	25.8 feet	24.6 feet	23.3 feet	22.0 feet
Bridle Makeup:	5B/35.2	5B/34.4	5B/33.6	5B/32.7	5B/31.8	5B/30.9	5B/30	5B/29	5B/28.1	5B/27.1	5B/26	5B/24.9	5B/23.8	5B/22.6	5B/21.3	5B/20
Bridle Angle:	54	55	57	59	61	63	64	66	68	70	73	75	77	80	83	86

The Bridle Chart

When it comes to calculating bridle lengths it is hard to beat the Pythagorean Theorem. However, the math is certainly more complicated that anything we have done in this lesson. A Bridle Chart is Pythagorean Theorem "cheat sheet" that allows you to look-up the length of the hypotenuse of any right triangle without having to do any math. Below is an example of Bridle Chart.

	DEPTH												
SPAN		2	4	5	6	7	8	9	10	11	12	13	14
	10	10.2	10.8	11.2	11.7	12.2	12.8	13.5	14.1	14.9	15.6	16.4	17.2
	15	15.1	15.5	15.8	16.2	16.6	17	17.5	18	18.6	19.2	19.8	20.5
	20	20.1	20.4	20.6	20.9	21.2	21.5	21.9	22.4	22.8	23.3	23.9	24.4
	25	25.1	25.3	25.5	25.7	26	26.2	26.6	26.9	27.3	27.7	28.2	28.7

Using it is simple. First, find the Span (horizontal) distance of Leg 1 in the SPAN row. Let's choose 10 feet for this example, so look across the SPAN row until you find "10." Put your finger on it. Next, select the Depth (vertical distance that the apex is below the beam). Let's use 15 feet. Run your finger down the column until you get to the number that aligns with the "15" in the DEPTH column. Your finger should be on "18." This is the length of the leg - 18 feet.

Notes:

1) I set my Bridle Chart up a little differently than the one in *Bridle Dynamics for Production Riggers,* so do not be confused by this.

2) A more extensive Bridle Chart can be found in Appendix 3-1 and 3-2 of *Entertainment Rigging* by Harry Donovan.

Lesson 23:

How much load can I put on a truss?

The "worst" location to hang a heavy point load on a truss or batten is in the center of a span because this creates the greatest deflection. Truss manufacturers typically specify both the Maximum Allowable Center Point Loads and the Maximum Allowable Uniform Point Loads for their truss, and sometimes the Maximum Deflection of their truss (see http://jthomaseng.com/general-purpose-truss.html or http://www.mainlight.com/pdf/products/truss/tomcat/12x18lightdutyplated.pdf). These charts, which show for load data for each type of truss, are based on the span between the lift points. For many truss, you can expect the Maximum Allowable Center Point Load to be approximately half of the Maximum Allowable Uniform Point Load, however, it is always best to check the manufacturer's data for the truss you are using.

The question that most riggers want answered is "how do you know if you have overloaded the truss?" Good question. Clearly, the answer is based on where the load(s) is/are placed on the truss and their weights.

For the example below, let's assume that we are using a GP 12" X 12" truss from James Thomas Engineering, and that the truss has a 40-foot span between the lift points. The manufacturer tells us that the Maximum Allowable Center Point Load for this truss is 428 pounds. So this is the number that we want be sure that we do not exceed. If we were hanging a single point load on center, this would be really easy to calculate, but what if our load is not on the center? In this case, we need to determine downward force at the center point for a point load that is hung at a location other than the center of the span.

Before we look at the formula, let's look at the data that you will need to know:

- Load equals Weight of the Point Load
- Location of Point Load equals Where on the truss the Load is hung. In this case, it will be a number between 0 (one end of the truss) and 40 (the other end).
- Center of Truss equals Half of the Span distance. In this example it is 20.
- Distance from Location of Point Load to Center of Truss equals the Distance from Location of Point Load to Center of Truss

Let's make the Load = 500 pounds and the Location of Point Load = 12 feet. So,

Load = 500
Location of Point Load = 12
Center of Truss = 20
Distance from Location of Point Load to Center of Truss = 8

To make the calculation easier, let's break it into two parts. First, let's calculate a "Divisor." The formula for the Divisor is:

Divisor = Center Point / (Center Point - Distance from Location of Point Load to Center of Truss)

So,

Divisor = 20/(20-8)

Divisor = 20/12

Divisor = 1.6666667

Now that we have the Divisor, the second part of the formula is simple.

Downward Force at Center Point = Load/Divisor

So,

Downward Force at Center Point = 500/1.666667

Downward Force at Center Point = 300 pounds

Since 300 pounds is less than the Maximum Allowable Center Point Load of 428 pounds, it is safe to hang this load at this location on our truss.

    If you have two or more loads on the truss, calculated the Downward Force at Center Point for each load, then sum the forces to get the Total Downward Force at Center Point.

    After you have done a few problems, you will notice that the further the load is away from the center of the truss, the greater the Divisor, and therefore, the lower the percentage of the Load is transferred to the center of the truss. Also, if you enter a number that is less that 0 or greater than the Span distance as the Location of the Point Load, you will get a negative load as the Downward Force at Center Point. This is because the load is on a cantilevered portion of the truss. This concept was covered in Lesson 15. In fact, if this lesson sounds a bit similar to the material in Lessons 13, 14 and 15, it is because it is indeed similar. However, those lessons calculated the downward force at the lift points (at the ends of the beam in Lessons 13 and 14), while this lesson calculates the downward force at the center of the span/beam.

One more thing. As stated above, the further the load is away from the center point, the greater that load can be. However, based on the method described above, if the load will be very close to the end of the truss, the potential load could be enormous - hundreds of thousands of pounds. Clearly, this amount cannot be practical. So, what is the maximum point load that you can put anywhere on the truss? That answer depends on the truss, but one clue is to look at the Maximum Allowable Center Point Load for a 10-foot span. For the GP 12" X 12" Truss, that number is 4,497 pounds. That is a lot of weight to hang on a single point. My recommendation is that is you are planning to hang anything close to the Maximum Allowable Center Point Load for a 10-foot span as a point load on a truss, you need to contact the truss manufacturer or an engineer for assistance.

By the way, I have created an Excel spreadsheet that does these types of calculations. It is called Force_at_CenterPoint.xls and you can download it from www.SpringKnollPress.com/downloads.

Sample Problems – Lesson 23

1. What is the downward force at the center point of a 30-foot long truss with a 350 pound point load at 10 feet?

2. What is the downward force at the center point of a 40-foot long truss with a 500 pound point load at 17 feet?

3. What is the downward force at the center point of a 30-foot long truss with 315 pound point loads at 10 feet and 20 feet?

Lesson 24:

Chalk Markings and Arena Floor Layout

This chapter will examine rigger's chalk markings and the process of laying out an arena floor.

Chalk Marks

Chalk markings are drawn on the floor of a venue and refer to the specific location of rigging points. They give the rigger specific information on point locations and how to make up the bridles and baskets for these specific locations.

Rigging points

Rigging points refer to locations where the chain hoists will attach to the truss and eventually attach to the ceiling I-beams. The House Rigger begins by establishing the 0-0 reference point *usually* at the upstage end of the stage and centerline near the arena floor knee wall called the dasher. 0-0 may vary from production to production, but it does need to be determined before any of the floor layout begins. 0-0 is not always shown on the rigging plot.

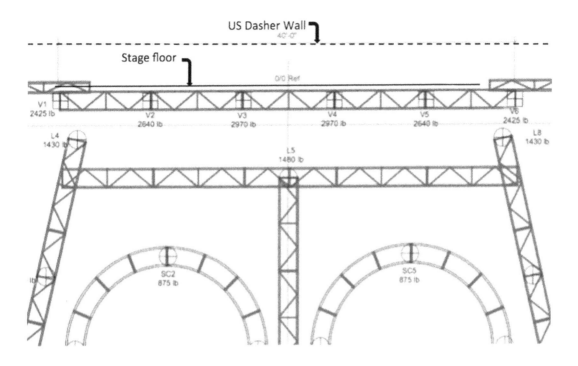

Upstage portion of a rigging plot

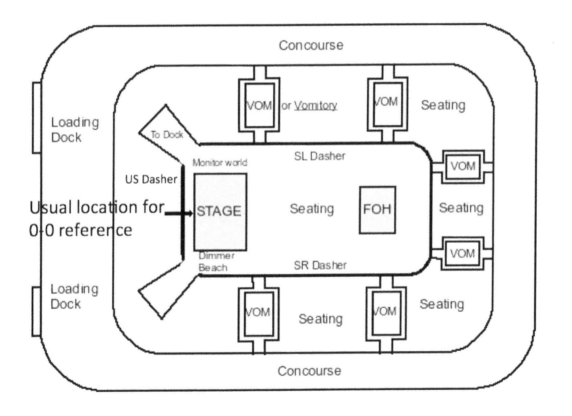

The 0-0 reference location may vary depending on the production, but its reference needs to be established. *Photo courtesy of IATSE local 470*

These are similar to the location of the centerline/ plaster-line in a theatre venue. The centerline of the arena is measured out downstage with a tape measure from the 0-0 reference. Horizontal references are measured off the centerline both SR and SL to the side dasher with measuring tapes. Rigging points are located off of these measurements by the Production Rigger. These points are marks on the floor where the motor hoists will go based on the production-rigging plot. The House Rigger will then come along and mark out the bridle information next to each point based on the I-beam configuration in the ceiling. Chalk markings may vary from venue to venue, but once you understand the basics, they are fairly easy to read.

The following illustrations show some basic rigging point markings. However, not every Head/Show Rigger follows these markings. The most basic marking is a simple circle with horizontal and vertical markings.

Basic Rigging Point

More specific markings maybe shown as follows:

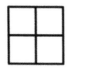

Sound Point   Video Point   Projection Point

The actual rigging "point" is the intersection of horizontal and vertical markings. It is this intersection that provides the up-rigger with a target to aim for with his rigging line.

Variations on Rigging Floor Marks- Hoist Markings

The illustrations below show how additional information can be added onto the floor markings for clarification.

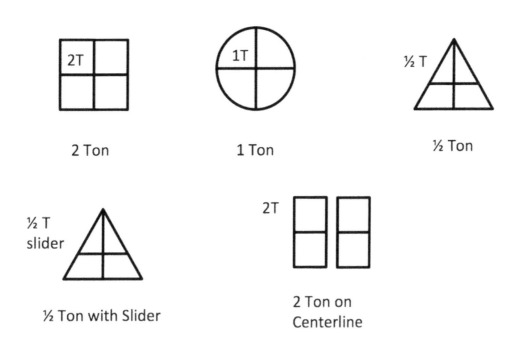

Variations on Rigging Floor Marks - Hoists

2 Ton   1 Ton   ½ Ton

½ Ton with Slider   2 Ton on Centerline

On the other hand, the rigging point symbols themselves may be found to represent hoists only as shown in the illustration below. This only goes to show that there is no standardization in the industry and how important it is for the new rigger to learn the markings as quickly as possible.

Another Variation Rigging Floor Marks for Hoists

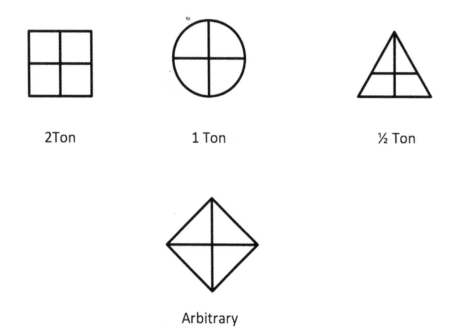

2Ton   1 Ton   ½ Ton

Arbitrary

In addition, dead-hangs can be identified by showing the basket and bridle markings together. The illustration below shows a 15-ft basket (a split basket) and a 30-ft leg or stinger. The centerline point shows the rigging point as split due to the tape measure that was laid out down the middle of the arena floor.

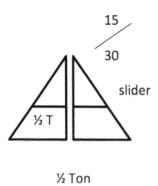

½ Ton

½ Ton Hoist with slider
on Centerline. Deadhang
with 15' split basket and 30'
stinger.

Bridle Markings

Bridle Markings provide the down-rigger with information on how to make up the bridle and basket for a specific rigging point. These are drawn next to the rigging point chalk marks.

   This Bridle Marking shows two split 15-foot baskets (SP 15), two 20-foot bridles, and a 5-foot stinger.

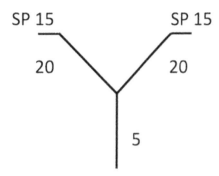

   Not every Bridle Marking will show the basket. For example, if the arena venue uses split 15-foot baskets for every point, then the basket will not be shown.

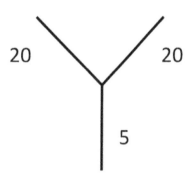

   The orientation of the Bridle Marking tells the up-rigger which I-beams to make the bridles. However, most bridles either run SR to SL or US to DS to avoid tangling bridles.

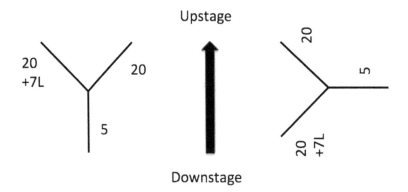

Upstage

Downstage

Bridle Legs are made
to the SR and SL I-Beams

Bridle Legs are made
to the US and DS I-Beams

STAC Chain

STAC chain stands for Special Theatrical Alloy Chain and is used to adjust the length of the bridle legs so that the bridle point or apex will fall at the rigging point chalk mark below on the floor. Adjusting the number of chain links can extend the bridle leg anywhere from an inch to several inches thus enabling the up-rigger to "make the point." These STAC chain links need to be indicated on the Bridle Markings. They tell the down-rigger how many chain links to add to the long leg of the bridle being sent up to the up-rigger. If there needs to be any adjustment of the bridle point, the up-rigger can adjust the links accordingly. The chain is attached between the long leg and the long leg basket. This illustration shows two 20-foot bridle legs with one of the legs having 7-links of STAC chain.

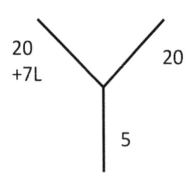

Venue Specific Chalk Markings

There are always "venue specific" floor markings. It is very important for riggers new to the venue to quickly learn these markings.

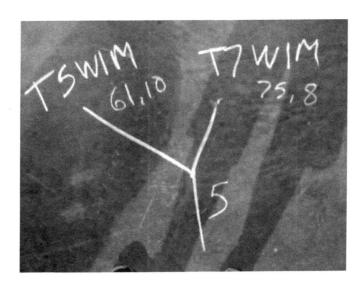

The "basket notations" T5W1M and T7W1M are really location references. The first notation is Truss 5 Window 1 Mississippi. Mississippi refers to one of the streets running outside the building. Rather than referring to SR or SL, the riggers there use the street names for easy reference; Mississippi for SR and Georgia for SL. T5 and T7 refer to Ceiling Beams called "Trusses" that are numbered starting upstage to downstage. The "Trusses" all have windows. Starting at the centerline moving toward the Mississippi side, the windows count 1,2,3,4,5 and so on. From the centerline moving toward the Georgia side, the windows again start 1,2,3,4,5 and so on.

So, T5W1M tells both the up and down-rigger that the bridle point needs to be send up to Truss 5, Window 1, on the Mississippi side. The other bridle point will be sent up to Truss 7, Window 1, Mississippi.

The baskets are all pre-hung in the windows, so all that needs to be send up are the bridle legs. The numbers 61.10 and 75.8 refer to the lengths of the bridle legs that need to be made up by the down-rigger. The number 5 is the stinger.

Arena Floor Layout

A good House Rigger will be able to accurately lay out the floor in as short a time as possible. Wasting time trying to work bridles out at the last moment takes time and is frustrating for everyone. Obviously, a House Rigger will have a good, working knowledge of the venue and the spacing distance between the I-beams so that he can quickly write the bridle markings on the floor in as little time as possible.

How it begins

Floor layout begins with establishing 0-0. As mentioned earlier, this is similar to finding the centerline and plaster line in a theatre venue. 0-0 is usually located at the very rear of the stage (or up-stage truss) near the dasher. Once established, a tape measure is laid out on the arena floor running downstage. Positioned horizontal to this are two tape measures running off the centerline tape. Three or five point lasers can be extremely useful in making sure that the tapes run perpendicular to each other. Next, the Production Rigger will come along and mark out the location of each rigging point in wet-chalk usually with reference to whether the point is for video, audio, projection, rigging or cable pick. Other show specific markings such as hoist type may be indicated at this time. The House Rigger then follows and marks out the bridle and basket information next to the point. But, how does the House Rigger gather this information?

House Riggers *know* their facility. It is best to work out as much of the bridle information based on I-beam bay sizes ahead of time using spreadsheets. Ben Kilmer, who is House Rigger for the Prudential Center and creator of the website *RigWorld,* has created one such chart for the south side of his facility. The Prudential Center has 13'6" bays and is 108 ft. from floor to beams. They use 10-ft bridle legs with 15-ft split baskets. The bridle apex falls 14'6" from I-beams. The chart below illustrates how many links of STAC chain is required with each foot of movement off center. For example, 1-ft off center would require 2 links of chain, 6'-9" is a Dead-hang, and 5 feet off center would require 11 links (or a *dog bone* + 4). This is marked out in wet-chalk next to the established rigging point. With a chart worked out like this, it is extremely fast and easy to write out the necessary bridle information for the down-riggers.

Pru Roof South Side

1' 2L	22' 11L or DB+4	40'8" +3
2' 4L	23' 9L	41'3" +4
3' 7L	24' 7L	41'8" +5
4' 9L	25' 4L	42'3" +6
5 11L or DB+4	26' 2L	43' +7
6' 14L or DB+6	27' Even	43' 9" DH
6'9" DH	28' 2L	44'9" 22+7
8' 12L or DB+5	29' 4L	45'9" 22+5
9' 10L	30' 7L	46'9" +9

10' 8L	31' 9L	47'9" +7
11' 6L	32' 11L or DB+4	48'9" +5
12' 3L 33' 13L or DB+6	33'9" DH	49'9" +3
13' 1L	34'8" +7	50'9" +2
13'6' Even	35'3" +6	51'9" Even
14' 1L	35'9" +5	52'9" +2
15' 3L	36'4" +4	53'9" +3
16' 5L	36'9" +3	54'9" +5
17' 8L	37'4" +2	55'9" +7
18' 10L	38'7" +1	56'9" +9
19' 12L or DB+5 +1	38'9" Even	57'9" 22+5
20'3" Even	39'7" +1	58'9" 22+7
21' 13L or DB+6	40'3 +2	60'3" DH

Chart courtesy of Ben Kilmer

The arena floor following layout.
photo courtesy of Ben Kilmer

The next step in this process will be for the down-riggers to "make up the steel" for each one of the bridles according to the information laid out in chalk.

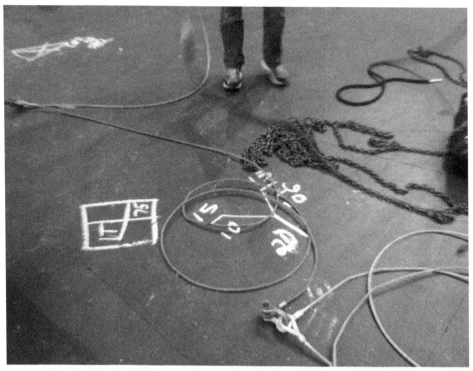

Steel comes in 2-ft and 2.5-ft lengths (called "dog bones"), 5-ft, 10-ft, 20-ft, 30-ft and 50-ft lengths. Color-coding of the steel is *usually* black for 2.5's, red for 5's, white for 10's and blue for 20's. However, some rental houses may color their steel to identify it as theirs in order to keep it separate from other companies. *Usually (but not always)*, 30-ft steel is green and 50-ft steel is yellow. Again there is no standardization in the industry for any of this. In the United States, red white and blue tends to be the norm for only 5's, 10's and 20's. Other countries have a totally different color-coding for their steel. In addition, steel comes in 3/8" and 1/2" thicknesses - 3/8" for 1 Ton Hoists and 1/2" for 2 Ton Hoists. Shackles come in two sizes, 5/8" and 3/4" depending on the size steel being used. The illustration below shows 15-ft split basket with 20-ft legs and a 5-ft stinger.

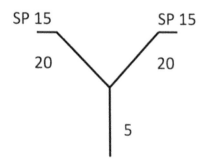

Based on the rigging floor mark shown above, the down rigger would make up a bridle consisting of two 20-ft legs, two 15-ft split baskets consisting of 10-ft and 5-ft steels (to wrap each I-beam), and 7 shackles or 3 shackles for each basket and one shackle for the working shackle making 7 shackles. The illustration below shows one leg of a 15-ft basket ready to send to the up-rigger. Remember, it is important to ask the up-rigger for the size of the bowline loop desired.

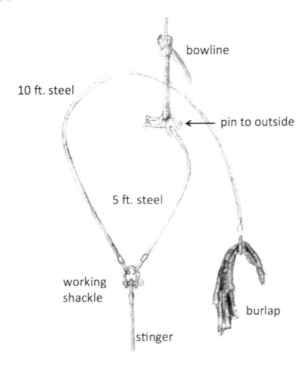

Up-riggers ready to haul up the bridles. Note most up-riggers often work in pairs.

Photo courtesy of Ben Kilmer

Baskets sent up may vary from venue to venue just like the floor markings. The illustration below shows the addition of an extra shackle to the basket hitch. This extra shackle most likely adds an additional 2 inches to the ELOH.

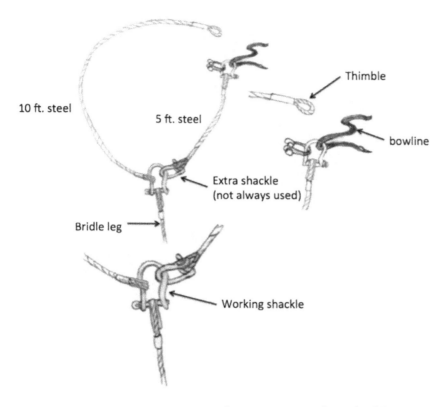

10 ft. steel

5 ft. steel

Thimble

bowline

Extra shackle
(not always used)

Bridle leg

Working shackle

photo courtesy of Mick Alderson and IATSE Local 470

The illustrations below show a 5-ft basket consisting of one 5-ft steel and two shackles based on the floor marking shown below.

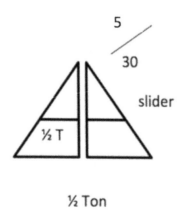

5

30

slider

½ T

½ Ton

The down-rigger would make up a 5-ft basket with a 30-ft leg and three shackles - two for the basket and one for the end of the 30-ft steel. The marking indicates a dead-hang so there would be no bridle. A slider is a steel tube added to the hoist chain to takes up cable slack when the hoist is raised. This will be found with the hoist and does not need to be added by the rigger.

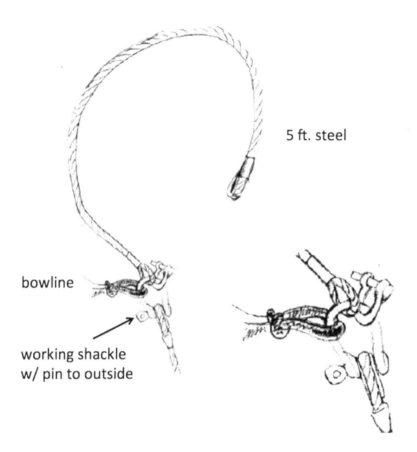

5 ft. steel

bowline

working shackle
w/ pin to outside

photo courtesy of Mick Alderson and IATSE Local 470

Sample Problems – Lesson 24

Read the following chalk marks.

Problem 1

Problem 2

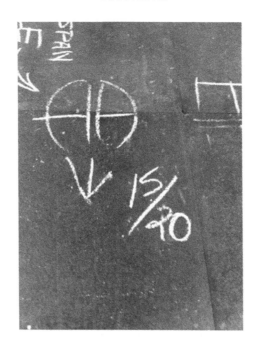

Problem 3

Problem 4

5. What length steel is a "dog bone"?

6. How many shackles would you use to make up a 20-ft bridle with two split 15-ft baskets?

7. True/False. The color-coding of steel is uniform throughout the industry.

8. STAC chain is usually attached to the *long* leg of the bridle leg for ease of adjustment by the up-rigger.

9. True/False. Floor markings will *always* indicate what size basket is to be made up.

10. True/False. Chalk markings are drawn on the floor of a venue and refer to the specific location of rigging points.

Lesson 25:
Angled Truss

It may seem strange to begin a Lesson on Angled Truss by saying; *"standard truss is only to be used in the horizontal position. Entertainment truss is not engineered to be suspended at angles,"* but this statement is true. Trans Siberian Orchestra (TSO) started the craze by designing their truss to be suspended at different angles, thus allowing for a stage design that uniquely changes shape. However, their truss *is* specifically designed and engineered for use in these configurations. It is not your average, "off-the-shelf" truss. In addition, angling truss may put stress loads on the hoist chains, shackles and round slings that may result in failure. Again, it is best to consult with the manufacturers of all components.

Truss, in a horizontal position, is engineered such that roughly 50% of its members are in compression and 50% in tension at any given time. Panel points are placed so that while in compression the load can be spread along the diagonals. Forces placed on the chords may be in tension or a combination of both. When a truss is angled - no matter how many degrees - the forces applied to the entire truss and its members are changed. Many structural members that were intended to be in compression may now be in a state of tension and vise versa. This change may or may not be within the limits of the structure.

ANSI E1.2 2012 covers the Design, Manufacture and Use of Aluminum Trusses and Towers. Section 3.3.1 of this document states, *"Engineering analysis of the truss or tower structures for the intended loading conditions shall be performed by calculation, modeling, or physical testing or by a combination of two or more of these methods."* If truss is to be loaded or suspended in any manner, an analysis needs to be performed by a *qualified* engineer. If the intension of the concert stage designer is to angle truss, then a qualified engineer MUST evaluate and certify that the truss and system components will be able to withstand the forces placed upon it. This needs to be done by the truss manufacturer. A totally re-designed and engineered truss may be in order as in the case of TSO.

This lesson will examine the calculations for angled truss with the assumption that the truss has been designed and engineered to be loaded in that configuration. In Lesson 15, we discussed how to calculate *Multiple Loads on a Beam* and in Lesson 13 we discussed *Dead-hang Tension on One End of a Beam.* We will be using both lessons in this chapter. It is recommended for angled truss that you stay with a Uniform Distributed Load or UDL as much as possible. As you will see, weight distribution on the L1 and L2 points will change as the truss angles change and the leg angles increase.

> *Important: When hanging any truss, it is important to consult the manufacturer's load data charts. When hanging truss at any angle, the manufacturer's engineer should be consulted. The angle of the truss may will also put stress loads on the hoist chains and components that result in chain and component failure.*

Angled Truss

The illustration below shows a 20-ft box truss that is 20.5" x 20.5" suspended from I-beams spaced at 20 ft. Truss weight is 10 pounds per foot. Movers weigh 90 pounds each. Hoist weight is 114 pounds. Chain is 80 feet at 1-lb per foot. The load consists of four movers; two spaced together at 5 feet and the other two spaced at 15 feet. Cable runs are removed for simplicity.

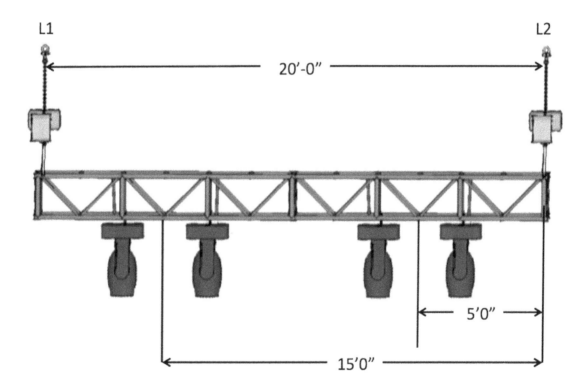

The formula *for Multiple Loads on a Truss* (see Lesson 15) is:

$$Tension\ on\ L1 = \frac{(Load\ 1 \times D1) + (Load\ 2 \times D2)}{Span}$$

$$Tension\ on\ L2 = (Load\ 1 + Load\ 2) - Tension\ on\ L1$$

Using this formula, we get a static load on L1 and L2 of 474 lb each. (or with a UDL, just add the loads and divide by two).

The next step in this process will be to angle the truss at 30-degrees. When working out these measurements, it is best to draft on graph paper or with a CAD program such a VectorWorks or AutoCAD. Scale is extremely important.

Thirty-Degree Angle

The next illustration shows the same truss angled at 30-degrees with new measurements taken from the mid-section of the truss plates. These vertical lines are then dropped down to a horizontal plane and measured. Note that the length of span has changed and the spacing of the movers has changed. When spacing changes, the UDL is affected. The illustration below shows how these measurements configure to those used for calculating *Multiple Loads on a Truss*; the Span is now 17'-3", D1 is 13'-6", and D2 is 4'-10".

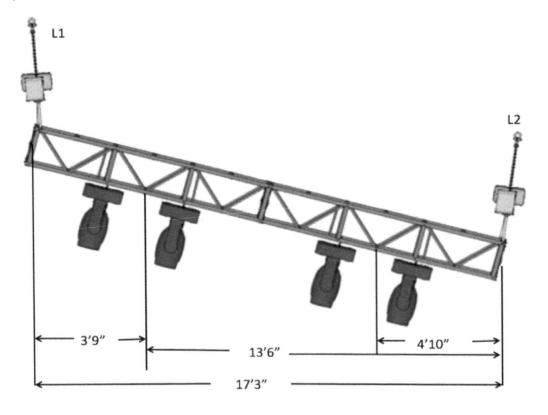

Before we begin, let's convert our measurements into decimals so that our math will be accurate. The following conversion chart will be helpful.

Inch	Decimal of a Foot
1 inch	0.0833
2 inches	0.167
3 inches	0.250
4 inches	0.333
5 inches	0.417
6 inches	0.500
7 inches	0.583
8 inches	0.667
9 inches	0.750
10 inches	0.833
11 inches	0.917
12 inches	1.000

With the conversions in place 17'-3" = 17.250 feet, 13'-6" = 13.5 feet, and 4'-10" = 4.833 feet. Now the Span is 17.250 feet, D1 will be 13.5 feet, and D2 will be 4.833 feet. Load 1 is 180 pounds (two 90-lb movers) and Load 2 is 180 pounds (two 90-lb movers). Find the tension on L1 and L2.

$$Tension\ on\ L1 = \frac{(Load\ 1 \times D1) + (Load\ 2 \times D2)}{Span}$$

$$Tension\ on\ L2 = (Load\ 1 + Load\ 2) - Tension\ on\ L1$$

or

$$Tension\ on\ L1 = \frac{(180 \times 13.5) + (180 \times 4.833)}{17.250}$$

$$Tension\ on\ L1 = \frac{2430 + 869.94}{17.250}$$

$$Tension\ on\ L1 = \frac{3299.94}{17.250}$$

Tension on L1 = 191.30 pounds

and

Tension on L2= (180 + 180) - 169.615

Tension on L2= 360 - 191.30

Tension on L2 = 168.7 pounds

Next, we will add the truss and the hoist weight onto both L1 and L2.

Truss weight is 10 pounds per foot. Truss length is 20 feet.

20 x 10 = 200 lb

200 / 2 = 100 lb each per point

Hoist weight is 114 pounds each plus 80 pounds each for the chain.

114 + 80 = 194 lb each per point.

Tension on L1 = 191.30 pounds + 100 truss + 194 hoist = 485.3 pounds

Tension on L2 = 168.7 pounds + 100 truss + 194 hoist = 462.7 pounds

Dead-Hang Tension

The final part to the problem will be calculating the dead-hang tension on point L1 and L2 with the truss raised to its final trim. In the illustration below, you will have noticed that as our 20-ft truss angled to 30 degrees, the span decreased to 17'-3".

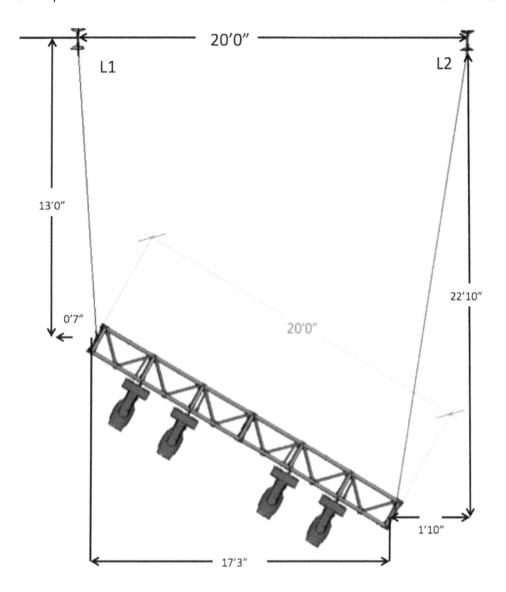

As a result, the slope of the motor chains or legs changed from vertical to angled. It will now be necessary to calculate the increased load on points L1 and L2 caused by the increase in angle. To do this, we will use the formula from Lesson 13 *Dead-hang Tension on the End of a Truss*. Again, it will be best to draft this in VectorWorks or AutoCAD.

$$Tension\ on\ L1 = Load \times \frac{L1}{V1}$$

We know the load on L1 is 485.3 pounds and L2 is 462.7 pounds. Working from the illustration above, the length of H1 is 0'-7" and V1 is 13'-0". The length of H2 is 22'-10" and V2 is 1'-10".

Using the Pythagorean theorem as discussed in Lesson 13, we need to find the length of the bridle legs. We will convert these numbers to decimals as before. First, H1 = 13.0 feet, V1 = 0.583 feet.

Leg 1 = $\sqrt{0.583^2 + 13^2}$

Leg 1 = $\sqrt{0.3398 + 169}$

Leg 1 = $\sqrt{169.3398}$

Leg 1= 13.01 feet

Next, V2 = 22.833 feet and H2 = 1.833 feet

Leg 2 = $\sqrt{1.833^2 + 22.833^2}$

Leg 2 = $\sqrt{3.359 + 521.345}$

Leg 2 = $\sqrt{534.704}$

Leg 2= 22.906 feet

Now we put this length into the equation

$$Tension\ on\ L1 = Load \times \frac{L1}{V1}$$

$Tension\ on\ L1 = 485.3 \times \dfrac{13.01}{13}$

$Tension\ on\ L1 = 13.01$

Tension on Leg L1 = 485.67 pounds

Next, The length of Leg 2 is 22.906 feet and V2 is 1.833 feet.

$Tension\ on\ L2 = 462.7 \times \dfrac{22.906}{22.833}$

$Tension\ on\ L2 = 464.17$ pounds

These changes do not seem to have produced much of a change in loads for a 30 degree angle at 13-foot trim on the high end, but *there indeed is* change. This will become magnified if the truss is raised and the bridles flatten - something to be avoided. *It will always be important to work these calculations out when working with angled truss so as to avoid overloading the points.* **Load cells are always recommended.**

Forty-five Degree Angle

The next problem will take the same truss and angle it to 45 degrees. Note that as the degree of incline increases, so will the load on L1. Note again, the spacing on the movers has shifted. The loads on the truss are no longer a UDL.

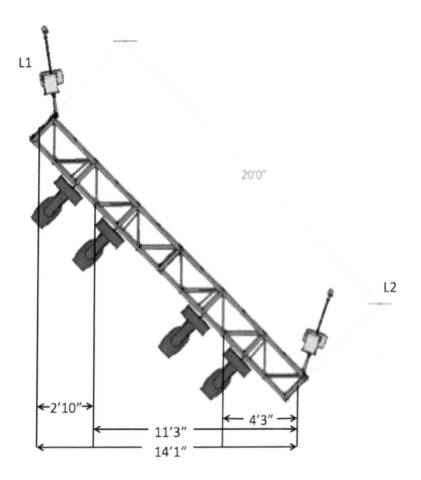

Let's convert these measurements to decimals as before. The Span will be 14.0833 feet, D1 will be 4.250 feet, and D2 will be 11.250 feet. Now, let's plug the numbers into our formula.

$$Tension\ on\ L1 = \frac{(Load\ 1 \times D1) + (Load\ 2 \times D2)}{Span}$$

$$Tension\ on\ L2 = (Load\ 1 + Load\ 2) - Tension\ on\ L1$$

or

$$Tension\ on\ L1 = \frac{(180 \times 4.250) + (180 \times 11.250)}{14.0833}$$

$$Tension\ on\ L1 = \frac{765 + 2025}{14.0833}$$

$$Tension\ on\ L1 = \frac{2790}{14.0833}$$

Tension on L1 = 198.10 pounds

and

Tension on L2= (180 + 180) - 198.10

Tension on L2= 360 - 198.10

Tension on L2 = 161.9 pounds

Next, we will add the truss and the hoist weight onto both L1 and L2.

Truss weight is 10 pounds per foot. Truss length is 20 feet.

20 x 10 = 200 pounds

200 / 2 = 100 pounds per point

Hoist weight is 114 pounds each, plus 80 pounds each for the chain.

114 + 80 = 194 lb each per point. So...

Tension on L1 = 198.10 pounds + 100 truss + 194 hoist = 492.1 pounds

Tension on L2 = 161.9 pounds + 100 truss + 194 hoist = 455.9 pounds

Dead Hang Tension

Again, the last part of this problem will be to calculate the dead-hang tension on the ends of the truss. The illustration below shows the problem with the truss brought to trim height of 9 feet. Note the I-beams are still 20 feet apart, the length of the truss remains at 20 feet, and the span remains at 14'-1" (14.0833'). However, due to the increased angle of 45 degrees, V1 is 9'0", H1 is 1'-8" (1.667'), V2 is 23'-1"(23.0833') and, H2 is 4'-3" (4.250').

Using Pathagoras as before, we need to find the length of each of the bridle legs. V1 is 9'-0", H1 is 1'-8" (1.667').

$$\text{Leg 1} = \sqrt{1.667^2 + 9^2}$$

$$\text{Leg 1} = \sqrt{2.778 + 81}$$

$$\text{Leg 1} = \sqrt{83.778}$$

Leg 1= 9.15

Next, V2 is 23'1"(23.0833') and, H2 is 4'3" (4.250').

$$\text{Leg 2} = \sqrt{4.250^2 + 23.0833^2}$$

$$\text{Leg 2} = \sqrt{18.062 + 532.838}$$

$$\text{Leg 2} = \sqrt{550.9}$$

Leg 2 = 23.471 feet

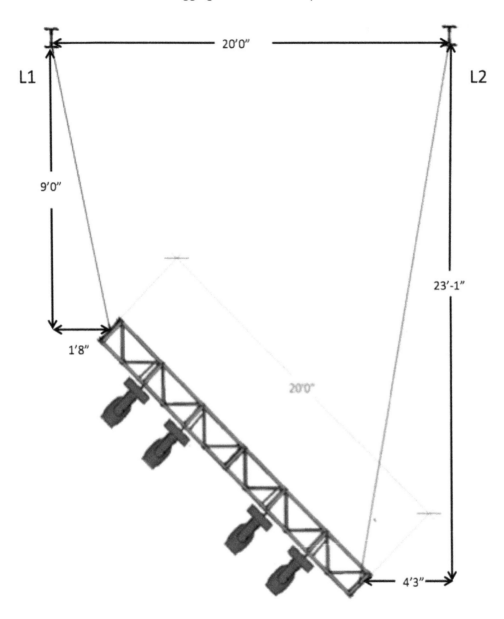

Using the same formula that we used for the 30 degree truss, we get:

$$Tension\ on\ L1 = Load \times \frac{L1}{V1}$$

Tension on L1 = 492.1 pounds

Tension on L2 = 455.9 pounds

V1 is 9'0", Leg 1 is 9.15', V2 is 23.0833' and Leg 2 is 23.471

$$\text{Tension on L1} = 492.1 \times \frac{9.15}{9}$$

Tension on L1 = 500.30 pounds

$$\text{Tension on L2} = 455.9 \times \frac{23.471}{23.0833}$$

Tension on L2 = 463.557 pounds

Warning: the answers represented are close approximations. Actual tensions could vary. Load cells are highly recommended. Manufacturer's engineers should be consulted.

Lesson 25 - Sample Problems

1. A 30-foot long 20.5" x 20.5" box truss weighs 10 pounds per foot. It will be angled at 50 degrees and suspended from two I-beams spaced 35 feet apart. There will be two uneven loads, one at 650 pounds and the other at 975 pounds. There will be two hoists mounted at the truss ends. Span is 19'-3" (19.250 feet), D1 is 12'-3" (12.250 feet), and D2 is 5'7" (5.583 feet). Hoist weight is 112 pounds. Chain is 60 feet at 1 pound per foot. Calculate the load on L1 and L2.

2. The same truss will be suspended from the 35-foot I-beams at a trim height of 9'-3" from the L2 end. Calculate the "dead-hang" load on points L1 and L2.

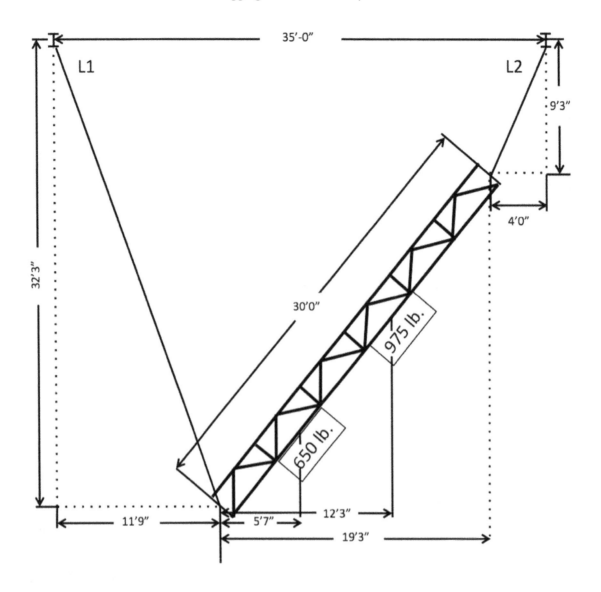

Unit VI:

Static and Dynamic Forces

Static and Dynamic Forces:

Introduction

The equation for finding Force is:

$$Force = Weight \times \frac{acceleration\ of\ gravity + acceleration\ rate}{acceleration\ of\ gravity}$$

We know that the acceleration of gravity is 32 feet per second^2, but what is the acceleration rate?

Finding the acceleration rate involves applying a specific force for a length of time.

Example: If an object takes 4 seconds to accelerate from a stationary position to moving at 16 feet per second, then: $\frac{16\ feet\ per\ second}{4\ seconds}$ = 4 feet per second, per second, or **4 feet per second^2** is the acceleration rate.

So, if the object weighs 500 pounds, then:

$$Force = Weight \times \frac{acceleration\ of\ gravity + acceleration\ rate}{acceleration\ of\ gravity}$$

$$Force = 500\ lb \times \frac{32\ feet\ per\ second^2 + 4\ feet\ per\ second^2}{32\ feet\ per\ second^2}$$

$$Force = 500\ lb \times \frac{36\ feet\ per\ second^2}{32\ feet\ per\ second^2}$$

$$Force = 500\ lb \times 1.125$$

$$\mathbf{Force = 562.5\ lb}$$

This means that the objects weighs 500 pounds when at rest, but 562.5 pounds of force are exerted during the first 4 seconds as the object accelerates. After the acceleration period, the object finishes its acceleration and is traveling at a constant 16 feet per second with a force of 500 pounds.

As you can see, the acceleration rate and time are multipliers of the static load. So, the shorter the acceleration/deceleration time, the greater the dynamic force. When the rate of acceleration or deceleration is very rapid, the dynamic force created can be significant. We often call this a shock load, which was mentioned briefly at the end of Lesson 17 and will be discussed in greater detail in Lesson 28.

Remember, shock forces only occur when an object accelerates or decelerates. When an object is motionless or moving at a constant speed, there is no shock force.

Dynamic forces are not easy to calculate because we do not always know all the data that we need to know to calculate them. Also, it gets much more complicated when a structure is supported by more than two points. For these reasons, load cells are becoming more common, especially on rigs with a "mother grid" that supports a lower grid. Load cells can constantly monitor the forces on each point so that the "true" static or dynamic force for each point is known.

Lesson 26:
Forces and Design Factors

Tension (a pulling force) is the most common type of force we experience in rigging. It is often associated with the use of fiber rope, wire rope, or chain and the suspension of objects. Also, hardware used in rigging (shackles, quick links, turnbuckles, etc.) is designed for the load to occur on a specific axis, and it is load-rated based on its tensile strength.

A truss is strongest when in **compression**, the presence of two opposing forces, which is why we hang box truss from its bottom chords and not the top chords. We also wrap the truss at panel points where the truss is strongest in order to avoid collapsing the truss at the chords. It is also why, if we are hanging something from/below the open web truss in a building, we want to wrap the sling over the top of the truss.

Torque, a twisting force, is probably the most deceiving force because most structures are not designed to take much torque, so a little torque can do a great deal of damage.

Shear and **Double shear** are forces usually associated with a pin or bolt. Below are examples of both shear and double shear forces.

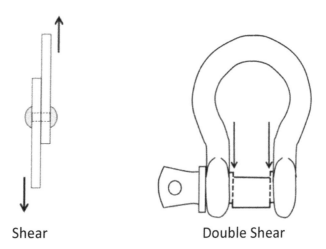

Shear   Double Shear

A shear force occurs when a bolt or pin is used to attach two objects that are being pulled or pulled in opposite directions, and the opposing forces are in the same plane on the bolt or pin. The bolts used to attach a hanger plate to a flat are in shear when the flat is suspended. Double shear is when the force on the bolt or pin are in two distinct planes, such as when a load hangs on a shackle.

Design Factors

Most industrial hardware is rated with a Working Load Limit (WLL), Safe Working Load (SWL) or Recommended Working Load Limit (RWLL). This is the maximum force that the manufacturer recommends be applied to this piece of hardware. The WLL (the most commonly seen designation) is a fraction of the breaking strength and is based on the application of a Design Factor.

Design Factors are a percentage of the breaking strength and are often expressed as a ratio, such as 5:1, or sometimes as a single number, such as 5. This is similar to the mechanical advantage described in Lesson 3.

Example: What is the working load limit (WLL) of a piece of hardware with a breaking strength of 2,500 pounds based on a Design Factor of 5:1?

$$Working\ Load\ Limit = \frac{Breaking\ Strength}{Design\ Factor}$$

$$Working\ Load\ Limit = \frac{2500}{5}$$

Working Load Limit = 500 lb

The Design Factor creates a margin of safety to compensate for normal wear and less than optimal working conditions. Design Factors do NOT compensate for extreme shock loads, extensive wear/damage or other factors that might cause the hardware to fail. All hardware used in rigging should be inspected before every install to ensure that it is not damaged.

All hardware does not have the same Design Factor. Below is a list of common design factors that are used by manufacturers of different types of hardware for determining the working load limit.

Minimum Design Factors For Use
Synthetic Slings: 5:1
Wire rope slings: 5:1
Stage rigging (counterweight rigging system, including the wire rope): 8:1
Shackles: 6:1
Base mounted drum hoists: 7:1
Personnel lifts: 7:1 to 10:1
Fiber ropes: 7:1 to 12:1

Chain (except grade 43): 4:1
Grade 43 chain: 3:1
Ratchet straps: 3:1

General Rules of Thumb
DF of 5:1 for Standing Rigging (i.e.: rigging that does not move)
DF of 8:1 for Running Rigging (rigging that moves)
DF of 10:1 for rigging used in flying of people or moving over the heads of people

    The Design Factor that the WLL is based on is not commonly displayed on the hardware's packaging or even in literature from the manufacturer. Therefore, it is important that riggers be familiar with the common design factors above.

    It should be recognized that recreational hardware, such as carabiners, is marked with its breaking strength (usually in kiloNewtons) instead of a WLL. This is a situation where knowing how to convert kiloNewons to pounds will be very useful. Note: Newtons and kiloNewtons are a measurement of Force. Sometimes weight and force are given in pounds, which can be confusing to the beginner or expert alike.

    If you are not sure of the Design Factor used to derive the WLL, you need to check with the manufacturer. Knowing the Design Factor for all rigging hardware is very important.

Lesson 27:

Estimating the Stretch of Wire and Fiber Rope under a Static Load

Everything is a spring. Everything stretches or bends (deflects) under a load. Some materials, such as bungee cord, stretch a lot. Others, such as steel chain, stretch very little. The stretch of a material will be very important in Lesson 28, when we discuss shock loading. However, in this lesson we want to calculate the length that a wire or fiber rope will stretch under a static load.

Elastic Stretch is the physical elongation of the material under load. Different materials have different amounts of stretch. Humidity can change the ability of some materials to stretch, and some natural fibers lose their elasticity with age.

New wire rope has both Elastic Stretch and Constructional Stretch. Constructional Stretch is the "settling-in" of the wires of new wire rope when put under a load. After some use, the Constructional Stretch will cease to exist, but Elastic Stretch will always exist unless the wire rope is put under tension that is equal to or greater than the "yield point" (approximately 55% of breaking strength of the wire rope).

Wire Rope

An estimate of the elastic stretch of wire rope can be calculated by using the following formula:

$$Elastic\ Stretch = \frac{Weight \times "G"\ Factor}{Diameter\ of\ Wire\ Rope^2}$$

"G" Factor = See Chart Below

180

Cable/Wire Rope	"G" Factor	Cable/Wire Rope	"G" Factor
1x7 302/304 SST	0.00000735	1x7 Galvanized	0.00000661
1x19 302/304 SST	0.00000779	1x19 Galvanized	0.00000698
7x7 302/304 SST	0.0000120	7x7 Galvanized	0.0000107
7x19 302/304 SST	0.0000162	7x19 Galvanized	0.0000140
6x19 302/304 SST IWRC	0.0000157	6x19 Galvanized IWRC	0.0000136
6x25 302/304 SST IWRC	0.0000160	6x25 Galvanized IWRC	0.0000144
19x7 302/304 SST	0.0000197	19x7 Galvanized	0.0000 178

Note: A "G" Factor or General Factor is a mathematical constant used in an equation. "G" Factors are found in varying disciplines and used to represent different types of data.

The last piece of information that you need is the length of the wire rope (in inches).

Example: If you hang a 200-pound load on a 50-foot long piece of 1/4" carbon steel 7x19 GAC, how long will it stretch?

$$\text{Elastic Stretch} = \frac{\text{Weight} \times \text{"G" Factor}}{\text{Diameter of Wire Rope}^2}$$

$$\text{Elastic Stretch} = \frac{200 \times 0.0000140}{0.25^2}$$

$$\text{Elastic Stretch} = \frac{0.0028}{0.0625}$$

Elastic Stretch = 0.0448 percent

Now that you know the percent of stretch, use the equation below to determine the amount of stretch in inches.

$$Stretch = \frac{Elastic\ Stretch}{100} \times Length\ of\ Wire\ Rope$$

$$\text{Stretch} = \frac{0.0448}{100} \times 600$$

$$\text{Stretch} = 0.000448 \times 600$$

$$\text{Stretch} = 0.2688 \text{ inches}$$

Fiber Rope

The stretch of fiber ropes can be far more difficult to calculate than the stretch of wire rope, for several reasons:

- Fiber ropes are made from many different types of fiber or combinations of types of fibers.
- There are many construction types.
- Humidity affects the stretch of some fibers.
- The stretch factor of many fibers is not linear – some get less stretchy as the tension increases while some fibers get more stretchy as the tension increases.
- Manufacturers of fiber ropes do not always provide information for calculating the stretch of their ropes. Fortunately, one manufacturer of ropes that are commonly used in the entertainment industry, New England Ropes, does provide very good information on stretch.

The table below contains elongation information on a few ropes manufactured by New England Ropes at 10, 20, and 30 percent of the rated tensile strength of the rope. For example: placing a 350 pound load on a length of 3/8" diameter Multiline II rope (10 percent of the tensile strength) would cause it to stretch 1.7 percent (0.017) of its length. If you used a 50-foot rope (600 inches) then:

$$\text{Stretch} = 0.017 \times 600$$
$$\text{Stretch} = 10.2 \text{ inches}$$

Product Name	Elongation at 10% of TS	Elongation at 20% of TS	Elongation at 30% of TS	Tensile Strength (lb)	
Multiline II	1.7%	3.7%	5.4%	3/8":	3,500
				7/16":	4,300
				1/2":	6,700
				5/8":	9,800
				3/4":	13,300
				7/8":	15,200
				1":	19,100

Product Name	Elongation at 10% of TS	Elongation at 20% of TS	Elongation at 30% of TS	Tensile Strength (lb)	
3-Strand Spun Poly	3.0%	5.6%	7.3%	3/16":	1,200
				1/4":	1,330
				5/16":	2,000
				3/8":	2,650
				7/16":	3,250
				1/2":	4,700
				5/8":	6,700
				3/4":	10,000

Product Name	Elongation at 10% of TS	Elongation at 20% of TS	Elongation at 30% of TS	Tensile Strength (pounds)	
Premium 3-Strand Nylon	5.3%	10.4%	13.1%	3/16":	1,300
				1/4":	2,100
				5/16":	3,000
				3/8":	4,250
				7/16":	6,000
				1/2":	7,500
				9/16":	8,800
				5/8":	11,650
				3/4":	17,150
				7/8":	22,300
				1":	27,700
				1-1/8":	35,800

Product Name	Elongation at 10% of TS	Elongation at 20% of TS	Elongation at 30% of TS	Tensile Strength (pounds)	
Sta-Set (white)	0.7	2.0	3.4	3/16":	1,400
				1/4":	2,350
				5/16":	3,850
				3/8":	5,100
				7/16":	7,000
				1/2":	10,100
				9/16":	11,700
				5/8":	16,900
				3/4":	23,500
				7/8":	33,800
				1":	40,900

Sample Problems – Lesson 27

1. If you hang a 500-lb load on a 25-foot long piece of 1/4" carbon steel 7x19 GAC, how long will it stretch?

2. If you hang a 200-lb load on a 75-foot long piece of 1/8" carbon steel 7x19 GAC, how long will it stretch?

3. If you hang a 1000-lb load on a 50-foot long piece of 1/2" carbon steel 7x19 GAC, how long will it stretch?

4. How much stretch (elongation) would occur if you place a 1,010 lb weight on a 50-foot length of 3/8" diameter Sta-Set rope?

5. How much stretch (elongation) would occur if you place a 2,250 lb weight on a 50-foot length of 1/2" diameter Premium 3-Strand Nylon rope?

Lesson 28:
Shock Loads

When most people think of the cause of a line (chain, wire or fiber rope) failing, they think of the load exceeding the tensile breaking strength of the line. While this situation can certainly cause the line to fail, there is another possible cause – the dynamic load (or shock load) exerted on the line is greater than the line's energy-absorbing capacity.

A shock load is the force that results when an object suddenly accelerates or decelerates, but we most often associate it with the abrupt stop of a falling object. Remember the old adage – "it is not the fall that kills you, it is the sudden stop at the end." A shock load force is exerted on both the object and whatever stops the object's fall. While this force is momentary, it can be tremendous.

Three factors determine the magnitude of the shock load: the weight of the object, the speed that the object is traveling before it starts to decelerate, and the rate of deceleration (the Stopping Distance).

With a free-falling object, the Stopping Distance (or time it takes for the object to stop falling) is critically important in determining shock loads, and the amount of stretch/elasticity in the material stopping the fall determines this distance. The more a material stretches, the more energy it absorbs. Bungee cord (a.k.a. shock cord) has a great deal of elasticity and is an excellent shock absorber. Therefore, falls on bungee cord typically result in relatively low shock loads. On the other hand, steel cable, and especially chain, has very little elasticity. Falls involving these materials usually result in extremely high shock loads.

The tensile breaking strength of a line is not related to its energy absorbing capacity. In fact, many lines with very high tensile strengths that allow them to hold extremely heavy loads have very low energy-absorbing capacities and can break easily when subjected to dynamic shock load.

A common situation where we might want to calculate a shock load relates to fall protection. How much shock load results when a technician falls a specified distance, is caught by his harness and lanyard, and stops over a specified distance as the lanyard stretches or the shock absorber on the lanyard extends?

The equation for solving this problem is

$$Force = Weight \times \left(\frac{Free\ Fall\ Distance}{Stopping\ Distance} + 1\right)$$

Note: The "1" represents the weight of the falling object. Without it there would be no load on the line AFTER the initial shock occurs, so do not forget to include it. If both the free fall distance and the stopping distance are zero (there is no fall and therefore no shock load) then these two zeros cancel each other out and Force = Weight x 1 or just the weight of the object. If the stopping distance is zero, and the free fall distance is greater than zero, then force would be infinite, which is not possible. So, the stopping distance MUST be greater than zero.

Example: A 200-pound man wearing a safety harness and lanyard falls six feet. As he stops, the harness and lanyard stretch 6 inches (or .5 feet). What is the force on him and the rigging that supports him?

Note: Remember to keep all measurements in the same unit of measurement – FEET.

$$Force = Weight \times \left(\frac{Free\ Fall\ Distance}{Stopping\ Distance} + 1\right)$$

$$Force = Weight \times \left(\frac{6}{0.5} + 1\right)$$

$$Force = 200 \times (12 + 1)$$

$$Force = 200 \times 13$$

Force = 2,600 lb

If this number seems large to you, it is. However, it is also correct. It would also probably be fatal. Shock loads can be huge; that is why you want to avoid them at all costs.

Shock load on wire rope

The equation used above to calculate the shock load of a falling object is pretty simple, and it is easy to see how most of the numbers were derived. But, where did the Stopping Distance come from? To be honest, it was pretty much just a made up number. The reason is that the Stopping Distance is determined by the elasticity of the material stopping the fall.

The equation for calculating the shock load when a wire rope "catches" a falling object is:

$$Shock\ load = Load \times \left(1 + \sqrt{1 + \frac{2 \times Falling\ Distance \times Area \times Modulus\ of\ Elasticity}{Load \times Length \times 12}} \right)$$

where

Load is the weight of the falling object in pounds

Falling Distance is in inches

Length of wire rope is in feet

Modulus of Elasticity is in pounds per square inch (psi) – and is 15,000,000

Note: This is the Modulus of Elasticity for wire rope that had the structural stretch removed, either through pre-stretching or through use. New wire rope has a Modulus of Elasticity of 11,500,000 psi.

Area (Equivalent Metallic Area in square inches) = *Diameter of wire rope (in inches) × Diameter of wire rope (in inches) × Area Factor*

(See table below to find the area factor for the wire rope construction)

Construction of Wire Rope	Area Factor
7x7 GAC	0.471
7x19 GAC	0.472
6x19W with fiber core	0.416
6x19W with IWRC	0.482
6x36WS with fiber core	0.419
6x36WS with IWRC	0.485
8x19W with fiber core	0.366
8x19W with IWRC	0.497

So, a 200-pound object is connected to a 10-foot length of ¼" diameter 7x19 GAC, and free-falls 1 foot (12 inches). What is the shock load on the wire rope and the beam to which it is attached?

Area $= 0.25 \times 0.25 \times 0.472$

Area $= 0.0295$ square inches

$$\text{Shock load} = \text{Load} \times \left(1 + \sqrt{1 + \frac{2 \times \text{Falling Distance} \times \text{Area} \times \text{E}}{\text{Load} \times \text{Length} \times 12}}\right)$$

$$\text{Shock load} = \text{Load} \times \left(1 + \sqrt{1 + \frac{2 \times 12 \times 0.0295 \times 15{,}000{,}000}{200 \times 10 \times 12}}\right)$$

$$\text{Shock load} = \text{Load} \times \left(1 + \sqrt{1 + \frac{10{,}620{,}000}{24{,}000}}\right)$$

$$\text{Shock load} = \text{Load} \times \left(1 + \sqrt{1 + 442.5}\right)$$

$$\text{Shock load} = \text{Load} \times \left(1 + \sqrt{443.5}\right)$$

$$\text{Shock load} = \text{Load} \times \left(1 + 21.059\right)$$

$$\text{Shock load} = 200 \times 21.059$$

Shock load $= 4{,}411.88$ lb

Shock loads on fiber rope

Accurately calculating the shock load of fiber ropes can be more difficult than calculating the shock load on wire rope for three reasons:

- Because humidity can change the ability of some materials to stretch, and some natural fibers lose elasticity with age.
- Because there are many different blends of materials.
- Because different manufacturers of rope supply different data about the energy absorbing capacities of their ropes. Despite this, it is possible to get a "good idea" of the shock load of a falling object being caught by a fiber rope.

As stated earlier, different companies supply different data on the elasticity of their ropes. We will look at the data provided by two rope companies, New England Ropes and Yale Cordage, and show how to calculate shock loads on each.

Method #1

Ron Reese, an arborist in Chattanooga, TN, developed the first method we will look at. His equation is:

$$Shock\ Load = \frac{-B + \sqrt{B^2 - (4 \times A \times C)}}{4 \times A}$$

where

A = (0.005 × Rope Stretch × Rope Length)/ Rope Load
B = -2 × A × Load
C = - Load × Fall Distance (in feet)

Rope stretch – rope stretch in percent as specified by the manufacturer. Put the number in as a percent – i.e. New England Ropes KMIII 7/16" rope stretches 5.1 percent, so put in "5.1" into the equation for calculating "A" above.

Note: You can find rope stretch (elongation) data for New England Ropes on pages 143 and 144.

Rope length – the length of the rope, in feet, between the Load and the termination point.

Rope load – the force that the manufacturer specifies will causes the stretch specified, e.g. for New England Ropes KMIII, the rope stretches 5.1% at 10% of the minimum breaking strength (MBS). The MBS is 7083 pounds, so the rope load is .1 x 7083 pounds = 708 pounds.

Load – weight of object that falls

Fall – distance in feet that the Load free falls

Let's use the same Load, Rope Length, and Fall Distance as we used in our wire rope calculation above, but replace the 1/4" GAC with 1/2" Multiline II – a fairly stretchy rope. So our problem is:

A 200-pound object is connected to a 10-foot length of 1/2" diameter Multiline II, and free-falls 1 foot. What is the shock load on the rope and the beam to which it is attached?

According to New England Ropes, Multiline II has an elongation rate of 1.7% at 10% of its tensile strength. Since the tensile strength of ½" diameter Multiline II is 6,000 pounds, 10% would be 600 pounds.

$$A = \frac{0.005 \times 1.7 \times 10}{600}$$

$$A = 0.000141667$$

$$B = -2 \times 0.000141667 \times 200$$
$$B = -0.056666667$$

$$C = -\ Load \times Fall\ Distance\ (in\ feet)$$
$$C = -\ 200 \times 1$$
$$C = -200$$

Plugging these numbers into our equation, we get

$$Shock\ Load = \frac{-B + \sqrt{B^2 - (4 \times A \times C)}}{4 \times A}$$

$$Shock\ Load = \frac{0.056666667 + \sqrt{-0.0566666667^2 - (4 \times 0.000141667 \times -200)}}{4 \times 0.000141667}$$

$$Shock\ Load = \frac{0.056666667 + \sqrt{0.003211111 - (-0.1133336)}}{0.000566668}$$

$$Shock\ Load = \frac{0.056666667 + \sqrt{0.116544711}}{0.000566668}$$

$$Shock\ Load = \frac{0.056666667 + 0.341386454}{0.000566668}$$

$$Shock\ Load = \frac{0.398053254}{0.000566668}$$

$$Shock\ load = 702.45\ lb$$

This is significantly less than the **4,411.88** pounds of shock load that occurred on the same fall using wire rope.

Method #2

Yale Cordage does not list the elongation of their ropes in percentages of the breaking strength as New England Rope does, so the equation above will not work. Instead, Yale Cordage provides energy absorption data that is based on the weight of each rope. Below is data on New England Rope's Double Esterlon rope.

Double Esterlon

Diameter	Working Load (lb)	Weight per 100 feet (lb)
1/2"	2,160	8.1
9/16"	2,740	9.6
5/8"	3,400	13.7
3/4"	4,160	16.3
7/8"	6,200	23.7
1"	8,800	35.2

Green working: 291 ft lb/lb
Red ultimate: 7,711 ft lb/lb

Yale Cordage's Double Esterlon rope, a low stretch rope, has a "green working energy absorption" of 291 foot-pounds per pound of rope. A 5/8" Double Esterlon rope weights 13.7 pounds per 100 feet (or .137 pounds for foot) and has a recommended working load limit of 3,400 pounds at 20% of its breaking strength (a 5:1 design factor). As before, let's use a 200-pound load falling 1 foot on a 10-foot-long piece of rope.

First, we need to calculate the force of the fall:

Force = Load x Falling Distance
Force = 200 lb × 1 foot
Force = 200 foot lb

Next we calculate the energy absorption capacity of our rope using Yale Cordage's equation:

Energy Absorption Capacity = Length of Rope × Green Working Energy Absorption × Weight of 1 foot of rope

Energy Absorption Capacity = 10 feet × 291 foot pounds² × 0.137 pounds per foot
Energy Absorption Capacity = 398.67 foot pounds

Since the force being placed on the rope (200 foot pounds) is less than the Energy Absorption Capacity (398.67 foot pounds[2]) of the rope, we know that the rope will be able to sustain the shock load without failing. However, to find the actual shock load on the rope, we use the equation:

$$Shock\ Load = \frac{Force}{Energy\ Absorbing\ Capacity} \times Recommended\ Working\ Load$$

So, for Yale's 5/8" diameter Double Esterlon rope (which has a working load limit of 3,400 pounds at 5:1):

$$Shock\ Load = \frac{200}{398.67} \times 3,400$$

Shock load = 1,705.67 lb

As we can see, Yale Cordage's 5/8" diameter Double Esterlon has less elasticity than New England Ropes Multiline II, but a great deal more elasticity than 1/4" dia. GAC.

Shock loads on Chain

The steel in an alloy chain has a modulus of elasticity of 30,000,000 psi, so it has even less elasticity than wire rope, and, therefore, potentially greater shock loads. This is why the shock load on the beam supporting a load being lifted by a 16-fpm chain hoist can be 20 to 50 percent greater than the load being lifted, simply due to the starting and stopping of the hoist. A 64-fpm chain hoist can create a shock load that is 200 percent greater than the load being lifted, by starting and stopping the hoist.

According to Phil Braymen, Engineering Manager at Laclede Chain Manufacturing Company, "… the chain industry does not test, certify or condone shock loading" of chain. The NACM (National Association of Chain Manufacturers) states, "Manufacturers do not accept any liability for injury or damage which may result from dynamic or static loads in excess of the working load limit."

To help understand how static loads affect chain, I ran several tensile tests using 1/4" Grade 30 proof coil chain. At its working load limit, 25 percent of its breaking strength, this chain stretches only about one-half of one percent of its length. At approximately 60 percent of the breaking strength of chain, the yield point of the steel, the chain stretches approximately 1 percent of its length. However, when the force on the mild steel chain reaches the yield point, two things happen. First, the shape of the links begins to deform, causing the links to get narrower and longer. Then, the metal enters its "plastic stage," where the metal stretches significantly under slight increases in force. During this stage, the growing tension on the chain slows dramatically as the deforming and elongating chain absorbs the energy. The tension grows even slower as the tension surpasses 90 percent of the breaking strength of the chain. In the final 40 percent of the breaking strength of the chain, the stretch of the chain is approximately 7.5 times greater than in the first 60 percent. This nearly constant changing of the rate of stretch under different amounts of force makes accurately calculating shock loads on chain, using a mathematical equation, a near impossibility.

Note: While the tests described above were done with Grade 30 proof coil chain, this grade of chain is not recommended for overhead lifting. Even the major manufacturers of counterweight rigging systems now use alloy chain for trim chains on linesets. The description above is only intended to demonstrate the behavior of chain under an extreme load.

The bottom line is that shock loads on chain can be quite high and can very easily exceed the working load limit of the chain, especially given the low design factor used for chain. Shock loading chain should be avoided whenever possible.

Chain Hoists and Shock Forces

Because most chain hoists start and stop suddenly (very little "ramp-up" or "ramp-down" to the speed), the starting and stopping of a chain hoist can produce a significant amount of shock load. How much? That depends on the acceleration and deceleration speed of the hoist. The starting and stopping of a 16-foot per minute (fpm) chain hoist does not produce as much shock load as the starting and stopping of a 64-fpm chain hoist.

As a "general rule of thumb," we say that a 16-fpm chain hoist produces a shock load of between 20 and 25 percent of the weight of the load it is lifting when it starts or stops. A 16-fpm chain hoist lifting a 2,000-pound load would produce a shock load between 400 and 500 pounds. So, the total force on the point would be between 2,400 and 2,500 pounds, plus the weight of the hoist and chain.

The faster the hoist speed, the greater the shock force. Again, as a general rule, a 32-fpm chain hoist produces a shock load of approximately 50 percent of the load, while a 64-fpm chain hoist produces a shock load of approximately 100 percent of the weight of the load it is lifting when it starts or stops. You could look at the shock loads this way:

$$Shock\ Load\ of\ a\ 16\ fpm\ chain\ hoist\ =\ Load \times 1.25$$

$$Shock\ Load\ of\ a\ 32\ fpm\ chain\ hoist\ =\ Load \times 1.5$$

$$Shock\ Load\ of\ a\ 64\ fpm\ chain\ hoist\ =\ Load \times 2$$

A simple formula for quickly calculating an approximate shock force of a chain hoist starting and stopping is:

$$Shock\ Load\ =\ Load\ +\ \left(\frac{Speed\ of\ hoist\ in\ fpm}{60}\times Load\right)$$

So, if a 64-fpm chain hoist was used to lift a 1000-pound load, the approximate shock load would be:

$$Shock\ Load\ =\ 1000\ +\ \left(\frac{64}{60}\times 1000\right)$$

$$Shock\ Load\ =\ 1000\ +\ (\ 1.0666667\times 1000)$$

$$Shock\ Load\ =\ 1000\ +\ 1066.67$$

Shock Load $=\ 2,066.67$ lb

This formula produces slightly higher results than our "general rules" specifies, but given the fact that on a rig with three or more chain hoists, the load on some hoists will be greater than calculated, this is not a bad thing.

Chain Grades

The National Association of Chain manufacturers categorizes welded chain by grades: Grade 30 (Proof Coil), Grade 43 (High Test), Grade 70 (Transport), Grade 80 (Alloy) and Grade 100 (Alloy). A chain's grade is determined by the following formula:

Grade = (0.000689 x MBS) / (0.5 x 3.14159265 x (Dia. of chain link x Dia. of chain link))

If you do not know the Minimum Breaking Strength (MBS) of the chain, it can be calculated using the following formula: Working Load Limit (WLL) x the Design Factor (DF) used to create the WLL. Note: all grades of chain, except Grade 43, have a DF of 4, while Grade 43 has a DF of 3.

You can download specification tables for welded chain from the NACM at http://www.nacm.info/Downloads/NACM_Welded.pdf.

Now you might be thinking, "How can I know if I need to use a design factor of 3 or 4 if I don't already know the grade of the chain?" or "Why would I need to do this when I already know the grade of the chain I have?" Good questions. Understanding how chain classes are determined will help you understand the strength relationship of one class of chain when compared to another. For example, assuming everything else is equal, a Grade 80 chain is a little more than 2.5 times stronger than a Grade 30 chain. While you may never use this equation, the more you know about chain, the better the choice you can make when choosing one for your applications.

Conclusion

Shock loads are not the same as static loads. The stiffness of the line (elasticity or lack of elasticity) amplifies the static load of a falling object when it decelerates. The less elasticity in the line, the greater the amplification. Technicians must consider the elasticity (energy absorbing capacity) of lines whenever a shock load is possible. As we have demonstrated, calculating the actual shock load on a wire or fiber rope is possible and can help you understand the results of dynamic forces involved in rigging.

Sample Problems – Lesson 28

1. A 175-pound man wearing a safety harness and lanyard falls four feet. As he stops, the harness and lanyard stretch 3 inches (or .25 feet). What is the force on him and the rigging that supports him?

2. A 75-pound lighting instrument falls one foot. As it stops, the safety cable stretches one inch. What is the force on the instrument and rigging that supports it?

3. A 150-pound object is connected to a 250-foot length of 1/4" diameter 7x19 GAC, and free-falls 2 feet (24 inches). What is the shock load on the wire rope and the beam to which it is attached?

Lesson 29:
Wind and Water

<u>How to Calculate Wind Loads</u>

When a structure is erected outdoors, it is subjected to the lateral force of wind in addition to other forces. The American Society of Civil Engineers' ASCE7-10 document contains precise information on how to calculate potential wind force on structures. This method requires the use of a wind force map for the area in which the structure is being erected and is extremely complex. There are, however, simpler formulas that can be used to get a rough estimate of the wind force on a structure. The method below is one such formula.

For this method, you will need to know the wind speed, the square footage of surface area of the structure, and its general shape (flat or curved).

Step 1. Calculate the force exerted by the wind on the structure by first squaring the wind speed (in miles per hour) and then multiplying the answer by 0.00256.

For a 30 mph wind the calculation would be

$$30 \times 30 \times 0.00256 = \textbf{2.304 lb per square foot}$$

Step 2. Multiply the force determined in Step 1 by the structure's surface area. With a 30 mph wind and a structure with a surface area of 100 square-feet, the calculation is

$$2.304 \times 100 = \textbf{230.4 lb}$$

Step 3. Multiply your answer from Step 2 by the structure's drag coefficient. For a flat square structure, multiply by 2.0. For a rounded structure, use 1.2.

For a flat structure with a surface area of 100 square feet, a 30 mph wind would create a wind load of

$$230.4 \times 2.0 = \textbf{460.8 lb}$$

196

IMPORTANT: The design of lateral forces upon structures, including wind forces are extremely complex and are dependent upon location, height, structure configuration and other factors. The formula given above is for general 'rule of thumb' calculations and should only be used to estimate the approximate lateral force on a structure caused by wind. A structural engineer should be consulted whenever large outdoor structures are erected or wherever you are unsure that your structure can withstand the potential wind force. Remember, uplift on a structure due to wind is often greater than the live and dead loads holding the structure down.

It should also be noted that ASCE7-10 requires all wall structures to be designed to withstand a minimum wind force of 16 pounds per square foot and "vertically projecting roof structures" to withstand a minimum of 8 pounds per square foot. So, the 100 square foot area in the previous problem should be designed to withstand a minimum force of 1,600 pounds.

Weight of Water

People often grossly underestimate the amount of standing water on a surface, and therefore underestimate its weight. A one-inch deep puddle of water weights 5.202 pounds per square foot (or 62.428 pounds per cubic foot). So, the weight of one inch of standing water on a 100' x 100' surface (such as a roof) would weight **52,020 pounds.**

Weight of Ice and Snow

Water expands approximately 9 percent when it freezes, so a one-inch thick sheet of ice is 0.92 inches of water. Combining this information with the information above, the equation for calculating the weight of a slab of ice is:

$$\text{Weight} = \text{Thickness of ice} \times 0.92 \times \text{area} \times 5.202$$

So, how much would a one-inch thick slab of ice on a 100' × 100' roof would weight?

$$\text{Weight of water} = 1 \times 0.92 \times 10,000 \times 5.202$$
$$\text{Weight of water} = 0.92 \times 10,000 \times 5.202$$
$$\text{Weight of water} = 0.92 \times 52,020$$
$$\textbf{Weight of water} = \textbf{47,860 lb or 4.786 lb/square foot}$$

The equation for calculating the weight of snow is very similar, except that the amount of water in snow can vary from 3 percent for dry snow to 33 percent for wet snow.

To determine the amount of water in the snow, gently push an empty metal can (open end down) into the snow. Push your hand into the snow and place it directly under the open end of the can, sealing the opening. Being careful not to compress the snow into the can, gently remove the can full of snow. Measure the height of the snow in the can. Now melt the snow and calculate the percentage of water in the can by comparing to the height of water in the can to the amount of snow you started with. Now put this number into the following equation.

Weight of snow = Depth of snow on surface × percentage of water × area × 5.2

So, if the snow is 1 foot deep and the percentage of water is 10 percent, and the area is 100' x 100', the weight of the snow is:

Weight of snow $= 12 \times 0.10 \times 10,000 \times 5.2$
Weight of snow $= 1.2 \times 10,000 \times 5.2$
Weight of snow $= 1.2 \times 52,000$
Weight of snow = 62,400 lb or 6.24 lb per square foot

Sample Problems – Lesson 29

1. What is the wind force on a flat 20' x 30' surface when the wind speed is 30 mph?

2. What is the wind force on a rounded 20' x 35' surface when the wind speed is 25 mph?

3. What is the weight of a pool of water 20' x 50' that is 2 inches deep?

4. What is the weight of a pool of water 24' x 24' that is 24 inches deep?

Lesson 30:
Motor Calculations

More and more, manual rigging systems are being replaced with automated, motorized rigging systems. Because of this, it is important for riggers to understand the math related to motorized rigging. Let's begin by defining some of the terms used in this lesson.

The most important variables in motorized rigging are horsepower, load, inertia, maximum speed, time needed to reach maximum speed, and distance needed to reach maximum speed. If you know three of these, you can calculate the other three.

Load – The weight of the object being lifted

Maximum speed – The maximum speed of travel needed for the object being lifted, measured in feet per second

Acceleration time – The time, either measured in feet per minute (fpm) or feet per second (fps), for the object to go from a resting position to Maximum speed

Adjusted weight – It might help you understand the "Adjusted weight" by relating it to *wind chill,* something you are probably familiar with if you live in an area that gets cold. With wind chill the temperature seems lower than it really is because the moving air takes away the body's heat. The faster the wind blows the faster the heat is taken away and the colder it seems. The Adjusted weight does the same for a moving object. While an object weighs a specific amount, the faster you try to get it to accelerate, the more in seems to weigh and the more power it takes to move it. The Adjusted weight is always greater than the weight of the load.

Horsepower – The strength of the motor required to move an object at a specific speed in a given time.

Horsepower is what we most often need to calculate, but as stated above, we need to know the Load and the Maximum speed, and the Acceleration time to calculate it. Let's solve the following problem:

What horsepower motor is needed to lift a 250 lb load at 30 feet per minute (.5 feet per second) with an acceleration time of 1.5 seconds?

The first step is to calculate the Adjusted weight. The formula to do this is:

Adjusted weight = (Load / 32.2) × (32.2 + (Speed in fps / Acceleration time))

So, plugging in the numbers from the problem we get:

Adjusted weight = (250 / 32.2) × (32.2 + (.5 / 1.5))

Adjusted weight = (7.763975155 × (32.2 + 0.333))

Adjusted weight = 7.763975155 × 32.533

Adjusted weight = 252.59 lb

The adjusted weight is very low because the Maximum speed is very slow and the acceleration time is fairly long.

To calculate the Horsepower of the motor, use the formula:

Horsepower = (Speed *Adjusted weight) / 550

So ...

Horsepower = (.5 x 252.59) / 550

Horsepower = 126.295)/ 550

Horsepower = 0.23

What would happen if we changed the Maximum speed from .5 fps to 10 fps? Plugging in these numbers you get:

Adjusted weight = (250 / 32.2) × (32.2 + (10 / 1.5))

Adjusted weight = (7.763975155 × (32.2 + 6.6666666667))

Adjusted weight = 7.763975155 × 38.8666666667

Adjusted weight = 301.18 lb

and

Horsepower = (10 x 301.18) / 550

Horsepower = 3011.8 / 550

Horsepower = 5.48

Wow, that made a huge difference. Now what would happen if we shortened the acceleration time from 1.5 seconds to 0.5 seconds?

Adjusted weight = (250 / 32.2) × (32.2 + (10 / 0.5))

Adjusted weight = (7.763975155 × (32.2 + 20))

Adjusted weight = 7.763975155 × 52.2

Adjusted weight = 405.28 lb

and

Horsepower = (10 x 405.28) / 550

Horsepower = 4052.8 / 550

Horsepower = 7.37

As you can see, changing the Maximum speed or the Acceleration time has a major impact on the Adjusted weight and therefore the Horsepower of the motor required to move the load at the specified speed. It is never a bad idea to have a motor that is a little more powerful than the <u>minimum</u> horsepower calculated. In fact, since motors are built in "standard" amounts, pick the one that is closest, but not less than the minimum amount calculated.

Sample Problems – Lesson 30

1. What horsepower motor is needed to lift a 500 lb load at 60 feet per minute (1 foot per second) with an acceleration time of 1.5 seconds?

2. What horsepower motor is needed to lift a 350 lb load at 5 feet per second with an acceleration time of 1 second?

3. What horsepower motor is needed to lift a 200 lb load at 10 feet per second with an acceleration time of 0.5 seconds?

4. What horsepower motor is needed to lift a 1500 lb load at 16 feet per minute (0.266666667 feet per second) with an acceleration time of 2 seconds?

5. What horsepower motor is needed to lift a 250 lb load at 15 feet per second with an acceleration time of 0.75 seconds?

Lesson 31:
Counterweight Bricks

Mechanical counterweight systems are a mainstay in many theatres. They allow us to easily "fly" scenery and lighting instruments that weigh hundreds of pounds by counterbalancing the load that we put on the battens with an equal load of weight placed on the arbor (assuming a single-purchase counterweight system). Of course, before you can know how much counterweight to load on the arbor, you must know the weight of the load you are wanting to fly. There is no simple way calculate this, so we will not try. We will just assume that you know the weight that you need to fly and we will deal with the counterweight.

Counterweight bricks come in many different sizes, so there are no "standard weights" to consider. Instead, you need to know the weight (or weights) of the counterweight bricks that you have in your theatre. Most theatre have at least two sizes (thicknesses) of bricks, but I have seen theatres with as many as six different sizes of bricks. In addition to size, the material that the bricks are made from must be considered. Most counterweight bricks are made of cast steel which weights approximately 0.2836 per cubic inch. Cast iron weights approximately 0.2604 pounds per cubic inch; and lead bricks (which should be replaced for health reasons) weight approximately 0.410 pounds per cubic inch.

So, how much do your bricks weight? In many theatres, technicians just guess, or the weight of the bricks have been passed from TD to TD through the years, and no one really knows for certain where the numbers came from. Of course, just bringing in a bathroom scale and weighing them is a good way to know the actual weight. Some theatres have signs at loading positions on the counterweight system that shows the weights of the counterweight bricks that the manufacturer or installer provided. If your theatre does not have such signs, you should consider making some.

The purpose of this lesson is to teach you how to calculate the weight of your counterweight bricks (so you do not have to bring in scales). This is done by calculating number of cubic inches in the bricks and them multiplying that number by the weight of the material. Lets get started by looking at a typical counterweight brick.

The drawing below is of a fairly typical counterweight brick. In addition to its width, length and thickness, we also have the width and length of the slots used to hold it in place on the arbor

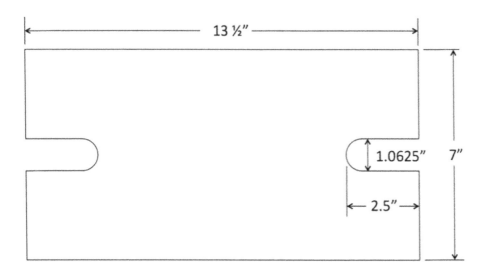

To calculate the number of cubic inches of material in the brick, we first calculate the total area of the brick based on the outside dimensions of the (its width, length and thickness). Next we calculate the area of the two slots, and subtract this area from the overall area we calculated first. Now that we know the area of the actual area of the material, we simply multiply this by the weight of the material, per cubic inch. Done.

Let's calculate the weight of the counterweight brick based on the specifications listed below.

Width	Length	Thickness	Slot width	Slot length	Weight of material per CI
7"	13.5"	1.25	1.0625"	2.5"	0.2836 lb

Begin by calculating the overall area of the brick. To do this we multiply the width by the length by the thickness. So,

$7 \times 13.5 \times 1.25 = 118.125$ cubic inches (ci)

That was easy. Now we need to calculate the area of the slots and subtract this amount from the overall area of the brick. Although the inside end of the slot is rounded, we can simplify our calculation be pretending that it is a rectangle. This shortcut will mean that our calculation is off slightly, but not enough to be stressed about. Let's use the formula:

$Area \; = \; (Width \; of \; Slot \times Length \; of \; Slot \times Thichness \; of \; Brick) \times 2$

So...

$Area \; = \; (1.0625 \times 2.5 \times 1.25) \times 2$

$Area \; = 3.32 \times 2$

$Area \; = \; 6.64 \; ci$

Next, subtract the slot area from the total brick area to the the area of the material.

Material area = 118.125 ci - 6.64 ci

Material area = 111.48 ci

Finally, multiply the Material area times Material Weight.

Brick weight = 111.48 × 0.2836

Brick weight = 31.6 pounds

Note: When I weighed a steel counterweight with these dimensions, it weighed 31.4 lb. For simplicity
    sake, I would just call this weight 32 pounds to make it easy to keep track of when loading
    weight.

If all of your bricks have the same outside dimensions and the same slot dimensions, you can
calculate the weight of the brick by the linear inch. The bricks used above weight approximately 25
pounds per inch, stacked on the arbor. So if you needed to add 300 pounds of counterweight to the
arbor, you need to add 12 inches of counterweight on the arbor.

Finally, there is a Brick Weight calculator that is a part of the *RigCalc* app, and I have created an Excel
workbook for doing these calculations that can be download from
http://www.springknollpress.com/RiggingMath/downloads/index.html.

Sample Problems – Lesson 31

If Slot Width = 1.0625", Slot Length = 2.5" and Weight per CI = 0.2826 lb (steel), calculate the weight of the counterweight brick when...

1. Length = 13.5", Width = 6" and Thickness = 1.5"

2. Length = 13.5", Width = 3" and Thickness = 2"

3. Length = 13.5", Width = 5" and Thickness = 1"

Lesson 32:
Pullout Capacity of Lag Screws

Every once in a while you may need to anchor something to wood. If you cannot bolt through the entire piece wood, you may have to use lag screws to attach to the wood. While it may not be the desired option, sometimes it is your only option. Fortunately, there is a way to calculate the pullout capacity of lag screws in wood. That formula is:

$$Pullout\ capacity\ =\ 1,800 \times Specific\ Gravity^{1.5} \times Bolt\ diameter^{0.75} \times Inches\ of\ thread$$

The first thing that might strike you as unusual about this formula is the term "specific gravity." Every type of wood has its own density or specific gravity - a number between 0 and 1. The specific gravity for many types of wood can be found in the table at the end of this lesson.

The next odd thing that you may notice is that the exponents in this equation are not whole numbers. This means that you will have to use a key on your calculator that you may not have used before - the y^x key. To find the result of $.5^{1.5}$, enter .5, then press the $[y^x]$ key, and enter 1.5, and finally press the [=] key. The result is 0.353553391.

Assuming you put 1.5" of thread of a 3/8" lag screw, into a beam of Eastern Hemlock (Specific gravity of 0.41) its pullout capacity would be:

$Pullout\ capacity\ =\ 1,800 \times 0.41^{1.5} \times 0.375^{0.75} \times 1.5$

$Pullout\ capacity\ =\ 1,800 \times 0.262528094 \times 0.479207328 \times 1.5$

$Pullout\ capacity\ =\ 339.67\ pounds$

Multiple lag screws would multiply the pullout capacity.

This equation assumes that the wood is dry and in good condition, that the lag screw(s) are perpendicular to the wood surface, and that the pullout force is in line with the lag screw(s).

Important: As in any rigging situation, always use an appropriate design factor for rating the load on any point.

Specific Gravities For North American Wood Species

Species Combination	Specific Gravity
Aspen	0.39
Alaska Cedar	0.47
Alaska Hemlock	0.46
Alaska Spruce	0.41
Alaska Yellow Cedar	0.46
Balsam Fir	0.36
Beech-Birch-Hickory	0.71
Coast Sitka Spruce	0.43
Cottonwood	0.41
Douglas Fir-Larch	0.50
Douglas Fir-Larch (North)	0.49
Douglas Fir-South	0.46
Eastern Hemlock	0.41
Eastern Hemlock-Balsam Fir	0.36
Eastern Hemlock-Tamarack	0.41
Eastern Hemlock-Tamarack (North)	0.47
Eastern Softwoods	0.36
Eastern Spruce	0.41
Eastern White Pine	0.36

Engelmann Spruce-Lodgepole Pine	0.38
Hem-Fir	0.43
Hem-Fir (North)	0.46
Mixed Maple	0.55
Mixed Oak	0.68
Mixed Southern Pine	0.51
Mountain Hemlock	0.47
Northern Pine	0.42
Northern Red Oak	0.68
Northern Species	0.35
Northern White Cedar	0.31
Ponderosa Pine	0.43
Red Maple	0.58
Red Oak	0.67
Red Pine	0.44
Redwood, close grain	0.44
Redwood, open grain	0.37
Sitka Spruce	0.43
Southern Pine	0.55
Spruce-Pine-Fir	0.42
Spruce-Pine-Fir (South)	0.36
Western Cedars	0.36
Western Cedars (North)	0.35
Western Hemlock	0.47
Western Hemlock (North)	0.46
Western White Pine	0.40
Western Woods	0.36

White Oak	0.73
Yellow Cedar	0.46
Yellow Poplar	0.43

Specific Gravities For Non-North American Wood Species

Species Combination	Specific Gravity
Austrian Spruce – Austria & The Czech Republic	0.43
Douglas Fir/European Larch – Austria, The Czech Republic & Bavaria	0.47
Montane Pine – South Africa	0.45
Norway Spruce – Estonia & Lithuania	0.43
Norway Spruce – Finland	0.42
Norway Spruce – Germany, NE France, & Switzerland	0.42
Norway Spruce – Romania & the Ukraine	0.38
Norway Spruce – Sweden	0.42
Scots Pine – Austria, The Czech Republic, Romania & the Ukraine	0.50
Scots Pine – Estonia & Lithuania	0.45
Scots Pine – Finland	0.48
Scots Pine – Germany	0.53
Scots Pine – Sweden	0.47
Silver Fir (Ables alba) – Germany, NE France, & Switzerland	0.43
Southern Pine – Misiones Argentina	0.54
Southern Pine – Misiones Argentina	0.45

Sample Problems - Lesson 32

Calculate the pullout capacity of a lag screw given the following conditions:

1. Wood = Eastern Spruce, Bolt Diameter = 3/8" and screw penetrates 4 inches into the wood.

2. Wood = White Pine, Bolt Diameter = 1/4" and screw penetrates 3 inches into the wood.

3. Wood = Mixed Oak = 1/4" and screw penetrates 2 inches into the wood.

4. Wood = Eastern Softwoods, Bolt Diameter = 5/16" and screw penetrates 4 inches into the wood.

5. Wood = Mixed Southern Pine, Bolt Diameter = 3/8" and screw penetrates 3 inches into the wood.

Lesson 33:
Drawbridge Problem

Twice in my career as a scenic designer, I have designed sets for *The Man of La Mancha*. Both of these productions have included drawbridges. The unique problem with rigging a drawbridge is the fact that the tension on the lift lines changes as the drawbridge is raised and lowered. While there is the temptation to use a winch and not worry about it, understanding how the placement of a critical pulley can change the load and what the loads are and can help make running this effect much easier when using the "old school" method of operation. In this lesson, we will look at how to calculate the tension on the line supporting the drawbridge.

The drawbridge for our production might look something that the one in the diagram below.

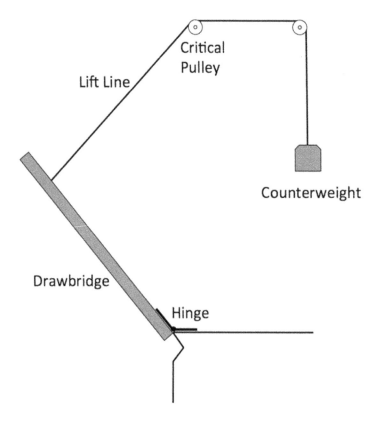

A lift line (actually two lines, but since we want to calculate the total tension on the line we need to treat it as a single line), is connected to the drawbridge and will lift it. The first pulley that the line runs through is the "critical pulley" because its position is a determining factor in the angle of the line, which then helps determine the tension on the lift line.

When the drawbridge is "up" (closed), there is no tension on the lift line - the entire weight of the drawbridge rests in the hinge. But as the drawbridge lowers (opens), the load on the lift line slowly increases.

To calculate the tension on the lift line, we need to know:

W - Weight of the drawbridge

COG - Distance from the hinge to the center of gravity of the drawbridge

D2L - Distance from the hinge to the point on the drawbridge where the lift line is attached

DA - Angle of the drawbridge (0 = horizontal, 90 = vertical; a negative angle means that the top of the drawbridge is lower than the hinge)

LA - The inside angle between the drawbridge to lift line

To calculate the inside angle between the drawbridge and the lift line (LA) we must know the position of the "critical pulley" in relationship to the point where the lift line attaches to the drawbridge. We need to know "H" - the horizontal offset distance and "V" - the vertical offset distance, of this pulley. All of these variables are shown in the drawing below.

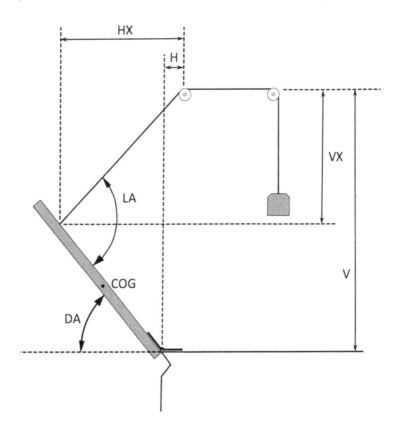

Let's begin by describing the specifics of the drawbridge rig. In this example, the drawbridge will be 10 feet long and completely symmetrical. This puts its COG at 5 feet from the hinge. (Note: If the drawbridge were not symmetrical - for example, if it were wider on one end, then we would have to calculate where the COG is located.) Let's place the lift line(s) 8 feet from the hinge(s). Next, lets put the top center of the "critical pulley" 5 feet offstage of the hinge, and 25 feet above the hinge.

Now, let's calculate the tension on the line when the drawbridge is raised to 20 degrees above horizontal. So,

W = 300 pounds
COG = 5 feet
D2L = 8 feet
V = 25 feet
H = 5 feet
DA = 20 degrees
LA = ? (this is the first thing we need to calculate)

To calculate the Line Angle (LA), we will use the equation:

$$LA \ = \ 20 \ + \ ATAN\left(\frac{VX}{HX}\right)$$

where,

$$VX \ = \ V \ - \ ((\ SIN(DA)) \times D2L)$$

and

$$HX \ = \ H \ + \ ((\ COS(DA)) \times D2L)$$

In order to calculate LA, we need to add two angles: the angle of the drawbridge (DA) and the angle from a horizontal reference line that is at the height of the point where the lift line attaches to the door to the line itself. Since we already know DA, we need to calculate this second angle; but to do this, we need to know two things: the horizontal distance from the point where the lift line attached to the drawbridge to the critical pulley (HX), and vertical distance from the the point where the lift line attached to the drawbridge to the critical pulley (VX).

To find these distances we use simple trigonometry. Lesson 34 explains how trigonometry works and how to figure-out exactly what these equations do (study the Trig Table in that Lesson).

So, plugging in the numbers we find that,

$$VX = 25 - ((SIN(20)) \times 8)$$

$$VX = 25 - (0.3420 \times 8)$$

$$VX = 25 - 2.73616$$

$$VX = 22.2638$$

and

$$HX = 5 + ((COS(20)) \times 8)$$

$$HX = 5 + (0.9396 \times 8)$$

$$HX = 5 + 7.5175$$

$$HX = 12.5175$$

Now that we know these lengths, lets calculate the angle of the lift line.

$$LA = 20 + ATAN\left(\frac{22.2638}{12.5175}\right)$$

$$LA = 20 + ATAN(1.7786)$$

$$LA = 20 + 60.6537$$

$$LA = 80.65 \text{ degrees}$$

Now that we know the Line Angle, we can calculate the force needed to support the drawbridge at a 20 degree angle. To do this we use the equation

$$Tension = (COG \times W \times COS(DA)) / (D2L \times SIN(LA))$$

Once again, this is basic trigonometry. Let's plug in the numbers and solve it.

$$Tension = (5 \times 300 \times COS(20)) / (8 \times SIN(80.65))$$

$$Tension = (1500 \times 0.9397) / (8 \times 0.9867)$$

$$Tension = 1409.9539 / 7.8937$$

$$\boldsymbol{Tension = 178.6\ pounds}$$

The following chart shows how this tension changes as you lift this drawbridge from -20 degrees to 90 degrees:

Drawbridge Angle	Angle of Lift Lines	Tension on Lift Lines
-20	46	246 pounds
0	63	211 pounds
20	81	179 pounds
45	106	138 pounds
60	124	112 pounds
75	143	80 pounds
90	164	0 pounds

Since it take a lot of math to calculate all of the tensions above, this seems to me to be a situation that would benefit greatly from being done in an Excel spreadsheet - so I created one - Drawbridge.xlsx. You can find this spreadsheet in the download page on the Spring Knoll Press website. This spreadsheet let you look at 10 different angles for any drawbridge setup. You can also change the location of "critical pulley" and compare the Line Angles and tensions, helping you select the best setup for your needs.

One more thing. Since there is very little weight on the lift line when the the drawbridge is close to vertical, putting a jack line on the sandbag makes it possible to control the drawbridge better. A jack line might look something like the one in the illustration below.

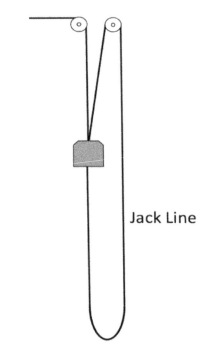

Jack Line

Sample Problems - Lesson 33

Using the specifications below, calculate the tension on the lift line.

1.

    W = 300 pounds
    COG = 6 feet
    D2L = 10 feet
    V = 12 feet
    H = 0 feet
    DA = 0 degrees

2.

    W = 300 pounds
    COG = 6 feet
    D2L = 10 feet
    V = 12 feet
    H = 0 feet
    DA = -20 degrees

3.

    W = 300 pounds
    COG = 6 feet
    D2L = 10 feet
    V = 12 feet
    H = 0 feet
    DA = 45 degrees

4.

    W = 200 pounds
    COG = 5 feet
    D2L = 8 feet
    V = 50 feet
    H = 15 feet
    DA = 60 degrees

Lesson 34:

Allowable Loads on Pipe Battens

Lesson 23 dealt with calculating the load on the center point of a truss and comparing that to the Maximum Allowable Center Point Load set by the truss manufacturer based on the size and span of the truss. This lesson will do something similar, but for pipe rather than truss. There is, however, one major complication. The steel pipe typically used for manual counterweight systems is intended to have the load or force applied to the inside of the pipe by gas or liquid pushing outward. Thus, this pipe is NOT a structural member designed to support vertical loads across a span and pipe manufacturers do not provide the kind of allowable load data provided for truss.

So, let's start by looking at the information on pipe battens that is part of ANSI E1.4-2014 Entertainment Technology — Manual Counterweight Rigging Systems. Section 3.9.1(c). This standard states,

> "The batten shall be capable of supporting at minimum 45 kg/m (30 lbs/ft) of uniformly distributed load. Battens shall be capable of sustaining a point load of 45 kg (100 pounds) at mid-span between any two lift lines with a maximum span deflection of 1/180 of the span."

This tells us two things: 1) when the pipe is uniformly loaded, it should hold a minimum of 30 pounds per linear foot without permanently bending; and 2) the force, placed on the center point of any span required to deflect the pipe 1/180 of the Span distance must be at least 100 pounds. Now that we know what requirements we are attempting to meet, let's look at how we calculate these numbers.

Before we start looking at equations, we need to know the physical/structural properties of pipe. Specifically, we need to know the pipe's Modulus of Elasticity (psi), Section Modulus (In^3), Moment of Inertia (in^3), Weight of pipe per linear inch) and Yield Strength (psi).

Luckily, it is not as complicated and confusing as it all sounds. In fact, pipe manufacturers supply this information in tables, so you just have to look it up. The ASTM A53 pipe that is typically used for pipe battens, has a **Modulus of Elasticity (E) of 29,000,000 psi**, and a **Yield Strength (Fy) of 30,000 psi**.

Below is a table that contains most of the other information you need for commonly used sizes of pipe.

Schedule 40 Pipe

ID	Weight per ft	Weight per inch (W)	Section Modulus (S)	Moment of Inertia (I)
1"	1.68	0.14	0.13	0.09
1-1/4"	2.27	0.192	0.23	0.19
1-1/2"	2.72	0.2267	0.33	0.31
2"	3.65	0.3042	0.56	0.67

Schedule 80 Pipe

ID	Weight per ft	Weight per inch (W)	Section Modulus (S)	Moment of Inertia (I)
1"	2.17	0.1808	0.161	0.106
1-1/4"	3.0	0.25	0.291	0.242
1-1/2"	3.65	0.3042	0.412	0.391
2"	5.02	0.4183	0.731	0.868

Now that we have the data, let's look at how to calculate the maximum force, per linear foot, that we can put on a Span of pipe without permanently deforming it. Since we do not want to load the pipe to its yield point, because that is the point when it will permanently deform, it is common to calculate the load at two-thirds (0.6667) of the yield point. So, the equation to do this is...

$$UDL \ = \ (12 \times Fy \times 8 \times S \ / \ (W\text{\textasciicircum}2) \times 0.6667) \ - \ Weight\ of\ pipe\ per\ foot$$

Using the information from the table above, let's calculate the UDL for 1-1/2" Schedule 40 pipe with a Span of 10. So...

$UDL \ = \ ((12 \times 30{,}000 \times 8 \times 0.326 \ / \ ((10 * 12)\text{\textasciicircum}2)) \times 0.6667) \ - \ 2.72$

$UDL \ = \ ((938{,}880 \ / \ 120\text{\textasciicircum}2) \times 0.6667) \ - \ 2.72$

$UDL \ = \ ((938{,}880 \ / \ 14{,}400) \times 0.6667) \ - \ 2.72$

$UDL \ = \ (65.2 \times 0.6667) \ - \ 2.72$

$UDL \ = \ 43.47 \ - \ 2.72$

$UDL \ = \ 40.7\ pounds$

Since 40.7 pounds is greater than 30 pounds minimum specified in this standard, a 10-foot Span is an acceptable span distance for this size pipe. Also, this calculation tells us the UDL that we can place on this pipe.

Next, we need to look at the maximum Center Point Load.

The second requirement of this standard is that the force, placed on the center point of any span, needed to deflect the pipe 1/180 of the Span distance, must be at least 100 pounds. Before we do this calculation, let's discuss the "1/180" part of it.

This number sets the stiffness required of the beam (or pipe, in this case). The higher the denominator, the stiffer the beam. For most beams, the denomination is either 120, 180, 240, 360 or higher. This number is not a safety matter. Rather, it is selected to ensure that the beam is rigid enough for the purpose it is used for. For example, a beam supporting a plaster ceiling or a tile floor needs a stiffness of at least L/120 in order to prevent the plaster or tile from cracking when the the beam bends under a load. (Note: "L" stands for "Length"). Stone needs a "fraction of deflection" of at least L/720. In this case, 180 was most likely selected because the pipe does not need to be exceptionally stiff. Jay Glerum discusses the allowable load for battens based on 1/240 of the span and J.R. Clancy's Allowable Batten Load table uses 1/360 of the span. Both of these allow less deflection than ANSI E1.4-2014.

The equation for calculating the max CPL on a pipe is:

$$Max\ CPL = \left(Fraction\ of\ deflection - 5 \times W \times (Span \times 12)^3 / (384 \times E * I)\right) \times 48 \times E \times I / (Span \times 12)^2$$

So, using the same 1-1/2" Schedule 40 pipe with a Span of 10 feet, let's calculate the maximum Center Point Load that can be placed on the beam when the deflection is 1/180 of the Span.

$$Max\ CPL = \left(0.005556 - 5 \times 0.226667 \times (120)^3 / (384 \times 29,000,000 \times 0.31)\right) \times 48 \times 29,000,000 \times 0.31 / (120)^2$$

$$Max\ CPL = \left(0.005556 - 5 \times 0.226667 \times 1,728,000 / (384 \times 29,000,000 \times 0.31)\right) \times 48 \times 29,000,000 \times 0.31 / 14,400$$

$$Max\ CPL = (0.005556 - 1,958,402.88 / 3,452,160,000) \times 431,520,000 / 14,400$$

$$Max\ CPL = (0.005556 - 0.000567298) \times 431,520,000 / 14,400$$

$$Max\ CPL = 0.004988702 \times 431,520,000 / 14,400$$

$$Max\ CPL = 2,152,724.687 / 14,400$$

$$\boldsymbol{Max\ CPL = 149.5\ pounds}$$

Because our result is greater than 100 pounds, that spacing of the lift lines allows the CPL to exceed the minimum requirement of ANSI 1.4, so it is "good to go."

If you know the CPL or UDL that you need to hang on a horizontal pipe, you can use the equations above to help you determine the size of pipe and the minimum spacing (span) between the lift lines for your needs.

Like other problems, this is one that would benefit greatly from being in a spreadsheet. You can download PipeLoad.xls from SpringKnollPress.com.

Sample Problems – Lesson 34

1. What is the CPL on a 1-1/4" Schedule 40 pipe with a Span of 8 feet when the deflection is L/180?

2. What is the CPL on a 2" Schedule 80 pipe with a Span of 12 feet when the deflection is L/180?

3. What is the Max UDL on a 1-1/2" Schedule 80 pipe with a Span of 10 feet at 2/3 of the yield?

4. What is the Max UDL on a 2" Schedule 40 pipe with a Span of 10 feet at 1/3 of the yield?

Unit VII:
Other Math Stuff

Lesson 35:
Trigonometry

Have you ever heard anyone say, "I am never going to have to use this stuff," when referring to math? Ever say it yourself? Students in math classes have been saying this for centuries. The problem with this statement is that it is probably not true. Trigonometry is used to solve many types of math problems; you have used it quite a bit in this book so far.

This lesson is not about rigging math - it will not directly help you solve any rigging problems. This lesson does not reference rigging in any way. This lesson teaches you about trigonometry, which in turn could help you with rigging math problems. Think of it as a "bonus lesson."

For many, many years I used trigonometry without really understanding it very well. I just plugged numbers into formulas and got the answers. I never knew why the formulas worked, they just did. The objective of this lesson is to help you understand a little more about trigonometry and trigonometric functions. The more you understand them, the more you can use them to solve lots of different types of math problems, not just rigging math problems.

Getting Started

The first thing to understand about trigonometry is that it most often (but not always) deals with right triangles. All right triangles must have a 90-degree angle (a right angle) as one of its three corners (vertices).

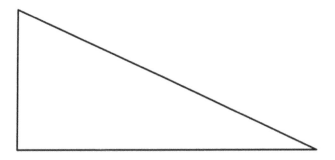

So what is so important about right triangles? First, the triangle is the simplest and most basic shape. And most complex shapes (those made up of straight lines) can be broken down into triangle. But what if the triangle is not a right triangle? Don't fear, because any triangle can be broken into two right triangles and trigonometry can then be used to help you understand them.

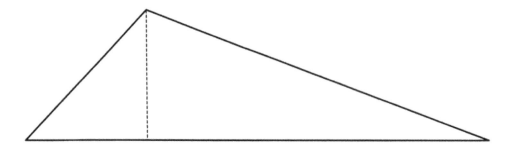

Remember, a complex problem that might seem impossible to solve can often be broken down into a number of simple problems. And that is the beauty of trigonometry – it helps you understand these simple shapes in ways that you did not think possible.

To do trigonometry, you will need a scientific calculator. I highly recommend the TI-30XA scientific calculator for doing most trigonometric problems. Do not fear, this is not an expensive graphing calculator. The TI-30XA is an inexpensive (under $15) calculator that is available at most department or office supply stores and is easy to use.

Finally, Trigonometry is a very "graphical" form of mathematics. As I started earlier, I find that diagramming the problem and labeling all of the parts makes understanding and solving it much easier. I highly recommend you do diagram the problems in this lesson as well.

The Pythagorean Theorem

Most people know, or have at least heard of, the Pythagorean Theorem. This is a simple equation that can be used to solve a great many trig problems. It is:

$$A^2 + B^2 = C^2$$

or put another way,

(A × A) + (B × B) = (C × C)

This equation is used find the length on one side of a right triangle when the lengths of the others two sides are known. Look at the right triangle below.

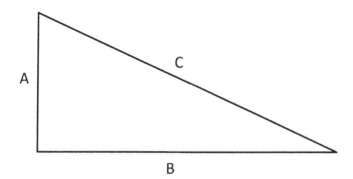

This equation refers to the two shortest sides of the triangle as labeled A and B, while the long side (the one opposite the right angle) is called C. The long side of a right triangle is known as the hypotenuse and is always the "C" part of this equation.

By squaring the lengths of the two short sides of the right triangle and adding them together, we get the square of the hypotenuse (C^2). Then, find the square root ($\sqrt{}$) of C^2 to find the length of C. Here is a simple example:

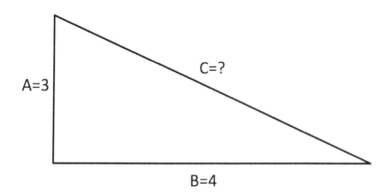

(C × C) = (A × A) + (B × B)

(C × C) = (3 × 3) + (4 × 4)

(C × C) = 9 + 16

(C × C) = 25

$C = \sqrt{25}$

C = 5

If you know the lengths of any two sides of a right triangle, you can use this equation, or a variation of this equation, to find the third. Here are two variations on this formula that can help you find the lengths of A and B, respectively, of you know the lengths of the other sides.

$$A = \sqrt{C^2 - B^2}$$

and

$$B = \sqrt{C^2 - A^2}$$

Examples

With this basic understanding of the right triangle and the simple formulas above, you can calculate a great many problems. Let's look at four problems and see how trigonometry can help us solve them.

Problem 1

You are a building contractor and you need to mark the layout the foundation of a new home that you are constructing. The house will be in the shape of a rectangle that is 40 feet wide (the front and back sides of the house) and 30 feet deep (the sides of the house). How do you do this so that the corners are perfectly square (90 degrees)?

Before we start solving this problem, let's discuss a special right triangle, sometimes called a "3-4-5 triangle." It is called this because the three sides are 3 units, 4 units and 5 units long. These are the smallest dimensions of a right triangle whose sides are all whole numbers. However, many right triangles can have sides whose lengths are all whole numbers (30, 40, 50 and 300, 400, 500 are two more examples. The key thing to remember is that triangles with these proportions are RIGHT TRIANGLES, and therefore, they have one vertex that is 90 degrees. So, how does that help us?

To solve this problem, drive two stakes in the ground that are 40 feet apart and are where you want the front of the house to be located. Next, take two measuring tapes (each at least 50-foot long) and placing the end of each tape at the two stakes you have positioned, measure 30 feet with one and 50 feet with the other, creating a triangle. At the point where these two points on the tapes cross, drive a stake to mark that point. This is one of the back corners of the house. Because the lengths of the sides of the triangle are 30, 40 and 50 feet, you have a right triangle and the corner is 90 degrees (exactly what you want).

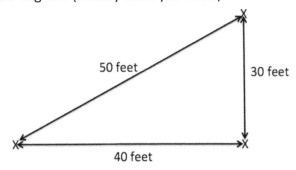

50 feet · 30 feet · 40 feet

Repeat this process and find the other corner.

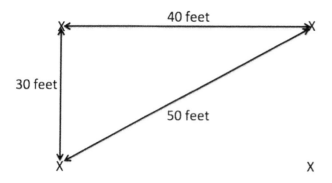

There, you have used trigonometry to lay out a large rectangle with perfect 90 degree corners. By the way, the ancient Egyptians used a similar method to lay out the foundations for the giant pyramids.

Problem 2

A variation on this method can be used to determine if a structure is square (has 90 degree corner). A carpenter building a window frame can measure diagonally from corner to corner. If the two diagonals (hypotenuses) are the same length, then the window unit is square.

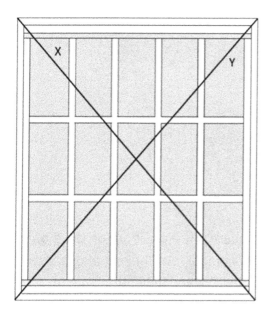

Problem 3

Let's say that you want to lay out a baseball diamond. It is 90 feet between the bases and the corners are all 90 degrees. Below is a diagram of a baseball diamond that has been divided into two right triangles, with the hypotenuse of each triangle running between home plate and second base.

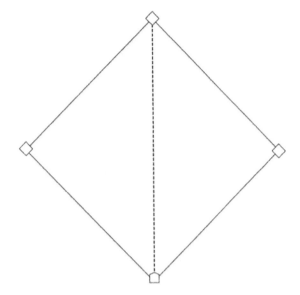

As you see, we already know a great deal about these triangles. What we do not know the distance from home plate to second base - the hypotenuse of both triangles. But we can calculate this distance very easily.

Hypotenuse = $\sqrt{opposite^2 + adjacent^2}$

Hypotenuse = $\sqrt{90^2 + 90^2}$

Hypotenuse = $\sqrt{8100 + 8100}$

Hypotenuse = $\sqrt{16200}$

Hypotenuse = 127.28 feet or roughly 127' 3-3/8"

Now that you know the distance from home plate to second base, measure it out on the ground (putting stakes at each location. Next, with two 100-foot measuring tapes, put the end of one at home plate and the other at second base, and measure 90 feet, just like you did in the Problem 1. Where they cross is where first and third base will be located.

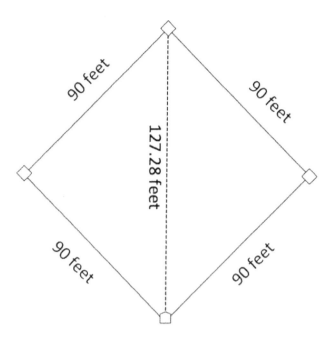

You have just created a perfect square for a baseball for a baseball diamond, using trigonometry.

Problem 4

An entertainment rigger uses steel cables to suspend lighting trusses for concerts. These cables are connected to I-beams above the arena floor. If a "point" needs to be between two beams, two cables, arranged in a "V" configuration called a bridle, are used to make the point at the desired location. The lengths of these two cables determines how far below the I-beams and how far away from each beam the apex (bottom of the "V") the point will be.

If two I-beams are 30 feet apart, and the rigger wants the apex to be 10 feet from Beam 1 and 20 feet from Beam 2, and to be 15 feet below the beams, how long is each cable?

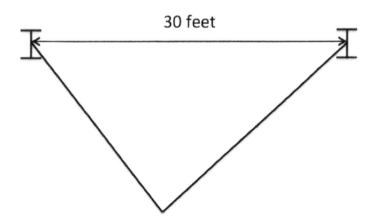

30 feet

Looking at this diagram you can see that we already have a natural triangle (the distance between Beam 1 and the apex being one side, the distance between Beam 2 and the apex being the second side, and the distance between the beams being the third side). However, this is not a right triangle. But remember, we can convert this triangle into two right triangles. When we do, our diagram looks like this.

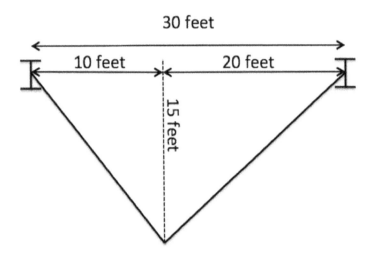

Perfect. Since we know the sides of each of our right triangles we just have to use the Pythagorean Theorem to find the hypotenuse of each triangle. So,

Bridle Leg 1 = $\sqrt{10^2 + 15^2}$

Bridle Leg 1 = $\sqrt{100 + 225}$

Bridle Leg 1 = $\sqrt{325}$

Bridle Leg 1 = 18.0277 feet

Bridle Leg 2 = $\sqrt{20^2 + 15^2}$

Bridle Leg 1 = $\sqrt{400 + 225}$

Bridle Leg 1 = $\sqrt{625}$

Bridle Leg 1 = 25 feet

Trigonometric Functions

The Pythagorean Theorem only deals with the sides of a right triangle, not its vertices (angles). This is where the Trigonometric function (Sine, Cosine and Tangent) helps us.

As you know, a right triangle has one vertex where the angle is 90 degrees. A small bracket that makes a square at this vertex is commonly used to denote this angle. The other two vertices are what I call the primary and secondary angles. A small arc often denotes the primary angle and the minor angle usually has no markings. Often these vertices are also given names. The Greek symbol θ (Theta), an X or the letter A are often used to name the primary angle. While the Greek symbol α (Alpha) or the letter B, is used to name the secondary. The right angle is sometimes called C or it is left un-named. Below is an example of one common way that the vertices are labeled (and the way they will be referenced in this book).

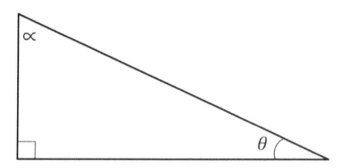

The sum of the three vertices is 180 degrees. And since the right angle is 90 degrees, the secondary is equal to the primary angle minus 90.

When using the Pythagorean Theorem, we labeled the three sides of the triangle A, B, and C. We are now going to rename them, based on their relationship to the primary angle Theta (θ). Because of this, it is very important that we know which vertex is Theta. While the sides can be given other names, the names described here will be very helpful as you delve a little deeper into trigonometry.

The diagram below indicates the new names of the three sides (along with the names of the vertices). The sides are: *opposite* (of Theta) and *adjacent* (to Theta) and the *hypotenuse.* Knowing the names of these sides (as they relate to Theta) is critical to the next section, so look at them carefully and remember them.

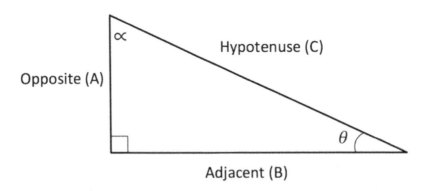

Old Harry And His Old Aunt

The three Trigonometric function that we will use in this book are: Sine (SIN), Cosine (COS) and Tangent (TAN). These functions are a mystery to most people (and they were to me for many years). It was not that I had not heard of them, it was just that I did not know how they related to the parts of the right triangle. That is where the phrase "Old Harry And His Old Aunt" comes in. They are the key to understanding this relationship and three simple, but very important, equations. Let's start by rearranging the words in pairs:

Old Harry

And **H**is

Old **A**unt

The fact that I made the first letter of each word **BOLD** will be explained shortly. But before I do that, let's throw in the functions:

Sin θ = **O**ld **H**arry

Cos θ = **A**nd **H**is

Tan θ = **O**ld **A**unt

Note: It will actually help you remember this is you say these out loud half-a-dozen times. (It may sound silly, but it works).

Finally, let's substitute the new names the sides of the right triangle (**O**pposite, **A**djacent and **H**ypotenuse) for **O**ld **H**arry **A**nd **H**is **O**ld **A**unt (now you understand the reason for making the first letter bold). Let's also include a divisor sign between the word. So, we have...

Sin θ = **O**pposite / **H**ypotenuse

Cos θ = **A**djacent / **H**ypotenuse

Tan θ = **O**pposite / **A**djacent

Along with the Pythagorean Theorem, these equations, or variations of them, can be used to solve problems involving all the parts of a right triangles.

For example: Let's say you know the lengths of the Opposite and the Hypotenuse of a right triangle. You can then use a variation of the Pythagorean Theorem to find the length of the Adjacent side. Then you divide the Opposite by the Hypotenuse to find the Sine of θ, or divide the Adjacent by the Hypotenuse to find the Cosine of θ, or divide the Opposite by the Adjacent to find the Tangent of θ. But how does that help you know what θ is?

Inverse functions

To find the angle from its Sine, you use its inverse function - the Arc Sine function. This is labeled as SIN-1 on most scientific calculators, and using it often involves pressing the 2nd key on the calculator, then the SIN key. For example, if the Sin of θ is .5, the angle is 30 degrees (be sure you have your calculator set to display Degrees and not Radians). Try it.

The inverse of the Cosine function is the Arc Cosine (COS-1) function. It is used to find the angle when you know the Cosine of θ. And the inverse the Tangent function is Arc Tangent (TAN-1). It is used to find the angle when you know the Tangent of θ. With this knowledge you can now find the angle if you know any two sides. And if you know the angle and the length of any side, use the "Old Henry And His Old Aunt" equations to find the lengths of the two unknown sides.

Trigonometric Equation Table

Remember, if you you know any two parts, you can solve for the others. Below is a table that shows what formula is used to solve the parts of a right triangle, based on any two "known" parts.

Trig Equation Table

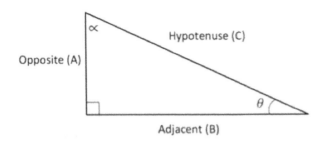

Theta (θ)	Alpha ($\propto$)	Opposite (A)	Adjacent (B)	Hypotenuse (C)
Known	90 - Theta	Known	$\sqrt{Hypotenuse^2 - Opposite^2}$	Opposite/SIN (Theta)
Known	90 - Theta	TAN(Theta)*Adjacent	Known	$\sqrt{Adjacent^2 + Opposite^2}$
Known	90 - Theta	SIN(Theta)*Hypotenuse	COS(Theta)*Hypotenuse	Known
ATAN(Opposite/Adjacent)	90 - Theta	Known	Known	$\sqrt{Adjacent^2 + Opposite^2}$
ASIN(Adjacent/Hypotenuse)	90 - Theta	Known	$\sqrt{Hypotenuse^2 - Opposite^2}$	Known
ACOS(Adjacent/Hypotenuse)	90 - Theta	$\sqrt{Hypotenuse^2 - Adjacent^2}$	Known	Known

For each option there are two "knowns" and three unknowns - that can be calculated.

This table was the basis for an Excel spreadsheet that I created for helping me do Trig calculations fast and easily. See Appendix C.

Degrees, Minutes and Seconds

So far, we have represented Theta and Alpha as "degrees" (and any fraction of a degree in decimal format). While this is a common practice, it is not the only way to represent angles. Instead of using a decimal number, angles can be represented in Degrees, Minutes and Seconds. This is commonly seen on GPS devices. Here are the stops for converting from angles from decimal numbers to Degrees, Minutes and Seconds. In this example we you use 121.135 degrees as our angle.

Step 1. The whole number of degrees will remain the same (121.135 degrees will be 121°).

Step 2. Multiply the decimal portion of the angle by 60 (0.135 * 60 = 8.1).

Step 3. Keep the whole number portion as the minutes (8').

Step 4. Take the remaining decimal and multiply by 60. (0.1 * 60 = 6).

Step 5. The resulting number becomes the seconds (6"). Seconds can remain as a decimal.

Step 6. Take your three sets of numbers and put them together, using the symbols for degrees (°), minutes ('), and seconds ("). This is your answer: 121°8'6".

To convert from Degree, Minutes and Seconds to a decimal number, follow the following steps (in this example we will use 27°12'45".

Step 1. Degrees remain the same, so write down 27.

Step 2. Divide the minutes by 60 to calculate the corresponding fraction of a degree. So, 12 (minutes) divided by 60 = 0.2 degrees. Write this number down.

Step 3. Divide the seconds by 3,600 to calculate the corresponding fraction of a degree. So, 45 (seconds) divided by 3,600 = 0.0125 degrees. Write this number down.

Step 3. Add up the three integer numbers of degrees and minute and seconds. So, 27 + 0.2 + 0.0125 = 27.2125 degrees.

Radians

Another way to represent an angle is in radians. The formula for converting from degrees to radians is to multiply the number of degree by Π /180°. So,

30 degrees = 30 * (3.141592654 / 180) or 0.523598776 radians

The formula for converting from radians to degrees to simply multiply the number of degree by 180°/(Π).

2.5 radians = 2.5 * (180 / 3.141592654) or 143.2394488 degrees

Doing these calculations is actually very easy on a scientific calculator.

Gradients

A gradient is 1/400 of a circle (0.9 degrees). This unit of measurement is rarely used and I only mention it here because it is mentioned in Appendix 2 on using a scientific calculator.

Examples

Let's now look at some problems that involve angles and see how these functions can help us solve them.

Problem 1.

For the right angle below, we know the lengths of the opposite and the adjacent sides, but nothing else. However, from these two lengths, we can calculate the Hypotenuse, θ and $\propto$. Let's do it.

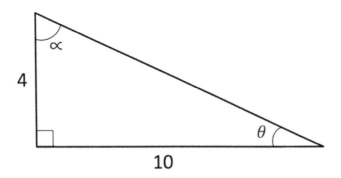

Hypotenuse = $\sqrt{opposite^2 + adjacent^2}$

Hypotenuse = $\sqrt{4^2 + 10^2}$

Hypotenuse = $\sqrt{16 + 100}$

Hypotenuse = $\sqrt{116}$

Hypotenuse = 10.77

Tan θ = **O**pposite / **A**djacent

Tan θ = 4/10

Tan θ = 0.4

θ = 21.8 degrees

$\propto$ = 90 - θ

$\propto$ = 90 - 21.8

$\propto$ = 68.2 degrees

See how easy this is? Now, that you understand how it works, let's look at some "real life" problems involving angles.

<u>Problem 2.</u>

An earlier problem had you calculate the lengths of cables for a bridle. Now, let's calculate the angle between the bridle legs (this is important because if the angle is greater than 120 degrees, it can create a dangerous situation). Here is what we know:

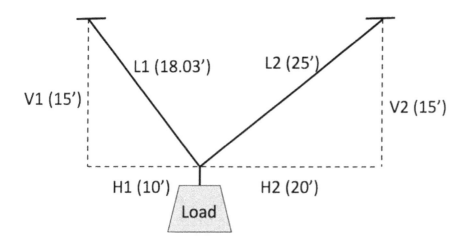

Because we divided our problem into two parts (right triangles) we need to calculate the angles of each and then add them together to get the total angle between the two legs of the bridle. Since we know the lengths of all three sides of each triangle, we can choose from several formulas for calculating the angle. Looking at the Trig Equation Table, we see that if we know the Opposite and the Adjacent, we can use the equation ATAN (Opposite/Adjacent) to find the angle of Theta. So, plugging in our values we get:

Theta 1 = ATAN (10/15)
Theta 1 = ATAN (6.6666667)
Theta 1 = 33.69 degrees

Theta 2 = ATAN (20/15)
Theta 2 = ATAN (1.333333)
Theta 2 = 53.13 degrees

Total angle = 33.69 + 53.13
Total angle = 86.82

Compass Heading

The next problem will involve a compass heading, so you need a little background information to get started. Below is a drawing (a Compass Rose) that shows compass headings. On a GPS device, positions are often given in terms of Degrees, Minutes and Seconds. In this problem, we will stick to Degrees only (at least until we get to the answer of the question).

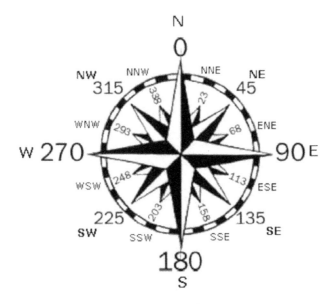

As you can see, North is both 0° or 360°. East is 90°, South is 180° and West is 270°. In the next problem you will be given compass headings and you will need to convert them into an angle (Theta) of a right triangle. In my diagrams of this problem, North will be at the top, South at the bottom, East to the right and West to the left, just like in the image above. You now need to use this direction to create a right triangle. The Hypotenuse will always be the compass heading, and the Adjacent side will always be on either the North, South, East or West coordinates (0 or 360, 90, 180 or 270 degrees lines). The length of the Hypotenuse will always be the distance traveled. And the Opposite side will be drawn either horizontally or vertically to connect the end of the Hypotenuse to the Adjacent line. This gives you your right triangle. Let's look an example.

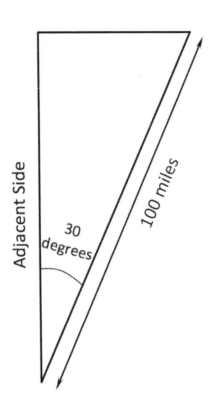

Look at the the triangle above. The hypotenuse of the triangle represents a compass heading of 30 degrees and a distance traveled of 100 miles. See this?

Next, look at the line that is the Adjacent side and figure-out what direction your Adjacent line runs from Theta – North (0), South (180), East (90) or West (270). In this case it is <u>North</u>, so write "0" on a piece of paper and call it "Start."

Next, compare the location of the Adjacent side to the Hypotenuse. To get from the Adjacent side to the Hypotenuse (and staying within the triangle) do you go clockwise or counter-clockwise. Based on the direction, use one of the following equations:

Clockwise: Angle = Compass Heading – Start

Counter-clockwise: Angle = Start – Compass Heading

In this example our equation is ...

Theta = 30 - 0
Theta = 30 degrees

Now that you know the angle (Theta) you can calculate the lengths of the Adjacent and Opposite sides. These will then tell you the distance North or South and the distance East or West traveled. These numbers will be important in calculating the final answer to the question. Using the Trig Equation Table above, we know that Adjacent = COS(Theta) x Hypotenuse, so ...

North (the Adjacent Side) = COS (30) x 100

North (the Adjacent Side) = 0.866025404 x 100

North (the Adjacent Side) = 86.6 miles

and

East (the Opposite Side) = TAN (Theta) x Adjacent

East (the Opposite Side) = TAN (30) x 0.866025404

East (the Opposite Side) = 0.577350269 x 0.866025404

East (the Opposite Side) = 0.5 miles

Note: If the compass heading was 210 degrees, the Adjacent line would have run South (180 degrees) and Theta would have still have been 30 degrees (210 - 180). But now your two directions would have been South and West.

Once you get the hang of this, the angle will seem obvious as soon as you look at the triangle.

Note: There are numerous free "compass" apps that you can get for a smart phone. I highly recommend that you get one and experiment with it. It will teach you a great deal about compass headings.

Problems 3

You have a private plane and fly from your home in Smallville to Mediumville. Your heading for this flight is 312 degrees and you fly a distance of 110 miles. The next day you fly from Mediumville to Largeville. Your heading for this flight is 75 degrees and you fly a distance of 225 miles. On the third day you fly from Largeville to Giganticville. Your heading for this flight is 330 degrees and you fly 57 miles. On the forth day you decide to fly back home to Smallville. What is the heading and distance of this flight?

Your combined flights might look something like this.

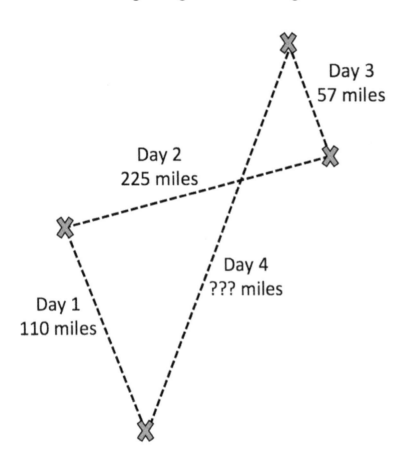

Wow, that seems very complicated. It is, but it can be divided into lots of small parts and solved using the formulas discussed above. Let's get going.

Here is a diagram of the first flight. I have added lines to create a right triangle and labeled the parts.

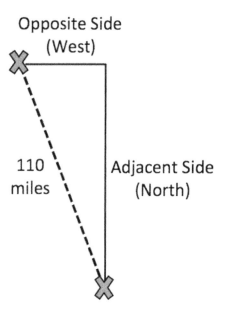

Since North is 360 degrees and the heading is 312 degrees, we know that Theta is 48 degrees (360 – 312). And, now that we know Theta, we can use it and the length of the Hypotenuse (110 miles) to calculate the Adjacent side by using the equation COS (Theta) * Hypotenuse.

Adjacent = COS(48) * 110
Adjacent = 0.669130606 * 110
Adjacent = 73.6 miles

This is the Northerly distance we traveled. Let's call it NS1. Write it down because we will need it later.

We also need to calculate the opposite side using the equation SIN(Theta)*Hypotenuse.

Opposite = SIN(48)*110
Opposite = 0.743144825 * 110
Opposite = 81.75 miles

This is the distance we traveled to the West. Let's call it EW1. One more thing, because the direction of the travel is to the left (West), EW1 = -81.75. Easterly distances will be positive numbers. It will make more sense a bit later.

Now look at the next leg of your trip.

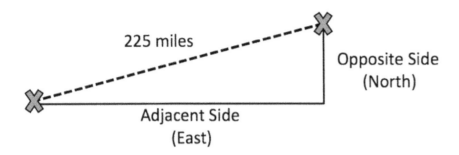

225 miles

Opposite Side
(North)

Adjacent Side
(East)

Again, we need to made a right triangle and calculate both the opposite and adjacent sides. Since the heading is 75 degrees, Theta is 15 degrees (90-75), and the Hypotenuse of our right triangle is 225 miles. Using the same equations as before, we calculate…

Adjacent = COS(15) * 225
Adjacent = 0.965925826 * 225
Adjacent = 217.33 miles

This is the distance we traveled East. Let's call it EW2. Remember, because the direction of the travel is to the right (East), EW2 will be a positive number.

We also need to calculate the opposite side using the equation SIN(Theta)*Hypotenuse.

Opposite = SIN(15) * 225
Opposite = 0.258819045 * 225
Opposite = 58.23 miles

This is the distance North we traveled. Let's call it NS2.

Next, let's look at the third leg of the trip.

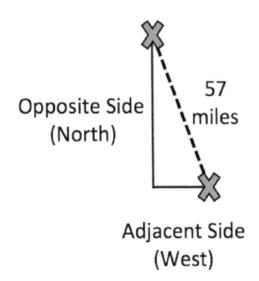

Opposite Side
(North)

57
miles

Adjacent Side
(West)

Again, we need to calculate the adjacent and opposite sides of our right triangle.

Since our heading was 330 degrees, Theta is 30 degrees (360 – 330), and the Hypotenuse is 57 miles. Again, we use the same equations to get...

Adjacent = COS(30) * 57
Adjacent = 0.866025404 * 57
Adjacent = 49.36 miles

This is the Northerly distance we traveled. Let's call it NS3.

We also need to calculate the opposite side using the equation SIN(Theta)*Hypotenuse.

Opposite = SIN(30) * 57
Opposite = 0.5 * 57
Opposite = 28.5 miles

This is the Westerly distance we traveled. Let's call it EW3. And like the first leg of the trip, the direction of the travel is to the left, so this will be EW3 = -28.5.

Now we are ready to calculate out trip home to Smallville. Lets begin by adding NS1, NS2 and NS3 to see how far North of Smallville we are. Since all of our travels were in a Northerly direction, all of these numbers are positive.

NS Total = 73.6 + 58.23 + 49.36
NS Total = 181.19 miles

Since legs 1 and 2 of our trip were Westerly and leg 2 was Easterly, we have both positive and negative number to combine to determine how far East or West we traveled.

EW Total = -81.75 + 217.33 – 28.5
EW Total = 107.08

Now, we are ready to draw and label the triangle that represents our trip home. It looks like this.

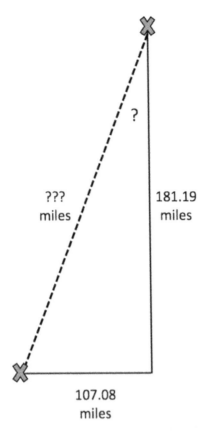

We know the Adjacent and Opposite sides, but the need to calculate the Hypotenuse (the distance from Giganticville to Smallville, and Theta (the angle that will allow us to calculate the heading).

We can calculate the Hypotenuse using the Pythagorean Theorem.

Giganticville to Smallville = $\sqrt{181.19^2 + 107.08^2}$
Giganticville to Smallville = $\sqrt{32829.8161 + 11466.1264}$
Giganticville to Smallville = $\sqrt{44295.9425}$
Giganticville to Smallville = 210.466 miles

And finally, we calculate the angle of our triangle.

Theta = ATAN (Opposite/Adjacent)
Theta = ATAN (107.08/181.19)
Theta = ATAN (0590981842)
Theta = 30.58 degrees

To get the heading, we add 180 and 30.58.

Heading = 210.58 degrees

We did it! That wasn't so bad.

Trigonometric functions are a very important part of Trigonometry, and the Trig Equation Table can help you know which function to use, depending on what you know and what you want to calculate.

Sample Problems - Lesson 35

1. Sam likes to hunt ducks with his dog Mabel. If a group of ducks fly directly over Sam's head at a height of 125 feet and Sam fires his rifle at an angle of 55 degrees (from horizontal) and kills a duck, assuming the the duck falls straight down, how far will Mabel have to go to retrieve the dead duck?

2. Three miners are trapped in a mine 2,200 feet below ground. Rescuers have determined the spot on the surface that is directly above the miners, but decide to move 660 feet to the East and drill the rescue shaft at an angle. How long will this shaft need to be to reach the miners and at what angle (to vertical)?

3. In a WWII video game, a bomber flies 10,000 feet above the ground and passes directly over an anti-aircraft gunner's position. The gunner's desire is the shoot-down the bomber when the bomber is 5,000 feet beyond his position (so that the debris falls in an uninhabited area). To do this, at what angle (to horizontal) will the gunner fire?

4. A fisherman leaves his dock and sails for 13 miles on a compass heading of 75 degrees. After fishing for an hour, he travels 8 miles on a compass heading of 14 degrees. After fishing at that location he sails for 22 miles on a compass heading of 180 degrees. At the end of his day of fishing, what would be his compass bearing to sail home and what compass bearing would he need to sail?

Lesson 36:

The ETCP Certified Rigger - Formula Table

Everyone who takes an ETCP rigging certification exam gets a list of formulas to help them with the exam. A note on the bottom of the Certified Rigger - Formula Table reads, "This list of formulas is provided by ETCP to aid candidates in completing the examination. However, it should not be considered a complete and exhaustive list of formulas that could be used in performing the calculations on the exam."

Until 2010, there were separate formula tables for the two different rigging exams. These have since been combined into one sheet to reduce confusion at the testing centers. The current includes 39 equations in two categories: "Standardized Formulas" and "Other Formulas." The vast number of formulas on this sheet, with many that do the same thing (the ETCP's Formula Table includes at least six variations of the Pythagorean Theorem), can be both confusing and intimidating.

My advice has always been for riggers to learn the formulas/methods that they can remember the easiest and not concern themselves with other methods. Many people believe that if you don't know how to solve the problem, this list will not help you. Still others believe the list of formulas is helpful. No matter what you believe, a little more information of these equations might be helpful, so I have included some on this lesson.

In this lesson, I will show the formulas on the current formula table and give a brief description of how each can be used. Also, since all of the formulas in the "Other Formulas" section on this sheets come directly from Harry Donovan's book *Entertainment Rigging*. I have cross-referenced the formulas to the page number in his book. You can download a copy of the Certified Rigger - Formula Table from: http://etcp.plasa.org/candidateinfo/riggingexams/docs/Formula_Sheet_2010.pdf.

While this table appears to be arranged in a series of columns, it is not. Actually, reading the formulas from left to right, top to bottom (like reading a book) puts the equations in their logical order. Also, while it might seem that the "Standardized Formulas" would be the most used, this is probably not true, as you will see, so I will begin by discussing the "Other Formulas" section first.

Most rigging problems involve calculating the force (tension) on a bridle leg or anchor point, while a few involve calculating the length of a bridle leg. Different formula contain different variables, and understanding what these variables represent is critical to being able to use the formula. Most of the variables contain subscripts. Some subscripts (1, 2, 3 or 4) indicate a particular leg or anchor point, while others (L, V, H and R) indicate the direction of the force (L = in line with the leg, V = Vertical force, H = Horizontal force and R = a Resultant force). The subscript "new" indicates that the problem involves bridle legs at different heights above the apex and a intermediate (new) value is needed before the final calculation can be done. For example:

$$D_{2Hnew} = D_{2H} \times \frac{D_{1V}}{D_{2V}}$$
and
$$S_{new} = D_{1H} + D_{2new}$$

Each of the sections below begin with a Legend of variables. You will probably be referring back to these legends many times as you look at the formulas in order to understand them.

Legend:
Δ = (Delta) Absolute difference
A = Either the opposite or adjacent side of a right triangle
B = Either the opposite or adjacent side of a right triangle
C = The hypotenuse of a right triangle
D = Horizontal Distance
D_F = Distance falling
F = Force
F_A = Applied Force (Weight)
F_R = Force (resultant)
F_H = Force (horizontal)
F_V = Force (vertical)
H = Horizontal distance
L = Length (of Leg)
P = Place of origin on a three-point bridle (Load on a rigging Point)
P sin<a = Load times the sine of the angle
V = Vertical distance
S = Span or horizontal distance between anchorages
T = Tension (same a Force)
W = Weight

X = Distance on X axis

Y = Distance on Y axis

Z = Distance on Z axis (height)

Other Formulas

$$A_1 : A_2 = B_1 : B_2 = C_1 : C_2$$

This equation will not help you solve any rigging problem - at least not any that I know of. It is an example of an "equivalent expression." Another example of an equivalent expression is $\frac{a}{\sin A} = \frac{b}{\sin B} = \frac{c}{\sin C}$ (the law of sines). Donovan: 11-3.

$$C = \sqrt{A^2 + B^2} \quad \text{and} \quad C = \sqrt{AA + BB}$$

The next two equations are variations of the Pythagorean Theorem. These equations are used to find the length of a bridle leg. Donovan: 20-8.

$$F_1 = \frac{D_1 W_1 + D_2 W_2 - D_3 W_3}{S}$$

This formula calculates the force (tension) on the vertical legs supporting a truss with two loads between the legs and one load cantilevered outside one of the legs Donovan: 16-11.

$$F = \frac{W D_F}{D_S} + W$$

This equation is used for calculating the shock load of a falling object. Donovan: 9-1.

$$F_1 = \frac{D_2 W}{S} \quad \text{and} \quad F_2 = \frac{D_1 W}{S}$$

These formulas are used to find the force (tension) on vertical legs on the ends of a truss with a single load or a uniformly distributed load. Donovan: 16-8.

$$F_2 = \frac{-D_1 W}{S}$$

This formula is used to find the force (tension) on a vertical leg on the end of a truss that is opposite a cantilevered end of the truss. Donovan: 16-8.

$$F_2 = \frac{D_5 W_2 + D_6 W_3 - D_4 W_1}{S}$$

This formula calculates the force (tension) on the vertical legs supporting a truss with two loads between the legs and one load cantilevered outside one of the legs Donovan: 16-11.

$$F_H = \frac{HW}{V}$$

This equation calculates the force on a horizontal breastline. Donovan: 19-10.

$$F_{H1} = \frac{WH_1 H_2}{V_1 H_2 + V_2 H_1}$$

This equation calculates the force on a horizontal on a leg attached to a beam. Donovan: 21-3.

$$F_{V1} = \frac{WV_1 H_2}{V_1 H_2 + V_2 H_1} \quad \text{and} \quad F_{V2} = \frac{WV_2 H_2}{V_1 H_2 + V_2 H_1}$$

These formulas calculate the vertical force on the beam to which a bridle leg is attached. Donovan: 21-1.

$$F_R = \frac{P \sin \angle a}{\sin \frac{\angle a}{2}}$$

This formula calculates the resultant force of a rope or cable running over a pulley. Donovan: 15-1.

$$L = \sqrt{V^2 + H^2}$$

This is another variation of the Pythagorean Theorem. This equation is used to find the length of a bridle leg. Donovan: 12-1 and 20-8.

$$L_1 = \sqrt{(V_1 - V_3)^2 + (H_1 - H_3)^2}$$

This is another variation of the Pythagorean Theorem. This equation is used to find the length of a bridle leg. Donovan: 20-12.

$$L_1 = \sqrt{(V_1 - V_3)^2 + (H_1 - H_3)^2 + (D_1 - D_3)^2} \quad \text{and}$$

$$L_2 = \sqrt{(V_2 - V_3)^2 + (H_2 - H_3)^2 + (D_2 - D_3)^2}$$

These formulas are used for calculating the length of bridle legs in three-dimensions. Donovan: 20-17.

$$P_1 = \sqrt{(X_1 - X_4)^2 + (Y_1 - Y_4)^2 + (Z_1 - Z_4)^2} \quad \text{and}$$

$$P_2 = \sqrt{(V_2 - V_3)^2 + (Y_2 - Y_4)^2 + (Z_2 - Z_4)^2} \quad \text{and}$$

$$P_3 = \sqrt{(X_3 - X_4)^2 + (Y_3 - Y_4)^2 + (Z_3 - Z_4)^2}$$

These formulas calculate the lengths of three-point bridle legs. Donovan: 22-3.

$$T_{L1} = \frac{WD_2L_1}{SH} \quad \text{and} \quad T_{L2} = \frac{WD_1L_2}{SH}$$

$$T_1 = \frac{WL_1H_2}{V_1H_2 + V_2H_1} \quad \text{and} \quad T_2 = \frac{WL_2H_1}{V_1H_2 + V_2H_1}$$

Note: An unusual alternative pair of equations (ones that appear at the end of this section) are:

$$T_{L1} = \frac{WD_2L_1}{H_1D_2 + H_2D_1} \quad \text{and} \quad T_{L2} = \frac{WD_1HL_2}{H_1D_2 + H_2D_1}$$

To use this pair of equations, exchange the variables "D" for "H" and "H" for "V."

$$T_1 = \frac{WL_1H_1}{V(Beam\ Span)} \quad \text{and} \quad T_{L2} = \frac{WH_1L_2}{V(Beam\ Span)}$$

These equations are used to calculate the tension on bridle legs for beams at the same height. Donovan: 21-3.

Standardized Formulas

These formulas are general physics/engineering equations and can be pretty confusing to most entertainment riggers. Many of these equations, but not all, can be found in Chapter 1: Forces and Formulas written by Rocky Paulson in *Entertainment Rigging for the 21st Century*, edited by Bill Sapsis. As above, I will note the book and page numbers (example: "Sapsis: 38").

$$F_1 = \frac{F_AD_2}{S} \quad \text{and} \quad F_2 = \frac{F_AD_1}{S}$$

are the same as

$$F_1 = \frac{D_2W}{S} \quad \text{and} \quad F_2 = \frac{D_1W}{S}$$

These formulas can be used to find the force (tension) on vertical legs on the ends of a truss with a single load or a uniformly distributed load. Sapsis: 4.

$$F_{1V} = \frac{F_A D_{2H}}{S} \quad \text{and} \quad F_{2V} = \frac{F_A D_{1H}}{S}$$

These equations are used to find the vertical force on the anchor point of a bridle leg. Sapsis: 36.

$$F_{1L} = \left(\frac{F_A D_{2H}}{S}\right)\left(\frac{D_{1L}}{D_{1V}}\right) \quad \text{and} \quad F_{2L} = \left(\frac{F_A D_{1H}}{S}\right)\left(\frac{D_{2L}}{D_{2V}}\right)$$

These formulas can be used to find the force (tension) on the legs of a bridle.

$$F_{1L} = \left(\frac{F_A D_{2Hnew}}{S_{new}}\right)\left(\frac{D_{1L}}{D_{1V}}\right) \quad \text{and} \quad F_{2L} = \left(\frac{F_A D_{1Hnew}}{S_{new}}\right)\left(\frac{D_{2L}}{D_{2V}}\right)$$

These equations are the same as the equations above, but are used when the anchors are not at the same height.

$$F_{1H} = \left(\frac{F_A D_{2H}}{S}\right)\left(\frac{D_{1H}}{D_{1V}}\right) \quad \text{and} \quad F_{2H} = \left(\frac{F_A D_{1H}}{S}\right)\left(\frac{D_{2H}}{D_{2V}}\right)$$

These formulas can be used to find the horizontal force on the anchor point of a bridle leg.

Note: Remember, $\left(\frac{F_A D_{2H}}{S}\right) = F_{1V}$. Sapsis: 38 and 43.

$$F_2 = \frac{-F_A D_1}{S}$$

is the same as

$$F_2 = \frac{-D_1 W}{S}$$

This formula can be used to find the force (tension) on a vertical leg on the end of a truss that is opposite a cantilevered end of the truss. Sapsis: 10 and 17.

$$D_{leg} = \sqrt{\Delta X^2 + \Delta Y^2 + \Delta Z^2}$$

This is another variation of the Pythagorean Theorem. This equation can be used to find the length of a bridle leg on a three-legged bridle. Sapsis: 49.

Lesson 37:
Other Rigging Stuff (that you need to know)

This lesson does not teach how to solve any particular math problem. Instead, it contains information that you might use to solve a variety of rigging problems that may arise. The information in this lesson could be very important, so study it carefully.

Shock Loads

Starting and stopping of chain hoist

16 fpm hoist = approx. 20% load increase (but can be as high as 50%)

64 fpm hoist = approx. 200% load increase

General Rules of Thumb for Total Load on a Support Member

For multiple-line block systems: Double load + Double weight of rigging

For single-line block systems: Double load + 15% of Load

Allowable Load

Allowable Loads = (Rigging Strength × Strength Reduction Factor) / (Design Factor × Load Increase Factor

Conversions

1 meter = 3.28 feet

1 cm = 0.3937 inches

1 mm = 0.03937 inches

1 kN = 224.8 lb

1 kip = 1,000 pounds of force

1 KpA = 145 psi

1 kilogram = 2.2 lb

Weight of Pipe

1.5" ID Schedule 40 pipe weighs 2.72 lb per foot

1.5" ID Schedule 80 pipe weighs 3.6 lb per foot

Knot Efficiencies

Bowline: 50%

Clove hitch around a 4" diameter pipe: 75%

Round turn and two half hitches around a 4" diameter pipe: 75%

Breaking Strengths

1/2" 3 strand manila rope: 2,650 lb

1/2" polypropylene rope: 4,000 lb

1/2" nylon rope: 6,000 to 7,000 lb

1/2" Dacron rope: 6,000 to 7,000 lb

The strength of a fiber rope in a sliding condition with a D:d ratio of 1:1 = 30% to 40%

Polypropylene, polyester, and nylon ropes can support a load of less than 20% of their breaking strength indefinitely.

1/8" 7x19 GAC: 2,000 lb

1/4" 7x19 GAC: 7,000 lb

3/8" 7x19 GAC: 14,400 lb

1/2" 7x19 GAC: 22,800 lb

1/2" 6x19 IWRC Bright XIP: 26,600 lb

1/2" 6x19 IWRC Bright XXIP: 29,200 lb

30 series or violet slings: 2.5 kip

60 series or green slings: 5 kip

D:d Ratio

A D:d ratio of 30:1 or greater is recommended for 6x19 wire rope (90% efficiency)

Allowable deflection on 1.5" ID steel pipe

Allowable Deflection = $\frac{\text{Length of Span}}{180}$

Working Load Limits

1/4" Galvanized Shackle: 1,000 lb

5/16" Galvanized Shackle: 1,500 lb

3/8" Galvanized Shackle: 2,000 lb

1/2" Galvanized Shackle: 4,000 lb

5/8" Galvanized Shackle: 6,500 lb

3/4" Galvanized Shackle: 9,500 lb

1/2" Alloy Shackle: 6,500 lb

5/8" Alloy Shackle: 9,500 lb

1/4" Grade 30 proof coil chain: 1,300 lb

1/2" Deck chain: 11,250 lb

STAC chain: 12,000 lb

Curtain Track

Max span between hanging points for ADC Silent Steel® 2800 (heavy duty) track is 7 feet

Max span between hanging points for ADC Besteel® 1700 (light duty) track is 6 feet

Termination Efficiencies

Wire rope socket (spelter or resin): 100%

Swaged socket: 100%

Manually Swaged eyes (Nicopress): 100%*

Mechanical spliced sleeve: 95%

Loop or thimble splice: 90% to 80%

Wedge socket: 90% to 75%

Properly installed wire rope clips: 80%

* Note: This reference is to oval copper swaging sleeves. There is great disagreement about the holding capability of aluminum sleeves. Mazzella Lifting Technologies issues the following warning in their catalog: "Aluminum sleeves may not develop 100% holding power (swaging efficiency). Testing is recommended prior to use to determine the holding power for any particular application, especially when the possibility of personal injury or property damage exists." And other experts question their ability to hold when subjected to shock loads. I do not use or recommend aluminum swaging sleeves for entertainment rigging.

Wire Rope Clip Table

Clip Size	# of clips	Turnback	Torque in foot pounds
1/8"	2	3-1/4"	4.5
3/16"	2	3-3/4"	7.5
1/4"	2	4-3/4"	15
5/16	2	5-1/4"	30
3/8	2	6-1/2"	45
7/16	2	7"	65
1/2"	3	11-1/2"	65

Fall Protection

- Three types of fall protection: guard rails, safety nets, and personal fall arrest systems
- Fall protection required for persons 6 feet or more above ground level
- Max fall distance: 6 feet
- Max arrest force: 1800 lb or 8 kN
- Max deceleration distance: 42 inches
- Minimum component strength for vertical system: 5,000 lb
- Fiber lifeline must have a breaking strength of at least 5,400 lb
- Personal Fall Arrest System (PFAS) designed for people between 130 and 310 lb
- Energy absorbers are designed to limit the arrest force to less than 900 lb (4kN)
- All connecting hardware must be proof tested to 3,600 lb
- Rigging systems that support people should have a 10:1 design factor

Conclusion

A good friend of mine says that you are always a student – you never stop your pursuit to learn more about your craft. This is a very good personal philosophy, and one that I strongly embrace. There are always things to learn, and hopefully, this book has taught you a few things.

I cannot emphasize enough the value of practice. The sample problems at the end of each lesson are just a starting point – you will want to create new problems that match the rigging problems that you face. One value in doing many calculations is that you soon start to see trends in the numbers, and you are able to closely estimate the results before you actually do the calculations. This is a skill that will be very handy in the field.

My friend also likes to say, "Safety is no accident," and math is an important part of the physics of rigging. Safe rigging is a result of always double-checking your work. Never be ashamed to ask another rigger to check after you or to show anyone your work. If you have done a good job, you should be proud of it and want people to see it.

Finally, one of the most important qualities of a good and competent rigger is to know when he or she does not know the answer. No one is perfect. When in doubt, seek out the advice of a qualified person or an engineer licensed in your jurisdiction. This will assure the accuracy of your work and perhaps save lives.

Happy (and safe) rigging!

References

Books

Breitfelder, Fred. *Bridle Dynamics for Production Riggers.* 1998.

Breitfelder, Fred. *Bridle Basics* (A Primer to *Bridle Dynamics*).

Donovan, Harry M. *Entertainment Rigging: A Practical Guide for Riggers and Managers.* 2002.

Glerum, Jay O. *Stage Rigging Handbook*, 2nd ed. Southern Illinois University Press. 1997.

Holden, Alys and Sammler, Ben. *Structural Design for the Stage.* Focal Press. 1999.

Sapsis, Bill, editor. *Entertainment Rigging for the 21st Century.* Focal Press. 2014.

Wire Rope Technical Board. *Wire Rope Users Manual*, 4th ed. 2005.

Web Sites

Automatic Devices Company. http://www.automaticdevices.com/

Calculating shock loads on ropes and TIPs...NEW CALCULATION. http://www.treeclimbercoalition.org/phpbb3/viewtopic.php?f=2&t=310

J.R. Clancey. http://www.jrclancy.com/Downloads/JRC_Allowable_Batten_Loads.pdf

Dynamic Energy in Arborist Rope. http://www.yalecordage.com/arborist-rope/dynamic-energy-in-arborist-rope.html

Electronic Theatre Controls. Knowledge Base: Source 4 Fixture and Shipping Weights. http://www.etcconnect.com/Community/wikis/products/knowledgebase-source-4-fixture-and-shipping-weights.aspx

Engineers Edge. http://www.engineersedge.com/fluid_flow/steel-pipe-schedule-40.htm and http://www.engineersedge.com/fluid_flow/steel-pipe-schedule-80.htm

James Thomas Engineering. http://www.jthomaseng.com/instructions.htm

LiftAll. Tuflex Roundslings. http://www.lift-all.com/

Line Pull Calculator. http://forestryforum.com/members/donp/linepullclc.htm

Mazzell Lifting Technologies. http://catalog.mazzellalifting.com/

McMaster-Carr. http://McMaster.com/

New England Ropes. http://www.neropes.com/

Riggers Page. http://www.rigging.net

Specialized Stage Engineer Pty Ltd. Rig it Right. http://www.stageengineering.com/

Universal Engineering, Inc. http://www.universalengineering.net/blog/?p=84

Vari-Lite Phillips Entertainment. http://www.vari-lite.com

Yale Cordage Double Esterlon. http://www.yalecordage.com/industrial-rope/double-braids/double-esterlon.html

Other

Much of the information in this book comes from the notes that I have made for myself over the last 30 years. These notes come from seminars I have attended, committees or workgroups on which I have served, catalogs, and information sent to me by friends and colleagues. Also, some photos and illustrations come from friends and other sources, as noted in the book.

Appendices

Appendix 1

Answers to Sample Problems

Important note: Because of the rounding of the decimal parts of numbers, your answers might be slightly different than the ones shown here. That is OK. If your answer is more than 1 percent off, check your math. Note: All lessons do not have Sample Problems.

Lesson 1: Converting between Imperial and Metric Units
1. 9.84 feet
2. 26.24 feet
3. 47.88 feet
4. 5.18 meters
5. 0.609 meters
6. 1.676 meters
7. 7.874 inches
8. 47.244 inches
9. 21.65 inches
10. 60.96 centimeters
11. 10.16 centimeters
12. 44.45 centimeters
13. 0.236 inches
14. 1.73 inches
15. 0.8267 inches
16. 38.1 millimeters
17. 9.525 millimeters
18. 20.32 millimeters
19. 2,700 lb (or more precisely 2,697.6 lb)
20. 157.5 lb (or more precisely 157.36 lb)
21. 5,175 lb (or more precisely 5,170.4 lb)
22. 22.22 kNs (or more precisely 22.24 kNs)
23. 0.777 kNs (or more precisely .778 kNs)

24. 16 kNs (or more precisely 16.01 kNs)
25. 30.8 lb
26. 319 lb
27. 715 lb
28. 1,590.91 kilograms
29. 95.45 kilograms
30. 204.54 kilograms

Lesson 2: Resultant Forces

1. 554.3 lb
2. 252.57 lb
3. 317.2 lb
4. 594.86 lb
5. 0 lb

Lesson 3: Mechanical Advantage

1. 66.67 lb
2. 33.33 lb
3. 33.33 lb
4. 33.33 lb
5. 33.33 lb
6. 16.67 lb
7. 16.67 lb
8. 16.67 lb
9. 6:1 MA

Lesson 4: Fleet Angles and D:d Ratios

1. 12.48 inches
2. 3.12 inches
3. 7.8 inches
4. 18.72 inches
5. 15.6 inches
6. 1.273 degrees
7. 2.385 degrees
8. 1.551 degrees
9. 2.147 degrees
10. 0.477 degrees

Lesson 5: Bridle Lengths

1. L1 = 6.324 feet and L2 = 7.211 feet
2. L1 = 12.36 feet and L2 = 12.64 feet
3. L1 = 17.08 feet and L2 = 14.86 feet

4. L1 = 11.4 feet and L2 = 9.486 feet

5. L1 = 13.03 feet and L2 = 14.76 feet

6. Angle = 52.125 degrees

7. Angle = 32.47 degrees

8. Angle = 40.21 degrees

9. Angle = 56.31 degrees

10. Angle = 60.77 degrees

Lesson 6: Tension on Bridle Legs

1. L1 = 6.32 feet and L2 = 7.21 feet, Tension on L1 = 351.36 lb and Tension on L2 = 200.3 lb

2. L1 = 12.36 feet and L2 = 12.64 feet, Tension on L1 = 294.5 lb and Tension on L2 = 225.87 lb

3. L1 = 17.08 feet and L2 = 14.86 feet, Tension on L1 = 182.34 lb and Tension on L2 = 190.35 lb

4. L1 = 11.4 feet and L2 = 9.48 feet, Tension on L1 = 152.02 lb and Tension on L2 = 295.14 lb

5. L1 = 13.03 feet and L2 = 14.76 feet, Tension on L1 = 325.96 lb and Tension on L2 = 369.12 lb

Lesson 7: Tension on a Horizontal Breastline

1. Horizontal Force = 60 lb

2. Horizontal Force = 250 lb

3. Horizontal Force = 500 lb

4. Horizontal Force = 62.5 lb

5. Horizontal Force = 77.77 lb

Lesson 8: Tension on a Deflecting Line

1. 173.87 lb

2. 153 lb

3. 655.2 lb

4. 361.32 lb

5. 427.25 lb

Lesson 9: Three-Point Bridle Lengths

1. L1 = 22.4 feet, L2 = 23.3 feet, L3 = 21.2 feet

2. L1 = 14.7 feet, L2 = 15.4 feet, L3 = 15.5 feet

3. L1 = 18.5 feet, L2 = 16.2 feet, L3 = 18.5 feet

4. L1 = 23.0 feet, L2 = 20.8 feet, L3 = 28.0 feet

5. L1 = 22.8 feet, L2 = 16.1 feet, L3 = 10.6 feet

Lesson 10: Tension on Three-Point Bridles

1. L1 = 136.65 lb, L2 = 129.7 lb, L3 = 282.84 lb

2. L1 = 54.99 lb, L2 = 181.73 lb, L3 = 316.23 lb

3. L1 = 110.8 lb, L2 = 129.24 lb, L3 = 110.8 lb

4. L1 = 190.76 lb, L2 = 62.82 lb, L3 = 211.46 lb

5. L1 = 136.31 lb, L2 = 325.81 lb, L3 = 518.22 lb

Lesson 11: Center of Gravity for Two Loads on a Beam

1. Side 1 = 1.67 feet and Side 2 = 8.33 feet
2. Side 1 = 3.75 feet and Side 2 = 6.25 feet
3. Side 1 = 5.526 feet and Side 2 = 9.4736 feet
4. Side 1 = 11.111 feet and Side 2 = 8.888 feet
5. Side 1 = 3 feet and Side 2 = 12 feet

Lesson 12: Uniformly Distributed Loads on a Beam

1. L1 = 300 lb, L2 = 937.5 lb, L3 = 300 lb
2. L1 = 200 lb, L2 = 570 lb, L3 = 570 lb, L4 = 200 lb
3. L1 = 250 lb, L2 = 712.5 lb, L3 = 625 lb, L4 = 712.5 lb, L5 = 250 lb
4. L1 = 120 lb, L2 = 342 lb, L3 = 300 lb, L4 = 300 lb, L5 = 342, L6 = 120 lb
5. L1 = 133.3 lb, L2 = 380 lb, L3 = 333.3 lb, L4 = 333.3 lb, L5 = 333.3, L6 = 380 lb, L7 = 133.3 lb

Lesson 13: Dead-hang Tension on One End of a Truss

1. Tension on L1 = 541.66 lb
2. Tension on L1 = 614.636 lb
3. Tension on L1 = 424.264 lb
4. Tension on L1 = 589.623 lb
5. Tension on L1 = 562.5 lb

Lesson 14: Simple Load on a Beam

1. Tension on L1 = 125 lb and Tension on L2 = 175 lb
2. Tension on L1 = 105 lb and Tension on L2 = 195 lb
3. Tension on L1 = 106.67 lb and Tension on L2 = 293.33 lb
4. Tension on L1 = 112 lb and Tension on L2 = 238 lb
5. Tension on L1 = 315 lb and Tension on L2 = 35 lb

Lesson 15: Multiple Loads on a Beam

1. Tension on L1 = 325 lb and Tension on L2 = 375 lb
2. Tension on L1 = 320 lb and Tension on L2 = 380 lb
3. Tension on L1 = 500 lb and Tension on L2 = 200 lb
4. Tension on L1 = 75 lb and Tension on L2 = 625 lb
5. Tension on L1 = 200 lb and Tension on L2 = 500 lb

Lesson 16: Cantilevered Load on a Beam

1. Tension on L1 = 425 lb and Tension on L2 = 675 lb
2. Tension on L1 = 655 lb and Tension on L2 = 445 lb
3. Tension on L1 = 341.67 lb and Tension on L2 = 408.33 lb
4. Tension on L1 = 360 lb and Tension on L2 = 540 lb
5. Tension on L1 = 440 lb and Tension on L2 = 560 lb

Lesson 17: Chain Hoists and Truss and Lights. Oh my!

1. Tension on L1 = 505 lb, Tension on L2 = 665 lb, and Tension on L3 = 340 lb
2. Tension on L1 = 448.75 lb, Tension on L2 = 496.25 lb, Tension on L3 = 627.5 lb, and Tension on L4 = 392.5 lb
3. Tension on L1 = 505 lb, Tension on L2 = 602.5 lb, and Tension on L3 = 652.5 lb

Lesson 19: Effective Length of Hitch

1. 3.7463 feet
2. 6.5612 feet
3. 6.0062 feet
4. 3.2546 feet
5. 5.9195 feet

Lesson 23: How much load can I put on a truss?

1. 233.3333 lb
2. 425 lb
3. 420 lb

Lesson 24: Chalk Markings and Arena Floor Layout

1. Sound point on center. Dead-hang. 15-ft basket, 20-ft leg.
2. Rigging point on center. Dead-hang. 15-ft basket, 20-ft leg.
3. Projection point on center with sliders. ½ Ton hoist. Dead-hang. 15-ft basket, 30-ft leg.
4. Rigging point on center. 20-ft legs, 20-ft stinger. 6 links of STAC on the left leg. C25 may refer to the hoist type. Baskets not shown.
5. A 2-ft or 2.5-ft steel.
6. Usually 7 (depending on the venue). Three for each of the basket hitches and one for the working shackle where the two bridle legs join.
7. False
8. True
9. False
10. True

Lesson 25: Angled Truss

1. L1 = 1,018.41 lb, L2 = 1,250.59 lb
2. L1 = 1,083.90 lb, L2 = 1,362.51 lb

Lesson 27: Estimating the Stretch of Wire and Fiber Rope under a Static Load

1. 0.336 inches
2. 1.6128 inches
3. 0.336 inches
4. 4.2 inches
5. 78.6 inches

Lesson 28: Shock Loads

1. Shock load = 2,975 lb
2. Shock load = 2,275 lb
3. Shock load = 3,412.28 lb

Lesson 29: Wind and Water

1. 2,764.8 lb
2. 1,344 lb
3. 1,040.4 lb
4. 71,917 lb

Lesson 30: Motor Calculations

1. 0.93 hp
2. 3.68 hp
3. 5.9 hp
4. 0.76 hp
5. 11.06 hp

Lesson 31: Counterweight Bricks

1. 32.54 lb
2. 21 lb
3. 17.28 lb

Lesson 32: Pullout Capacity of Lag Screws

1. 906 lb
2. 412 lb
3. 714 lb
4. 650 lb
5. 942 lb

Lesson 33: Drawbridge Problem

1. 234 lb
2. 195 lb
3. 157 lb
4. 100 lb

Lesson 34: Allowable Loads on Pipe Battens

1. 152 lb
2. 286 lb
3. 51 lb plf
4. 34 lb plf

Appendix 2

The TI-30XA Scientific Calculator

The TI-30XA scientific calculator is the one that I recommend, and this page covers the features of this calculator that you will use in this primer. Other calculators can be used to help solve the problems in this primer, but the instructions in this primer are written specifically for the TI-30XA.

The TI-30XA's keys

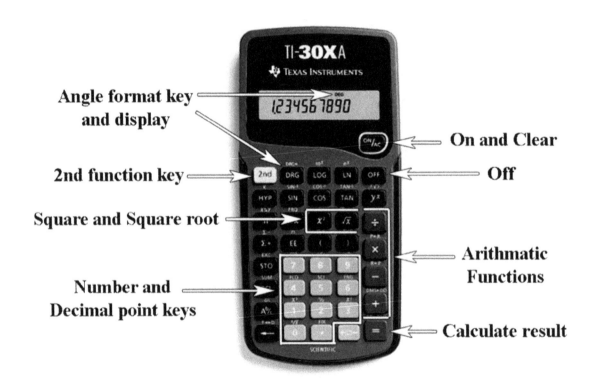

On and Clear – Turns the calculator ON and Clears the display.

Off – Turns the Calculator OFF.

Arithmetic function keys – Allows user to indicate which arithmetic function (division, multiplication, subtraction, or addition) should be performed.

Calculate results – The [=] key tells the calculator to compute the result of the equation that has been entered.

Number and Decimal point keys – Allow for the entry of numbers.

Square and Square root keys – The [X^2] key (pressed after a number has been entered) squares that number (multiplies it by itself). The [$\sqrt{x}$] key (pressed after a number has been entered) results in the square root of the number being displayed.

Scientific functions – These keys (pressed after a number, representing an angle, has been entered) and indicate which scientific function (SIN, COS, or TAN) should be performed.

2nd function key – When the [2nd] key is pressed, "2nd" appears in the display. Now when any other key is pressed, its second or alternate function, indicated in Yellow type above the key, is performed. The only time this key will be needed in this primer is when you need to use the arc tangent function (denoted as "TAN-1" on your calculator).

Angle format key – DRG stands for Degrees, Radians, and Grads; the three formats that angles can be represented. Since we will always be indicating angles by degrees, press the [DRG] key until "DEG" appears in the display. Done. You should never have to change it again (at least for the lessons in this book).

You may have already noticed that when I reference a particular key that is to be pressed, I have enclosed it in square brackets [ ]. This will be true in the early lessons of the primer, until you get used to entering data into your calculator. Numbers will NOT be enclosed in brackets, so if I want you to add 36 and 5.5, you will see "36 [+] 5.5 [=]. " After some example problems, you will see a number in parentheses ( ). This is the answer to the problem. You should get this answer when you do the calculation. If you get a different number, try again. Before you start a new calculation, you should Clear the display by pressing the [ON/C] key. This is easy to forget, and I will remind you to do this in the early lessons. Later on, you will have to remember it for yourself.

Before you start with the lessons, practice using your calculator (including using the scientific function keys – even if you do not know if the answers are correct).

Appendix 3
Cheat Sheet of Formulas

Conversions

Meters to Feet: Meters x 3.28 = Feet

Feet to Meters: Feet / 3.28 = Meters

Centimeters to Inches: CM x .3937 = Inches

Inches to Centimeters: Inches / .3937 = Centimeters

Millimeters to Inches: MM x .03937 =

Inches to Millimeters: Inches / .03937 = Millimeters

kiloNewtons to Pounds: kN x 224.8 =

Pounds to kiloNewtons: Lb / 224.8 = kiloNewtons

Kilograms to Pounds: Kg x 2.2 = Pounds

Pounds to Kilograms: Lb / 2.2 = Kilograms

$$\underline{Resultant\ Force} = Load \times \frac{sine\ of\ angle}{sine\ of\ (angle/2)}$$

Fleet Angles = Maximum Allowable Offset = Distance × 0.026

$$\underline{Bridle\ Angle} = Arctangent\ of\ \left(\frac{Offset}{Distance}\right)$$

$$\underline{Length\ of\ Bridle\ Leg} = \sqrt{H^2 + V^2}$$

$$\underline{Bridle\ Angle} = \left(Arctangent\ \left(\frac{H1}{V1}\right)\right) + \left(Arctangent\ \left(\frac{H2}{V2}\right)\right)$$

Tension on Bridle Legs

$$Tension\ on\ L1 = Load \times \frac{L1 \times H2}{(V1 \times H2)+(V2 \times H2)}$$

$$Tension\ on\ L2 = Load \times \frac{L2 \times H1}{(V1 \times H2)+(V2 \times H2)}$$

$$\underline{Horizontal\ Force\ on\ a\ Breastline} = Load \times \frac{H1}{V1}$$

Center of Gravity for two loads on a beam

$$Length\ of\ Side\ 1 = \frac{Load\ 2 \times Span}{Load\ 1 + Load\ 2}$$

$$Length\ of\ Side\ 2 = \frac{Load\ 1 \times Span}{Load\ 1 + Load\ 2}$$

or

Length of Side 2 = Span – Length of Side 1

Dead-hang Tension (on one end of a truss)

$$\text{Tension on L1} = \text{Load} \times \frac{L1}{V1}$$

Simple load on a beam

$$\text{Tension on L1} = \frac{\text{Load} \times \text{D1}}{\text{Span}} \qquad\qquad \text{Tension on L2} = \frac{\text{Load} \times \text{D2}}{\text{Span}}$$

or

$$\text{Tension on L2} = \text{Load} - \text{L1}$$

Multiple loads on a beam

$$\text{Tension on L1} = \frac{(\text{Load 1} \times \text{D1}) + (\text{Load 2} \times \text{D2})}{\text{Span}} \qquad \text{Tension on L2} = (\text{Load 1} + \text{Load 2}) - \text{L1}$$

Cantilevered (Complex) load on a beam

$$\text{Tension on L1} = \frac{(\text{Load 1} \times \text{D1}) + (\text{Load 2} \times \text{D2}) - (\text{Load 3} \times \text{D3})}{\text{Span}}$$

$$\text{Tension on L2} = (\text{Load1} + \text{Load 2} + \text{Load3}) - \text{L1}$$

Shock Load

$$\text{Force} = \text{Weight} \times \left(\frac{\text{Free Fall Distance}}{\text{Stopping Distance}} + 1 \right)$$

Wind Force

Force = ((((Wind speed $\times$ Wind speed) $\times$ 0.00256) $\times$ Area) $\times$ Drag coefficient)
*Drag coefficient = 1.2 for curved surface and 2 for flat surface

Weight of Water

Weight = Square footage $\times$ inches of depth $\times$ 5.202 or Weight = Volume in cubic feet $\times$ 62.428

Horsepower

Adjusted weight = (Load / 32.2) $\times$ (32.2 + (Speed in fps / Acceleration time))
HP = Speed $\times$ Adjusted Weight / 550

Tension on a Deflecting Line (Resultant Force)

$$Deflected\ Angle = Arctangent\left(\frac{H1}{V1} \right)$$

$$\textbf{\textit{Resultant Force}} = Load \times \frac{sine\ of\ angle}{sine\ of\ (angle/2)}$$

Weight of Counterweight Brick

$Area\ in\ ci = Width \times Length \times Thickness$
$$- ((Width\ of\ slot \times Length\ of\ slot \times Thickness) \times 2)$$

Weight = $Area\ in\ ci \times$ Weight of material

Steel = 0.2836 per cubic inch, Cast iron = 0.2604 pounds per cubic inch and Lead = 0.410 pounds per cubic inch.

Maximum Fleet Angle Offset (1.5 degrees)

Offset in Inches = Distance in feet $\times$ 0.314

Appendix 4
What Things Weigh

A. Chain Hoists

Columbus McKinnon Lodestar Half-Ton Hoist	Weight	1/4" Chain	5/16" Chain
Model F (16 fpm)	74 lb	.5 lb/ft	
Model J (32 fpm)	115 lb		1 lb/ft
Model JJ (64 fpm)	120 lb		1 lb/ft

Columbus McKinnon Lodestar One-Ton Hoist	Weight		
Model L (16 fpm)	114 lb		1 lb/ft
Model LL (32 fpm)	105 lb		1 lb/ft

Columbus McKinnon Lodestar Two-Ton Hoist	Weight		
Model R (8 fpm)	134 lb		1 lb/ft
Model RR (16 fpm)	112 lb		1 lb/ft

Verlinde Half-Ton Hoist	Weight		
Stagemaker (16 fpm)	51 lb		1 lb/ft
Stagemaker (32 fpm)	51 lb		1 lb/ft

Verlinde One-Ton Hoist	Weight	
Stagemaker (16 fpm)	104 lb	1 lb/ft
Stagemaker (32 fpm)	104 lb	1 lb/ft

Verlinde Two-Ton Hoist	Weight	
Stagemaker (16 fpm)	104 lb	1 lb/ft

B. Steel Pipe

Size (ID)	Schedule 40 Weight (lb/ft)	Schedule 80 Weight (lb/ft)
1/2"	0.85	1
3/4"	1.13	1.47
1"	1.68	2.17
1-1/4"	2.27	3
1-1/2"	2.72	3.65
2"	3.65	5.02

C. Truss

Total Fabrications

Generic Truss
Light Duty
12" x 12"
12" x 18"

Length	10'	8'	5'	2-way block	3-way block	4-way block	5-way block	6-way block
Weight	60 lb	48.5 lb	37.5 lb	26.5 lb	31 lb	35.2 lb	39.6 lb	44 lb

Generic Truss
Medium Duty
20.5" x 20.5"

Length	10'	8'	5'	2-way block	3-way block	4-way block	Concentric pivot
Weight	84 lb	70.5 lb	62 lb	44 lb	53 lb	62 lb	40 lb

Generic Truss
Heavy Duty
30" x 20.5"

Length	10'	8'	5'	2-way block	3-way block	4-way block
Weight	88 lb	73 lb	60 lb	53 lb	62 lb	70.5 lb

Generic Truss
Par Truss
Single 26" x 15"

Weight information Single PAR

Length	10'	8'	5'	2-way block	3-way block	4-way block
Weight	75 lb	55 lb	40 lb	33 lb	40 lb	46 lb

Weight information Double PAR

Length	10'	8'	5'	2-way block	3-way block	4-way block
Weight	121 lb	90 lb	64 lb	55 lb	66 lb	77 lb

James Thomas Engineering

General Purpose
GP 12" x 12"

Length	10'	8'	5'	2' 6"	2-way block	3-way block	4-way block	6-way block	Flat plate hinge section
Weight	55 lb	46 lb	35 lb	24 lb	15 lb	17.5 lb	19.5 lb	26.5 lb	14 lb

General Purpose
GP 12" x 18"

Length	10'	8'	5'	2' 6"	2-way block	3-way block	4-way block
Weight	61.5 lb	52.5 lb	37.5 lb	24 lb	17.5 lb	19.5 lb	22 lb

General Purpose
GP 20.5" X 20.5"

Length	10'	8'	5'	2-way block	4-way block	6-way block	0-90 pivot	0-270 pivot	0-180 Flat pivot
Weight	88 lb	75 lb	60 lb	33 lb	37 lb	42 lb	42 lb	43 lb	37 lb
Truss with castors	105 lb	92 lb	77 lb						

D. Lighting Instruments

Electronic Theatre Controls

ETC – Source Four

Fixture Name	Fixture Weight
5 Degree	19.2 lb
10 Degree	15 lb
19 Degree	19.3 lb
26 Degree	20 lb
36 Degree	20 lb
50 Degree	20 lb
70 Degree	23.4 lb
90 Degree	23.7 lb

ETC – Source Four jr

Fixture Name	Fixture Weight
26 Degree	10 lb
36 Degree	10 lb
50 Degree	10 lb

ETC – Source Four Zoom

Fixture Name	Fixture Weight
15-30 Degree	21 lb
25-50 Degree	17 lb

ETC – Source Four jr Zoom: 10 lb

ETC – Source Four PAR EA: 7.5 lb

ETC – Source Four PAR EMC: 7.5 lb

ETC – Source Four PARnel: 8 lb

ETC – Source Four HID

Fixture Name	Fixture Weight
5 Degree	23.3 lb
10 Degree	19.3 lb
19 Degree	18 lb
26 Degree	18 lb
36 Degree	18 lb
50 Degree	18 lb

ETC – Source Four HID jr

Fixture Name	Fixture Weight
26 Degree	13.6 lb
36 Degree	13.6 lb
50 Degree	13.6 lb

ETC – Source Four HID Zoom

Fixture Name	Fixture Weight
15-30 Degree	25 lb
25-50 Degree	20.7 lb

ETC – Source Four HID jr Zoom: 15 lb

Phillips Vari-Lite

Fixture Name	Fixture Weight
VL5	25 lb
VL6	22 lb
VLX Wash	62 lb
VL1000	72 lb
VL2500	59 lb
VL3000 Spot	91 lb
VL3500Q	94 lb
VL3500 Wash	96 lb

Appendix 5
Shackles

Of all the hardware that us used for rigging, shackles are probably the most common. Unlike bolts that come in different "grades" of steel, shackles come in four types: black-oxide steel, hot-dipped galvanized alloy steel, hot-dipped galvanized carbon steel, and stainless steel. Because there are so many different sizes of shackles, it is difficult to remember the measurements and working load limits of the different types of steel shackles. This Appendix can help.

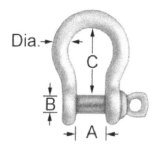

Black-Oxide Steel

Dia.	(A)	(B)	(C)	Work Load Limit, lbs.
1/4"	15/32"	5/16"	1-1/8"	1,000
5/16"	17/32"	3/8"	1-1/4"	1,500
3/8"	21/32"	7/16"	1-7/16"	2,000
7/16"	23/32"	1/2"	1-11/16"	3,000
1/2"	13/16"	5/8"	1-15/16"	4,000
5/8"	1-1/16"	3/4"	2-1/2"	6,500
3/4"	1-1/4"	7/8"	3"	9,500
7/8"	1-7/16"	1"	3-1/4"	13,000
1"	1-11/16"	1-1/8"	3-3/4"	17,000

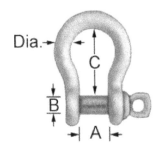

Hot-Dipped Galvanized Carbon Steel

Dia.	(A)	(B)	(C)	Work Load Limit, lbs.
3/16"	3/8"	1/4"	7/8"	666
1/4"	7/16"	5/16"	1-1/8"	1,102
5/16"	1/2"	3/8"	1-1/4"	1,500
3/8"	5/8"	7/16"	1-7/16"	2,204
7/16"	3/4"	1/2"	1-11/16"	3,306
1/2"	13/16"	5/8"	1-7/8"	4,409
5/8"	1-1/16"	3/4"	2-3/8"	7,165
3/4"	1-1/4"	7/8"	2-13/16"	10,471
7/8"	1-7/16"	1"	3-5/16"	14,330
1"	1-11/16"	1-1/8"	3-3/4"	18,739
1-1/8"	1-13/16"	1-1/4"	4-1/4"	20,943
1-1/4"	2"	1-3/8"	4-11/16"	26,455
1-3/8"	2-1/4"	1-1/2"	5-1/4"	29,762
1-1/2"	2-3/8"	1-5/8"	5-3/4"	34,000
1-3/4"	2-7/8"	2"	7"	50,000
2"	3-1/4"	2-1/4"	7-3/4"	70,000

Hot-Dipped Galvanized Alloy Steel

Dia.	(A)	(B)	(C)	Work Load Limit, lbs.
3/8"	5/8"	7/16"	1-7/16"	4,000
1/2"	13/16"	5/8"	1-7/8"	6,600
5/8"	1-1/16"	3/4"	2-3/8"	10,000
3/4"	1-1/4"	7/8"	2-13/16"	14,000
7/8"	1-7/16"	1"	3-5/16"	19,000
1"	1-11/16"	1-1/8"	3-3/4"	25,000
1-1/4"	2"	1-3/8"	4-11/16"	36,000
1-1/2"	2-3/8"	1-5/8"	5-3/4"	50,000
1-3/4"	2-7/8"	2"	7"	68,000
2"	3-1/4"	2-1/4"	7-3/4"	86,000

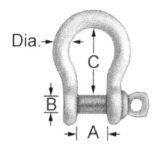

Type 316 Stainless Steel

Dia.	(A)	(B)	(C)	Work Load Limit, lbs.
1/4"	1/2"	5/16"	1-1/8"	1,000
5/16"	1/2"	3/8"	1-3/16"	1,300
3/8"	11/16"	7/16"	1-3/8"	1,500
7/16"	3/4"	1/2"	1-3/4"	2,000
1/2"	13/16"	5/8"	1-13/16"	3,000
5/8"	1"	3/4"	2-3/8"	4,000
3/4"	1-1/4"	7/8"	2-13/16"	6,000
7/8"	1-1/2"	1"	3-5/16"	8,000
1"	1-11/16"	1-1/8"	3-13/16"	10,000

Appendix 6

LiftAll Tuflex Roundslings

Code	Color	Capacity Vertical (lb)	Capacity Choker (lb)	Capacity Basket (lb)	Minimum Length (ft)
EN30	Purple	2,600	2,100	5,200	1.5
EN60	Green	5,300	4,200	10,600	1.5
EN90	Yellow	8,400	6,700	16,800	3
EN120	Tan	10,600	8,500	21,200	3
EN150	Red	13.200	10,600	26,400	3
EN180	White	16,800	13,400	33,600	3
EN240	Blue	21,200	17,000	42,400	3
EN360	Grey	31,000	24,800	62,000	3
EN600	Brown	53,000	42,400	106,000	8
EN800	Olive	66,000	52,800	132,000	8
EN1000	Black	90,000	72,000	180,000	8

NOTE: CAPACITY IS WLL (DESIGN FACTOR = 5)

Appendix 7
Spreadsheet Basics

This is a tutorial on the basics of how to start creating spreadsheets. It is nothing fancy, but it will help you understand how a spreadsheet is laid out, some spreadsheet terminology, and how to enter formulas. OK, let's get started.

Begin by opening Excel, or your spreadsheet program and open a New Workbook or spreadsheet (use the File dropdown menu). An empty or blank spreadsheet will appear. Spreadsheets are made up of a collection of cells (the rectangles you see on the screen). Each cell has an address based on its column letter (displayed at the top of the spreadsheet) and row number (displayed on the left side of the spreadsheet). The address of the cell in the upper left corner of the screen is A1. A spreadsheet can have many thousands of cells. Fortunately, we will not be using very many for this spreadsheet.

We can put different types of data in these cells, but we are going only deal with three: text, numbers and formulas. Excel is pretty good at automatically figuring out if the data you have entered into a cell is text or a number. However, it needs a clue if the data type is a formula. The clue that it is looking for is the equals sign ("=") at the beginning of the formula. For example, if you enter "1" unto cell A1, and "2" into cell A2, and want the result of adding these numbers to appear in cell A3, then you need to enter a formula into cell A3. The formula would be "=A1+A2" (do not include the quote marks). The "=" tells Excel that what followings is a formula, and "A1+A2" tell it to add the contents of these two cells. Since the formula is in cell A3, that is where the result, not the formula, will appear.

By using the buttons in the menus area, you can make the contents of a cell bold, underlined, italicized, or justified, just like you can do with a word processor. You can also change the color of the text or the background of a selected cell. At various times you will want to change the number of decimal places used in display a number. This can be done by using the Format>Cells>Number command.

You will also want to change the width of some columns in your spreadsheet to allow text to fit better. To change the width of a column, put your cursor on the line between two columns in the grey column row at the top of the spreadsheet. The standard arrow cursor should change to one with arrows pointing left and right. When it does, press and hold the left button on your mouse, and slowing move the mouse left or right. As you do the width of the column to the left of the cursor will change. When you have it the desired width, release the mouse button. Done.

Appendix 8
The InchCalc Add-In

Before you can use BridleCalc Pro, you need to download and install an "add-in" on your computer, and then "link" it to the BridleCalc Pro workbook. Each of these tasks involves several steps (although not difficult ones). Let's get going.

Download the InchCalc.xla add-in file and save it to a folder on your hard drive. Remember where you put it because you will need to find it very shortly.

Now, to install the InchCalc Add-In

For Excel 2013 and 2010

1. Click the **File** on the menu bar, and then click **Options** in the left panel.
2. Click the **Add-Ins** category.
3. In the **Manage** box, click **Excel Add-ins**, and then click **Go**.
4. Click **Browse**, and then locate the InchCalc.xla add-in file that you downloaded above.
5. Quit out and reload Excel. Now type =i2s(12) in the first cell and press enter!

For Excel for Mac

1. On the **Tools** menu, click **Add-Ins**.
2. Click **Select**, and then locate the InchCalc.xla add-in file that you downloaded above and click **Open**.
3. Quit out and reload Excel. Now type =i2s(12) in the first cell and press enter!

InchCalc is now installed. The functions i2s() and s2i() should be available just like any other Excel functions.

"Link" InchCalc to BridleCalc Pro

Now that InchCalc is loaded and working, you need to "link" it to BridleCalc Pro., so **Open** BridleCalc Pro (BC-Pro-1.xlsm).

<u>On the Mac</u>

Opening this file will open a series of pop-up windows. When prompted, make the following selections:

1. **Enable Macros** (Note: this option may or may not appear)
2. **Edit Links**
3. **Change Source**
4. Find and select the InchCalc.xla file, then click on **Change**
5. **Update Now**

It might take several seconds for file to update and the worksheet to refresh, so be patient.

When it does, hit **Close** and you are done. Save the file and you are ready to go.

<u>On a PC</u>

For Excel 2013

When Excel 2013 opens *BC-Pro 1.xlm*, it should recognize that the link to InchCalc in this workbook points to a different computer, and you should see the message "This workbook contains links to one or more external sources that could be unsafe. If you trust the links, update them to the latest data. Otherwise, you can keep working with the data you have.

1. Click on **Update**

Next you will see the message, " We can't update some of the links in your workbook right now. You can continue without updating their values, or edit the links you think are wrong."

2. Click on **Edit Links**
3. Next choose **Change Source**
4. Now, select the *InchCalc.xla* file and click on **Open**
5. The links in the workbook should now be updated, so **Close**
6. This is a good time to **Save** the file with its updated links.

Done.

Note: Different versions of Excel may not have the same prompts as described above, so be prepared to "adjust" the instructions above, if needed.

More about InchCalc

To learn more about how to use the InchCalc add-in, go to www.josh.com/InchCalc/. This site contains detailed information on this add-in and how to use it to its fullest.

Appendix 9

ANSI Standards for Entertainment Technology (Rigging)

The chart below shows the current versions (as of October 1, 2014) of ANSI Standards for entrainment rigging. Thanks to a partnership between ProSight Specialty Insurance and PLASA, these documents can be downloaded free from:

http://tsp.plasa.org/tsp/documents/published_docs.php

Note: *Documents offered through this website are copyrighted and their viewing and downloading is covered by an End User Licensing Agreement (EULA). All documents are provided in pdf format and are designed to be opened and read with a current version of Adobe Acrobat or Acrobat Reader.*

ANSI E1.1 - 2012
Entertainment Technology - Construction and Use of Wire Rope Ladders

Document Scope: ANSI E1.1 - 2012 describes the construction and use of wire rope ladders in the entertainment industry. It is a revision of the 2006 standard to raise the load rating to accommodate heavier workers. Wire rope ladders are distinguished from other ladders by having flexible rails, and are used in applications where ladders with rigid rails are impractical to use, or where a rigid ladder would pose a greater danger to the user or other workers in the area.

Standard Approved: June 19, 2012

ANSI E1.2 - 2012

Entertainment Technology — Design, Manufacture and Use of Aluminum Trusses and Towers

Document Scope: ANSI E1.2 describes the design, manufacture, and use of aluminum trusses, towers, and associated aluminum structural components, such as head blocks, sleeve blocks, bases, and corner blocks, used in the entertainment industry in portable structures.

Standard Approved: January 15, 2013

ANSI E1.4 - 2014

Entertainment Technology - Manual Counterweight Rigging Systems

Document Scope: ANSI E1.4 - 2014, Entertainment Technology - Manual Counterweight Rigging Systems, describes the design and construction of manually powered counterweight rigging systems to help assure the safety of these system. The standard does not cover motorized systems, systems for flying performers, or systems used for moving materials during building construction.

Standard Approved: January 21, 2014

ANSI E1.6-1 - 2012

Entertainment Technology – Powered Hoist Systems

Document Scope: ANSI E1.6-1 - 2012, Entertainment Technology – Powered Hoist Systems, establishes requirements for the design, manufacture, installation, inspection, and maintenance of powered hoist systems for lifting and suspension of loads for performance, presentation, and theatrical production. This standard does not apply to the structure to which the hoist is attached, to the attachment of loads to the load carrying device, to systems for flying people, to welded link chain hoists, or to manually powered hoists.

Standard Approved: October 16, 2012

ANSI E1.6-2 - 2013

Entertainment Technology — Design, Inspection, and Maintenance of Electric Chain Hoists for the Entertainment Industry

Document Scope: ANSI E1.6-2 - 2013 is part of the E1.6 powered entertainment rigging suite of standards. It covers the design, inspection, and maintenance of serially manufactured electric link chain hoists having capacity of 2 tons or less and used in the entertainment industry. This standard does not cover attachment to the load or to the overhead structure. Controls used for multiple hoist operation are excluded from the scope of this part of the standard.

Standard Approved: July 10, 2013

ANSI E1.6-3 - 2013

Selection and Use of Chain Hoists in the Entertainment Industry

Document Scope: ANSI E1.6-3 - 2012 is part of the multi-part E1.6 powered rigging standards project. It establishes minimum safety requirements for the selection and use of serially manufactured electric link chain hoists having capacity of two tons or less in the entertainment industry. This part does not address the design or maintenance of these hoists.

Standard Approved: July 03, 2013

ANSI E1.8 - 2012

Entertainment Technology--Loudspeaker Enclosures Intended for Overhead Suspension--Classification, Manufacture and Structural Testing

Document Scope: ANSI E1.8 is a standard for the structural integrity of loudspeaker enclosures that are suspended overhead. It is designed to ensure that flown speaker enclosures don't break and drop debris.

Standard Approved: January 15, 2013

ANSI E1.15 - 2006 (R2011)

Entertainment Technology--Recommended Practices and Guidelines for the Assembly and Use of Theatrical Boom & Base Assemblies

Document Scope: ANSI E1.15 - 2006 (R2011), Entertainment Technology--Recommended Practices and Guidelines for the Assembly and Use of Theatrical Boom & Base Assemblies, is a reaffirmation of the 2006 standard. It gives advice on boom and base assemblies, simple ground-support devices for lighting equipment and accessories. If the assembly is tall, not plumb, loaded unevenly, or likely to get run into by stage wagons or performers, there is substantial risk. This document offers advice to lower or eliminate that risk.

Standard Approved: December 06, 2011

ANSI E1.21 - 2013

Entertainment Technology — Temporary Structures Used for Technical Production of Outdoor Entertainment Events

Document Scope: This document establishes a minimum level of design and performance parameters for the design, manufacturing, use and maintenance of temporary ground supported structures used in the production of outdoor entertainment events. The purpose of this guidance is to ensure the structural reliability and safety of these structures and does not address fire safety and safe egress issues.

Standard Approved: December 19, 2013

ANSI E1.22 - 2009

Entertainment Technology - Fire Safety Curtain Systems

Document Scope: ANSI E1.22 - 2009, Entertainment Technology - Fire Safety Curtain Systems, describes the materials, fabrication, installation, operation, testing, and maintenance of fire safety curtains and fire safety curtain systems used for theatre proscenium opening protection. The requirements avoid cook-book descriptions of a fire safety curtain system; they specify how a fire curtain shall perform.

Standard Approved: April 21, 2009

ANSI E1.44 - 2014

Common Show File Exchange Format For Entertainment Industry Automation Control Systems – Stage Machinery

Document Scope: ANSI E1.44 is a standard for common show file requirements for automated stage machinery control systems used in entertainment venues. It establishes a minimum level of design and performance guidelines for the integrated software design of processor based machinery control equipment. The purpose of this guidance is to ensure that users will be able to transfer, modify and customize a 'least common denominator' show file for the data required to tour entertainment productions from one facility to another, even when the facilities' physical conditions, hoist inventories, and placements, and the machinery control consoles and data topology differ.

Standard Approved: February 06, 2014

CPSIA information can be obtained
at www.ICGtesting.com
Printed in the USA
LVHW052317180820
663559LV00018B/2136

9 780692 309896